Start Consulting—How to Walk the Talk

William L. Reeb, CPA

AICPA
American Institute of Certified Public Accountants

NOTICE TO READERS

Start Consulting: How to Walk the Talk does not represent an official position of the American Institute of Certified Public Accountants, and it is distributed with the understanding that the author and publisher are not rendering legal, accounting, or other professional services in this publication. If legal advice or other expert assistance is required, the services of a competent professional should be sought.

1 2 3 4 5 6 7 8 9 0 PP 9 9 8

Library of Congress Cataloging-in-Publication Data
Reeb, William L.
Start consulting : how to walk the talk / by William L. Reeb. Stephen L. Winters, Stanley E. Winters.
p. cm.
ISBN 0–87051–206–4
1. Accountants. 2. Business consultants. I. Winters, Stephen L. II. Winters, Stanley E. III. Title.
HF5627.R43 1998
001′.068—dc21 98–7431
CIP

Acknowledgments

I would like to thank a number of people who have supported me on this project. First is my wife, Michaelle Cameron, who not only helped me think through and organize this information, but had the patience to read this book more times than I have. As you see in the technical acknowledgments, Michaelle was the contributing author in the marketing material as well. Naturally, Steve and Stan Winters, shareholders in our CPA firm, have provided a great deal of input, both in content and financially, into this product. Todd and Lynda Denlinger, shareholders in our software development company, were not only financially involved in this project, but performed more than their share of my work so that I had the time to make this edition a reality.

Technical Acknowledgments

I would like to thank:

- *Larry McGinnes*, Senior Associate, Communispond, Inc., for his assistance in the area of presentation skills.
- *Michaelle Cameron, Ph.D.*, Assistant Professor of Marketing, Saint Edward's University, Austin, Texas, for guidance throughout the book and her role as a contributing author for chapters 7 and 9.
- *Rachelle Mazumdar*, Manager of Service Quality and Client Development for American Express Tax and Business Services, for her constant vigilance regarding material organization.

The following are members of the Management Accounting Services Committee and others who provided direction for and reviews of this book.

Janet G. Caswell, CPA
Janet G. Caswell, CPA, PC
Bloomfield Hills, Michigan

Robert Lynch, CPA
Benson & McLaughlin
Seattle, Washington

Dominic Cingoranelli, Jr., CPA
Grimsely, White, and Company
Pueblo, Colorado

Judith R. Trepeck, CPA
The Trepeck Group
Southfield, Michigan

Mike Gocke, CPA
Moss Adams LLP
Seattle, Washington

C. Cody White, Jr., CPA, APC
Heard, McElroy & Vestal, LLP
Shreveport, Louisiana

Lawrence R. Lucas, CPA
Lucas Company
Moscow, Idaho

AICPA Acknowledgments

Acquisitions Editor	Laura E. Inge
Editor	Margot Faivush
Production	Ingrid Anderson
Design	Kim Mangal
	AICPA Graphic Design Services

Table of Contents

Section 1

Consulting and the CPA Profession

Chapter 1
Introductory Issues

Most CPAs already provide consulting services. Many have even gone to the extra effort of formalizing this area. And a few, rapidly growing in number, are strategically shifting the image of their firms from that of traditional accounting to consulting practices with accounting expertise.

This text was written to assist those traveling the road of consulting, whether they are beginning to build a practice or just fine-tuning one. For CPAs with minimal consulting experience, this text will review the fundamental issues of consulting on a step-by-step basis. For those who are successfully delivering consulting services, our material offers a back-to-the-basics review to help you pinpoint possible weaknesses.

Regardless of where you are in your consulting journey, by the time you finish working through this publication, you should be able to begin designing a plan that will enhance your ability to provide profitable consulting services that add value to your clients' organizations. However, we ask for your indulgence in reading this book. Some of the concepts we introduce are like abstract pieces to a puzzle. Each concept by itself won't reveal a discernible picture or hold up to much scrutiny. But once all the pieces of the puzzle have been detailed and are in place, the picture will be clear and you'll have a structure and foundation from which to build or enhance your consulting practice. With this in mind, here are our comments concerning some of the most commonly asked questions regarding this subject.

I need to develop more technical expertise at a price clients can afford in order to consult. How will this help?

It is assumed by the vast majority of CPAs that technical expertise and price are critical to the formation and expansion of a consulting practice. However, two May 1995 *Accounting Office Management and Administration Report* (AOMAR) articles, "How Do Clients Define 'Quality' Accounting and Consulting Services?" and "Client Satisfaction," lead to a different conclusion. The first point was that clients assume their CPA's technical competence as a given, and additionally, that technical excellence is rarely discernible by clients. Second, more than 68 percent of clients in the survey agreed that their CPA or consulting firm's fees were about right. (Note: These articles were based on two surveys AOMAR conducts each year. The issues identified in the 1995 surveys have remained constant in subsequent surveys.)

If technical expertise and price are not the formidable hurdles slowing the expansion of consulting, what is? We believe it is the unconscious bundling of what we term the "consulting framework" and "consulting packages." In the article "Body of Knowledge" by F. Anne Drozd, printed in a recent edition of *CAmagazine* (published by the Canadian Institute of Chartered Accountants in Toronto, Canada), the author lists the following as the seven key skills all consultants should have:

1. Ability to learn quickly
2. Proficiency in asking questions
3. Ability to patiently listen and observe
4. Possession of people skills
5. Adeptness at analyzing information or situations and drawing conclusions
6. Creativity
7. Competence as a communicator

These skills are the essence of what we call the "consulting framework." Let's assume that your firm develops a twenty-two step program outlining the delivery of a new consulting service called "The Small Business Checkup." Let's further assume that it can be profitably delivered for $1,500.

It is our contention that while a consulting package such as this one is invaluable, it is useful only as long as the CPAs in your organization are comfortable and competent in—

- Identifying which clients have a need that this service could benefit.
- Convincing those clients of the value of having this service performed.
- Communicating and persuading management to take appropriate action.
- Taking on the role of the change agent facilitating this transition.
- Establishing an environment that is conducive to creatively resolving conflicts and overcoming obstacles.

Almost all CPAs do this to some degree on a regular basis. And for that reason, this capability may sound simple, straightforward, and common. However, few CPAs have fine-tuned the skill-set required (those skills identified above as essential to the consulting framework) to do this well. Because of the significance of these skills, this text is primarily focused on building the consulting framework. It is our experience that almost every CPA firm is loaded with consulting packages that are under-utilized and under-delivered. By better understanding and embracing the consulting framework, firms can quickly raise the utilization and delivery of their current competence by learning to identify new consulting opportunities. This in turn augments existing revenues while simultaneously improving client satisfaction.

I am not looking for today's quick fix to a stagnating or declining revenue problem. I am searching for a long-term solution. Why do you think consulting fits that description?

We believe that consulting is fundamental to our profession's future, and not just some quick fix to current revenue problems. Paraphrased, the AOMAR client satisfaction survey identifies some common complaints clients have regarding their CPAs:

- I'm looking for "services that spark new ideas or can save additional dollars."

- I want "customized advice, not 'boilerplate' recommendations."
- "Providing guidance and direction for the future" is the kind of help we need, "not just a slap for prior transgressions."
- My CPA needs to have an "interest in our business—not just our tax returns or financial statements."
- I want a better balance between "advice based on perceived opportunities versus fixing problems."
- My advisor should have "the presence to answer questions in a manner that can be understood by the lay person, and not be afraid to say 'I don't know, but I'll find out.'"

The AOMAR client satisfaction survey is just one of many such surveys that has been conducted in the past ten years that has revealed basically the same message: *that clients are looking for more than accounting from their CPA firm.*

And when they can't find the assistance they need, they are going elsewhere, often to other CPA firms. Consulting is *not* just another revenue source, it's the *client-demanded future of our profession.*

GOALS OF THIS BOOK

Many firms are ignoring the changing demands of their clients. And of those that have responded to the changing demand, many are unfortunately providing consulting services unprofitably, in a manner prone to litigation, and in a way that provides minimal value. This text can help make improvements in each of these areas.

We make no promises or guarantees that the ideas and approaches in this text will work for you. However, you do, at a minimum, have the opportunity to see what works well for us and for the firms we have counseled. By using this information as a starting point for reorganizing and planning your firm's consulting evolution strategy, you should be better able to consistently deliver consulting services which are both valuable to your clients and profitable to your organization.

HOW THE BOOK IS ORGANIZED

This book is broken into sections and chapters. The sections are *Consulting and the CPA Profession, The Consulting Framework, Identifying and Marketing Your Services, Administrative and Organizational Issues,* and *Consulting Packages.* We have presented this text, for the most part, in a format that allows you to build on the skills in the same order that you would use them in practice. For example, since it's not customary to prepare an engagement letter before you know what the engagement is all about, we cover the skills necessary to define the engagement before we worry about administering it. Another example is that we cover the skills necessary to identify services the client is interested in before we discuss how to motivate the client to hire you. Here is the way the book breaks down, some of the main focuses of each section, and the plan that this text follows to create an entire consulting methodology.

Consulting and the CPA Profession

Chapters 1, 2, and 3: Introductory Issues, Starting at Ground Zero,* and *Why Take the Risk?

- Why consult
- Definition of consulting
- Services versus packages
- Providing differentiated services
- Making the transition
- Organization implementation
- Global services
- Implementation strategies
- The evolution of the profession

The Consulting Framework

Chapters 4 and 5: Developing Your Self Skills* and *Refining the Most Important Consulting Tool: Communications

- Developing self skills
- Improving communication techniques
- Evolving investigative questioning
- Learning to facilitate the solution

Chapter 6: Delivering Value-Adding Services

- Consulting techniques
- Pricing techniques

Chapter 7: The Structure of the Calls

- Discovery calls
- Sales calls
- Consulting calls

Identifying and Marketing Your Services

Chapter 8: Two Approaches to Business Consulting

- Building the fortress
- Building the empire
- Determining the most appropriate services

Chapter 9: Marketing Your Consulting Practice

- The marketing plan
- The message
- Exposure alternatives
- Client service plans

Administration and Organizational Issues

Chapter 10: Billing and Engagement Considerations

- Billing issues
- Retainers and collection issues
- Being paid for your involvement
- Engagement considerations

Chapter 11: Client Communications

- Meeting management
- Presentation skills

Consulting Packages

Chapter 12: Facilitating Your Client's Planning Process

- Strategic planning
- Tactical planning
- Our role in planning
- Conducting the planning session

Section 1, "Consulting and the CPA Profession," focuses on why consulting is so important. It contains three chapters: "Introductory Issues," "Starting at Ground Zero," and "Why Take the Risk?" These chapters lay the groundwork as to why consulting is not just another service, but a new way of doing business. These chapters also cover why some strategies have been more successful than others.

Section 2, "The Consulting Framework," includes four chapters. The first two chapters, "Developing Your Self Skills" and "Refining the Most Important Consulting Tool: Communications," deal predominately with self-awareness, communication, persuasion, and listening skills. Without an in-depth understanding of how we act and react, as well as how to facilitate change, it will be difficult for us to ever get into a position to show very many clients what we can do. The third chapter is "Delivering Value-Adding Services." In addition to covering some critical techniques as to how to deliver consulting, it also includes direction regarding estimating projects. The last chapter in this section is "The Structure of the Calls," which covers three different call types: the discovery call, the sales call, and the consulting call. This chapter not only hones in on how to conduct each of these interactions effectively, but how to do a better job of qualifying, quantifying, and solving your client's problems.

By this time, the book has taken you through skills and techniques which augment selling and delivering consulting services. It's time now to focus on marketing. Building the best mousetrap doesn't mean anyone will buy it. That's where marketing comes in, so we created Section 3, "Identifying and Marketing Your Services." This section includes "Two Approaches to Business Consulting," which helps you determine what services your firm should be offering and why, and "Marketing Your Consulting Practice," which not only reviews the most commonly used exposure vehicles, but also covers how to create a marketing plan.

After you have been hired to perform consulting, there are a variety of administrative and organizational issues that come into play, hence Section 4. The topics include "Billing and Engagement Considerations" and "Client Communications."

Section 5, "Consulting Packages," takes you through a simple format for facilitating a goal setting or strategic planning session. The "Facilitating Your Client's Planning Process" chapter is laid out in a way that allows you to sell and deliver this service immediately.

Finally, the Appendix contains the AICPA's Statement on Standards for Consulting Services No. 1.

It's Time

With all of this in mind, it's time to get started. We ask that you be patient and read through the entire text. Much of this material will seem to be common knowledge, and at times, insignificant. But note this . . . while this review of the basics and the subtleties of this text might not jump off the page as important, by incorporating these ideas and techniques into your skill-set toolbox, you will find yourself in a new world with seemingly unlimited opportunities and the competence and confidence to deliver a higher level of value to the clients you serve. We hope you enjoy reading this as much as we did writing it!

Chapter 2
Starting at Ground Zero

What do audits, financial statements, and tax returns have in common? In addition to serving as the backbone of the CPA industry, they have unfortunately become commodities in the eyes of the public. Simplistically stated, this means that the general public views the traditional services CPAs perform, like tax preparation, as being the same regardless of the CPA's personal experience or knowledge. And, what happens to a commodity when it is left to stand on its own merits? When quality is considered a constant, then price becomes the most important buying criteria.

Many firms have already been confronted with this issue in the audit marketplace, where severe price discounting battles have been fought. Other firms have begun to feel this same fee pressure in areas such as financial statement and tax return preparation.

Why have so many traditional CPA services become commodities? The main reason is that our industry has done a great job of selling the value of a CPA's education, training, and skills. A long time ago, our profession focused on creating a distinction between the CPA and everyone else that worked in accounting. Because this was done very successfully, the marketplace now recognizes that in accounting those three initials after someone's name indicates an added value. But since CPA professionals in the last fifteen years have dramatically expanded the scope of services we offer (both in public and industry), we are finding the quality public relations job started fifty years ago is plaguing us. Why? Because during the fight to create distinction between the CPA and a non-CPA, we perpetuated the idea that all CPAs have the same skills set. This resulted in the idea that a CPA is a CPA is a CPA. This image went beyond the work performed; a unique accountant stereotype emerged. Just ask anyone you meet on the street to describe a CPA. This stereotype that we all think alike, act alike, and have the same skills is now part of the problem. Our marketplace tends to judge us as a profession rather than individually. As a result, the public often generalizes that the traditional services a CPA delivers (that is, audits, financial statements, and tax returns) are the same regardless of who performs the work.

This is a primary reason why consulting is so important to our profession. *Consulting is the value-adding service that converts a commodity into a unique offering. It helps differentiate one CPA's product from another based on that individual's experience and knowledge.*

To put this into perspective, consider how specialty stores succeed in selling many commodity-type items for more money than department stores. The answer is consulting. At the specialty store, a salesperson will be available to answer your questions about the product, to make suggestions, and generally to assist in the buying process. At the department store, you'll be lucky to find a warm body to talk to, much less someone who will take the time to help you make a more informed decision. The specialty store tries to create a hassle-free, advised buying experience, which costs a little extra, but is a price many don't mind paying.

This same analogy regarding differentiation holds true in our profession too. With some patience and just a little accounting knowledge, anyone can prepare a financial statement or tax return. And with the abundance of quality computer software, these products are getting easier to produce. You can rise above this flood of "me too" product offerings by creating unique new offerings which combine a commodity product (like a financial statement) with advice based on your personal knowledge and experience. Consulting is the forum which allows you to deliver advice and provide customized assistance, thereby differentiating your product from those of your competitors. For example, a financial statement is merely a compliance report until the information is analyzed, synthesized, and presented in a manner that management can easily understand and use. *Those CPAs who are not consulting with every client are delivering services which are destined to become price-sensitive commodities.*

Don't Preach to Me, I'm Already Advising My Clients!

Even if you are regularly advising your clients, if this service is not formalized as consulting and properly marketed, it will prove to be of little value. The American consumer has become savvy at distinguishing those goods in a stripped-down bare-bones package from those bursting with extras. While our profession will provide this delineation of services, it seems common practice to confuse the consumer by referring to both the bundled and unbundled versions identically. For example, let's say one of your clients calls you several times during the year with tax questions regarding the financial impact of various decisions. If you are like many CPAs around the country, you will record that time and bill it when you deliver the tax return. The bill received by the client will often read only, "Tax Return Preparation." So here's a case where tax consulting services were appropriately delivered, but since they were not labeled as such, the client will incorrectly assume that "Tax Return Preparation" includes quality advice throughout the year as part of the package.

This practice of bundling our services and generically referring to the work performed trains our clients to believe that our advice is free because we make our living selling paper products. This creates an impression that few CPAs would deem positive. The damage this misunderstanding causes becomes apparent when a competitor offers to do your clients' tax returns at half of what you have been charging. Based on this savings, and the feeling that they have been taken advantage of, a few of your clients decide to change CPAs. What these ship-jumping clients are likely to find is that the tax return is less expensive, but the overall bill will remain about the same. It's just that the new

CPA charges separately for advice. However, it's too late then; they are not likely to switch again until another significant issue arises. In this circumstance, the clients didn't change providers due to poor performance, but rather because quality services were delivered that they were *allowed* to take for granted.

The solution, once again, is consulting. Consulting provides you with a marketing tool that allows you to differentiate your personal knowledge and experience from that of your competitors. *Consulting is the application of knowledge*; it provides a forum to take information at least one step further. Consulting answers questions such as "How does this apply?" or "What can be done?" In other words, consulting often focuses on the future and attempts to predict outcomes of situations occurring and decisions being made today. That's why our definition of consulting is *that decision-making part of any project, task, or function that must be undertaken without sufficient information to predict a final outcome with any certainty.*

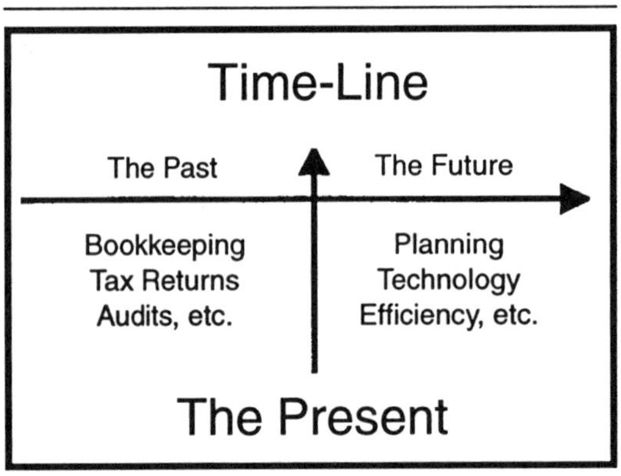

Consulting is the natural transition that occurs when the question, "What has happened?" is replaced by, "Based on what has happened, what is likely to occur next?" Consulting is the movement on the timeline from the past, through the present, into the future. With this in mind, the next time you prepare a tax return, incorporate some future focused aspect of that service such as tax, retirement, estate, or financial planning. If you perform bookkeeping services, no statement should be delivered without spending time with the client reviewing the meaning behind the numbers, and so on. This additional time should be classified as consulting and itemized and billed accordingly because it creates a distinction between the commodity (the financial statements) and the consulting (the advice given which requires your special skills and experience). The result is a distinctive service that gives you a competitive edge, both for building client loyalty and generating new business.

THE AICPA'S DEFINITION OF CONSULTING

Now, since we've shared our definition of consulting with you, it's only fair to include the AICPA's Management Consulting Section's (MCS) in-process definition. At the time this book went to print, it was:

Consultants provide businesses with professional services—

1. Characterized by the following qualities:
   - Two-party relationship
   - Disciplined objective
   - Independence rules do not apply
   - No known third-party reliance
2. Comprised of the following services:
   - Diagnosing
   - Strategizing
   - Constructing
   - Implementing
   - Operating
3. Applied in the following arenas:
   - Management services
   - Transactional services
   - Operational services

Why the extreme difference between the two definitions? Very simply, the MCS's definition has a much broader objective than ours. First, theirs tries to create a distinction between consulting (a two-party relationship) and assurance services (a three-party relationship), an important issue when it comes to standards, workpaper requirements, and liability issues, to name a few. As you know, in a two-party relationship (consultants and management), consultants are not hired to make representations to the public, they are retained to help management. But as soon as another party—the public, a bank, the SEC—becomes reliant on the information provided by the consultants, and especially if that third party is presuming independence on the part of the consultant's work, then the relationship becomes one of assurance rather than consulting.

Second, the MCS's definition has to consider the work performed by small, large, regional, national, and international CPA firms for clients ranging from "Mom and Pop" shops to the Fortune 100. This takes in a scope of work that more than 42,000 CPA firms around the country will never have (nor probably want) an opportunity to be involved. For example, very few of us will ever be asked to provide a million dollars worth of services over a week's period of time with three weeks notice. The MCS's consulting definition has to consider these types of services, which are not only projects our firm couldn't handle, but ones we don't want.

Third, the MCS's consulting definition includes the advisory function we highlight in this book in concert with an ever-expanding list of nontraditional services or consulting packages. While our definition says it much differently, ours primarily focuses on the first half of the MCS's definition. In the "comprised of the following services" section of the MCS's definition, by the time you get down to "constructing" and beyond, from our viewpoint, this work often falls to a specialist, a consulting package you offer, a third party, an alliance with another organization, and so on.

The point is, we agree with the AICPA's broader definition of consulting. We recognize the need and opportunity for our profession to offer a wide variety of business services. We also realize that many CPA organizations will find it extraordinarily lucrative to specialize in the delivery of certain consulting packages. Where the big difference regarding our two definitions lies is . . . we maintain that *consulting has to become the flagship service that forms the foundation of our evolving profession if we want to maintain and enhance the status of the CPA initials.*

This profession survival message is directed towards expanding the relationships with your clients as their trusted, valued advisor. This advisor by our definition is someone who can spark new ideas, deliver customized advice, provide guidance and direction for the future, show a genuine interest in the client's business, provide advice based on perceived opportunities, and so on (as pointed out by the AOMAR survey cited in chapter 1). These services are two-party in nature and have no expectation of independence (except maybe that of contributing a viewpoint from outside the organization). This is the value-add that we believe every CPA should be trained to deliver. Make no mistake about it—in our opinion, our profession's success in no way depends on whether your firm can install a computer network or perform a business valuation. These are merely two examples of literally hundreds of nontraditional services that your firm may or may not consider offering. So, for the sake of minimizing confusion, for the remainder of this text, unless we specify otherwise, when we refer to consulting, think about the diagnosing, strategizing functions of the MCS definition or our definition.

Incorporating Consulting Into Your Daily Routine

How hard is it to incorporate consulting into your daily routine? In theory, it is very simple. This is because we are discussing a change in philosophy more than a change in capability. However, everyone's habits need to be reexamined to ensure that those performing the work are motivated to look beyond the client's past and present, and into their future. Also, as professionals, we have to learn to become more comfortable, and at the same time more humble, when it comes to "guessing" what a client's future might hold.

The managing partners of most firms are typically not only marketing-oriented, but future-focused compared to the rest of the firm. This is partly true because their job descriptions require this perspective. Therefore, it stands to reason that these CPAs, because of what they do for their own firms, are more apt to enter into strategic level discussions with their clients. Including the managing partner, we've found (through our experience working with CPA firms across the country) that it is common for approximately 20 to 33 percent of the CPAs within any CPA organization to have a comfort level switching between services *constrained by facts, procedures, and regulations* to those services *laden with ambiguity and guesswork*. However, despite one's preferences, each member of a CPA firm is likely to have a specific client or two that forces him or her into this more ambiguous "tell me what is likely to happen tomorrow" role. Usually, the more mature the partner, the more often this role request is made by the client.

The point is . . . everyone can and does perform consulting, some more naturally than others. The trick is to get everyone to perform this service instinctively whenever possible. This transition is a logical place to encounter stumbling blocks. The good news is . . . in "The Consulting Framework" section of this book we will help you identify how to facilitate this change.

Who Should Become a Consultant?

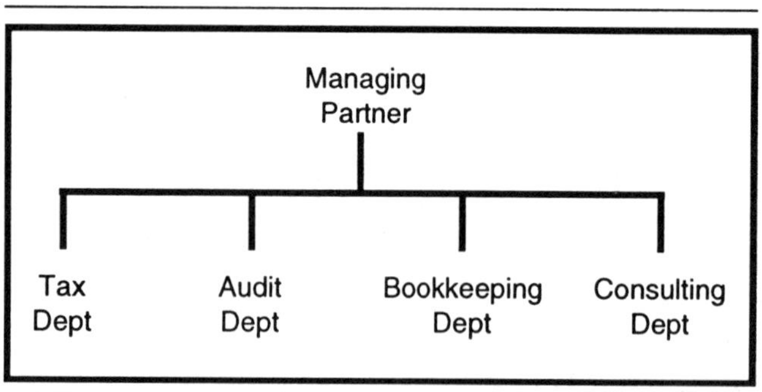

As to who should be involved in consulting, as you have probably already guessed, this is one area where our philosophy differs from the practiced norm. To most firms around the country, consultants are considered to be specialized people delivering specialized services within a specialized department. In these organizations, consulting is really just the catch-all word describing a variety of *consulting packages*. The focus is not on the "advisory" function of consulting, but rather on delivering highly specialized (nontraditional) niche services.

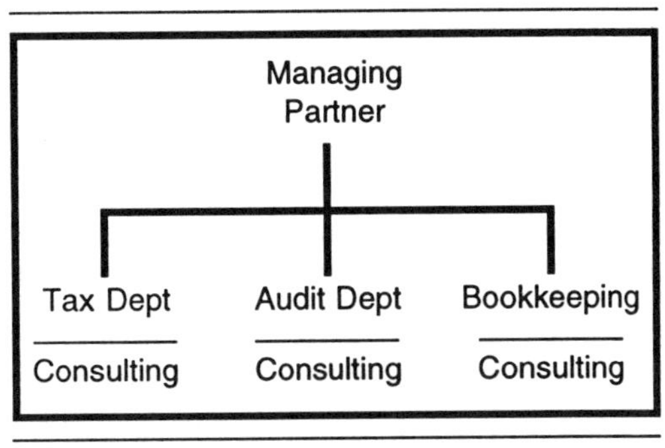

We feel the best place to start building a consulting practice is from an advisory perspective. As you can see from the diagram to the right, we believe strongly that every department (and service for that matter) should have a consulting or advisory element added to it. This means that *every member of every department should incorporate consulting into the current work being performed*. The main reason is the benefit derived by both you and your clients from spending just a little more time helping them determine how to best utilize whatever information is being delivered. Certainly, the more experience one has, the wider the range in the advice to be offered. But remember, consulting, simplistically speaking, is a philosophy which requires you to *interpret the meaning or impact* of the historical information with which you are familiar. This formalization of consulting—

- Is the easiest to implement.
- Has the fastest return on investment.
- Is the least risky.
- Provides the greatest value-add to the client.
- Is the most effective in transforming the culture of the firm.
- Is the least likely to be found.

If This Is Such a Good Strategy, Why Is It the Least Likely to Be Found?

It is the least likely consulting philosophy to be found because the largest CPA firms have successfully implemented a departmental strategy for consulting, even to the point of splitting off from the CPA firm itself. However, if you look closely, most of these firms would be more appropriately named "Smith Non-Traditional Services" rather than "Smith Consulting." The term consulting used by most CPA organizations does not refer to a holistic approach for providing business advice. It does not refer to services focused on finding out "what keeps the business owners awake at night" and then helping them resolve those issues. Instead, it refers to a variety of non-traditional services or consulting packages that are being offered, like system development, programming, re-engineering, and literally hundreds more. This translates into mass specialization, as large firms have the luxury of allowing generalists to become specialists purely due to volume of work. For example, instead of just having a tax department, these organizations might have a tax division with tax departments for the U.S., Canadian, Pacific Rim, European and NAFTA markets. This depth of knowledge becomes a competitive strength large firms can and should sell. And as long as demand is adequate, expansion through consulting packages (or non-traditional niche services) well suits their already-in-place management and organizational structure.

The Large Firm Approach to Consulting

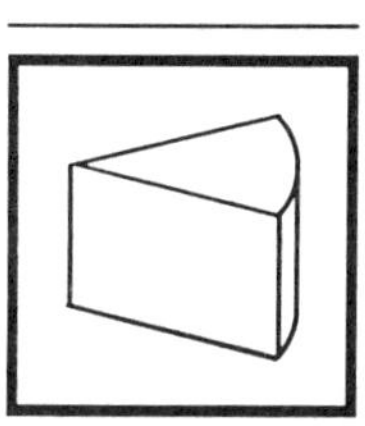

We call the approach large firms use the "Swiss cheese approach" to consulting package delivery. Here's why.

Assume the picture to the left represents a block of cheese. Also assume that this block of cheese pictorially represents the total potential demand for non-traditional services from a CPA firm's client base. Large firms jump right to the high dollar project opportunities by picking various nontraditional services, developing the required expertise and methodology, and offering them. As the demand for one nontraditional service dwindles, resources are shifted to poke new holes or deliver new services to the untapped opportunities which exist in the current client base. After periods of opportunistic service delivery, total potential demand begins to resemble a piece of Swiss cheese.

Once again, if your client base is large enough, then continually poking holes in the over-abundance of client demand is likely to be a profitable strategy. That's why the job description of the *consultant* in these organizations is often defined by the word *travel.* When consulting packages are launched, in order to maintain an acceptable volume of billable hours, a consultant has to work throughout the country (with all of the offices) in order to build a large enough demand base to consume the available expertise. As demand rises, more consultants with specialized knowledge are shifted from other work or hired, thereby either allowing the organization to respond to bigger and bigger projects or reducing the geographic area each consultant needs to cover. However, when smaller firms attempt this same strategy, because of their more limited client base size, under-utilized specialized expertise quickly results. This converts to idle time, expensive overhead, marginal profits (if at all), and often, abandoned specialties.

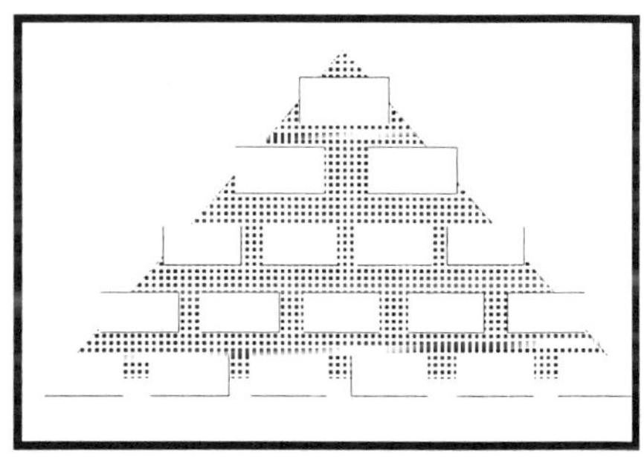

Another reason departmentalization of consulting works well for large firms is because they have acclimated their clients to the idea of *musical chair* service delivery. In other words, almost every service is delivered by other than the client service partner or account manager. And it is not uncommon for a client to have more than one client service partner. In other words, there might be a partner in charge of audit, another in charge of specific consulting services, etc. Why so many account managers? Because when performing huge projects, advice is not the key to the work. When you are looking for relationships that generate annually a minimum of $75,000 of revenue, or projects that range from several hundred thousand into the millions of dollars, the real profit comes from implementation. Often the clients large CPA firms serve have very high paid, high profile people driving strategy and advice. These clients turn to the CPA firms looking for ways to turn the identified vision into reality. The pyramidal organizational structure works well in this environment because it centers around delivering manpower; passing projects to the lowest paid, least experienced people who can accomplish the work.

The Small and Midsized Firm Approach to Consulting

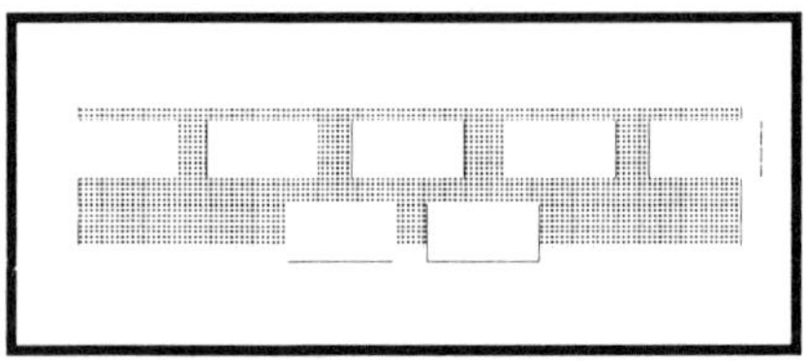

Unfortunately or fortunately, most small and many middle-market firms are not, and cannot be, structured this way. The smaller the CPA firm, the more boutique in nature it's organization, and the more "hands-on" the partner's approach. In the boutique firm, partners, managers and some staff are not only the main contacts, but the main workers on many of their clients' projects. This is partly due to the clients' levels of sophistication. For example, the smaller the organization, the more likely outside, objective, management level, forest-through-the-trees perspective and advice are seen as the mission critical services. That's why it is such a great match for smaller businesses (under $100 million in sales) to work with boutique firms where the contact person and the service provider is the same individual. Or at least, the same contact person is involved regardless of the project being performed. On the other hand, the larger the organization, the more these visionary and specialized skills are available through normal channels like advisory boards, directors, key stockholders, and internal management talent. Therefore, when Fortune 1,000 sized companies outsource help, they are often looking for specialized specialists. A simple example would be that with a smaller company, an advisor might be brought in to talk about the benefits and justification for allowing their people working outside the office to have the same access to systems as if they were in the office. In larger organizations, by the time the consultant is brought in, the discussion wouldn't be revolving around why or when, but how. Issues like identifying the pros and cons of communicating data-graphics-video through protocols such as asynchronous transfer mode (ATM), frame relay, integrated service data services network (ISDN), fiber digital data interconnection (FDDI), t-span, and satellite would more likely be the reason for requesting outside assistance. Or on an even grander scale (as the MCS consulting definition includes), the client might be looking to hire an organization that would take over the constructing, implementing, and operating of this communication network.

To summarize, the smaller the organization, the more advice and vision will open doors. The larger the organization, the more specialized and plentiful the labor-force, the easier it is to get management's attention. The great news is . . . small, regional, national and international CPA firms deliver a different product or service to different marketplaces. While it seems at times we compete with each other, in reality, each segment of firms is well suited for solving different problems. Therefore, for the most part, we tend to compete for business with those of a similar size or a slight step up or down in size from our own firms. With this in mind, recognize that according to the Small Firms Advocacy Committee of the AICPA that of the 44,500+ firms represented by AICPA membership, over 42,000 have 10 or fewer professionals. This book is focused on serving the 42,000+ firms that are predominately boutique in organization that serve $100 million businesses or smaller. And to compete with this group for this market, it makes both dollars and sense for your organization to focus on improving everyone's ability to deliver high level customized advisory services.

Consulting Services Versus Consulting Packages

So far, both consulting services and consulting packages have been mentioned several times in the same paragraph. Are these one-and-the-same or is there a distinction?

While there is a distinction between consulting services and consulting packages, the dividing point is gray. But generally, consulting services formalize into consulting packages as—

- The volume of work increases.
- The depth of knowledge required to perform the work intensifies.

- The work itself begins to proceduralize because you find yourself following a specific methodology.
- The work strays farther and farther from a business advisory capacity.

Consider this scenario: You are working with a $10 million business. The original services this company hired you for were financial statements and tax return preparation. Because your client's business has grown, the CEO has asked for your help in bringing the accounting function in-house. You provide this assistance. Now, you come in on a monthly basis to review the work being done by the client's staff. During one of your monthly visits, the client comments about their lack of goal setting and budgeting. Within a couple of months, you are facilitating a goal setting session, which is not only being done to help organize the operation, but to provide you with some basic information so you can help them prepare their first budget.

This describes the natural evolution and expansion of services a CPA is likely to encounter while working in an advisory capacity with businesses under $100 million in sales. This natural evolution has a name in the marketing text books called "service extension." As trusted business advisors deliver one service, logical extensions of that service are easily identified, sold, and then delivered. In the scenario above, we would describe all of these extended services as consulting. Why? Mostly because it appears the CPA is making up the approach as he or she goes; advice under fire if you will. We also would maintain that the work described, with the possible exception of the software installation, is comprised of services that everyone within a CPA firm should be comfortable delivering.

So how do consulting services metamorphose into consulting packages? Here's one way it might happen. After you finish the goal setting and budgeting process, the client is excited. She tells several of her CEO peers about how your work improved her organization. Before you know it, you have several more clients, some of them new, wanting the same service. You start having trouble squeezing in your traditional work and the consulting, so you start writing down exactly what you have been doing so others can help. On occasion, you overhear other partners in your firm talking to their clients about how they can benefit from this "goal setting budgeting" service. Clients continue to respond with interest. You begin to consider having someone specialize in this service in order to meet demand, to ensure that adequate focus is placed on expanding it into new markets and use it to create a differentiation between you and your competitors.

In this example, what started out as an on-site tailored consulting service, one that everyone should be capable of performing, has grown into a full-blown consulting package. How can we tell? Because—

- The work volume relative to this service increased.
- The service was proceduralized so others could perform it as well.
- The work has strayed from a make-it-up-as-you-go (customized) business advisory function, as demonstrated by management's consideration of packaging it up, to making it someone's priority focus, and selling it as a differentiating service.

The fact that the "goal setting and budgeting" session becomes a consulting package doesn't mean that every firm member should stop delivering this service. It's just that organizationally, by formalizing this advisory function into a consulting package, a more efficient marketing, management and delivery system can be implemented. Think of it this way, consulting services cultivate consulting packages. And consulting packages are just a broad category for nontraditional services.

We are attempting to delineate the distinction between consulting services and consulting packages early because, depending on which you are trying to implement, your road to success is different. The good news is . . . both can be very profitable for your organization. And we will address how to best chart your course throughout this text in a logical step-by-step fashion.

Global Functions

You've stated that everyone in a CPA organization should be capable of delivering consulting services (high level customized advisory services), which areas of a business does that include?

A clue as to where to start should be to consider broad categories of needs with which all businesses constantly struggle. These categories include:

- Planning
- Products or services
- Employee benefits
- Operational efficiency
- Operational profitability
- Marketing
- Technology
- Financing
- Information management

Because every business needs services to help it improve its capabilities in the areas listed above, we call them *global functions.* From our perspective, consulting revolves around the delivery of services around these global functions. And we believe that every business advisor within your firm should be able, at a moment's notice, to talk to any client about any of these areas. We maintain that a business advisor's (consultant's) basic tool kit should include—

- An ability to communicate with the client regarding each of these functional areas.
- An understanding of some of the common improvements and refinements organizations are making in these functional areas.
- Typical malfunctions or inefficiencies encountered in these areas.
- Your firm's general approach to enhancing performance in these areas.
- An ability to manage others who might assist in performing projects.

Note that specialized knowledge regarding *global functions* is not a required tool for a consultant. But a general knowledge is necessary, including knowing that—

- An organization with fifteen or more employees (generally) should not only have a policies and procedures manual, but also job descriptions in order to protect against discrimination lawsuits, as well as for employee motivation purposes.
- There are numerous types of computer networks, numerous ways networks communicate with each other, and numerous operating systems—all with their advantages and disadvantages. Also, that PC networks, minicomputers, and mainframes are all viable solutions, each with advantages and disadvantages. This leads to the fact that business problems have countless computer solutions and that experts should be brought in to advise both the CPA and the client as to what solution is best for that unique situation.
- Cost control is only one vehicle for helping businesses become more profitable. Each CPA should be equally ready and comfortable talking about ways to increase revenues, discussing typical advertising approaches, and reviewing pricing and compensation models in order to better stimulate sales.

And the stories go on. The point is, when a consultant walks into the client's office, he or she should mentally examine each area on the global functions list and look for ways to improve the operation. The answers to these mental questions may call for further discussion with the client, specific focus on a problem, or acquisition of specialists to facilitate technical changes. (See more on this in chapter 5.)

Specialized Services

OK . . . I buy the idea that our firm needs to build better advisory capability throughout the firm. However, isn't there still room for some specialized services?

Absolutely! However, before you offer any new service, you need to answer two questions: Who is the service targeted to serve? and Why it is important for you to serve that market? We have developed a methodology to help you in this analysis that uses the terms *fortress* and *empire*. Chapter 8 focuses on issues that should drive the decision as to whether or not to specialize as well as which specializations might be most appropriate.

If we focus on building the better advisory capability you are describing, will we lose out long term to those who put their emphasis in a couple of specialty areas?

We believe just the opposite will be true; those that focus on building better advisory skills will have much greater control over their own destiny than those firms concentrating in a few niche specialty areas. This is especially true for the more than 42,000 firms around the country with less than ten professionals. But before we defend our position, we want to tell you a story; our version of the evolution of the medical profession. We believe the practice of medicine serves as a good benchmark for the kind of changes our profession is likely to undergo.

How Specialization Changed the Medical Profession

Until about sixty years ago, most doctors entered the marketplace expecting to practice family medicine, and were often referred to as general practitioners—or "GPs." As the practice of medicine continued to become more involved, complicated, and just as important, litigious, doctors turned to specialization for relief. Specialization created a wealth of opportunity as new services were popping up everywhere due to clearer lines regarding expertise. This helped insulate doctors as their scope of work was dramatically narrowed. And due to the litigious environment, GPs were glad to refer their patients to these specialists. Specialists had a great situation. Not only did they enjoy a steady stream of patients from other doctors' referrals, their more highly specialized skills and training allowed them to demand greater fees.

It seems hard to believe now, but specialization was supported by many doctors, and fiercely contested by many others. Even in the early 1900s, those who held themselves out as "specialists" were considered "quacks" by their own industry. Those favoring specialization believed that it was in the public's best interest to clarify the fact that not all doctors had the same skills. Those doctors who had developed niche expertise were frustrated by a system that didn't recognize their unique capabilities. Many other doctors felt that the creation of a variety of designations would restrict individual doctors' service latitudes and thereby be disastrous to the profession. These doctors knew that once specialty designations were accepted, they would multiply exponentially. And once this occurred, not having a designation in a specific area would put a doctor at a competitive and litigious disadvantage.

Well, we all know how this story evolved. Board certified specializations were adopted and have become commonplace today. Those who had spent significant time working in a highly specialized niche area were the first to raise their new differentiation banner. Specialization also provided an interesting twist. While the most experienced doctors tended to specialize at first, specialization turned out to be an even greater windfall for new doctors. It provided them with a greater chance to compete and find employment opportunities. For example, years ago, significant opportunity could be found by associating with one of the few big medical practices that existed in every major metropolitan area. However, with a steady stream of new doctors constantly emerging from the educational system, the marketplace for the good jobs became more and more competitive. So, new doctors started becoming even more highly specialized; they became specialists in a specialty field so to speak. For instance, it wasn't that long ago when GPs would have X-rays done and perform the diagnoses themselves. Then, along came practitioners trained to devote all their time to reading X-rays (radiologists). Today, doctors don't just become radiologists, they specialize as neuroradiologists, pediatric radiologists, nuclear radiologists, and so on. What's odd is that the early adopters of the specialization radiology are now GPs in the specialty field of radiology.

Today, insurance companies are restricting access to many of the specialists as a cost control measure, and also capping the money they will pay for these unique services. Insurance companies are requiring patients to first seek attention from GPs, and if the GP feels a specialist's involvement is appropriate, a referral is made. Because GPs have become the "gatekeepers" for most services rendered within the medical profession, today there is growing demand for more general practitioners. Why has this job become more pivotal? Because GPs are the people with account control. They determine what other services should be called upon. And while the GPs can recommend specific practitioners, unless the recommended specialist is on the client's insurance company's constantly changing approved list, they will never see the referred patient.

The CPA-"GP" and the CPA Specialist

Much of the history of specialization in medicine is applicable to our profession and the changes it is likely to undergo. The scope of work that CPAs profess to perform is so vast (with many of those services being exceptionally complex, detailed, and constantly evolving), no human could maintain the bandwidth of knowledge required to be competent in all of these areas. Because we, as a profession, have used the CPA designation rather than the work being performed for differentiation, we have been promoting a growing litigious environment. When you consider all of this, as well as the ever-increasing competition within our profession, specialization quickly rises to the top as an alternative providing some relief in the battle of survival.

Just as with the medical profession, now that our profession has begun the landmark release of "business valuation" as a supported specialty designation, you can expect an explosion of additional designations over the next ten years. As each designation is released, not having a designation in that specific area puts a CPA professional at a competitive and litigious disadvantage. Specialization will create tremendous opportunity for new CPAs entering the profession as they will become more and more highly specialized in order to attract the interest of existing successful organizations. As in the medical profession, the more specialized firms become, the more dependent they will be on their alliances and referrals from mainstream CPA firms (general practitioners). And as more and more specialty designations are created, general practitioner CPAs will more commonly refer or subcontract with highly specialized CPAs for their unique services.

If we put this into a pictorial perspective, it might look like the graphic above. The entire circle represents market demand for the countless number of services our profession offers. The first inside ring represents an industry filter. For example, many CPA firms specialize in a specific industry, such as construction or health care. Inside the industry filter lies the CPA general practitioner (CPA-GP). Whether the CPA-GP specializes in an industry is not significant in this graphic. More than anything, displaying the industry filter merely denotes that we recognize that some markets are demanding that their advisors (GPs) have industry-specific expertise and commitment. The ring within the CPA-GP is divided into the *global function areas* that are or will be honeycombed with hundreds—

potentially thousands—of unique services (many of which have not even been thought of yet). Many of the specialty services will be delivered by the talent within the controlling CPA firm, or other strategically aligned specialized CPA and non-CPA firms will be brought in to assist. In this picture of our evolution, the CPA-GP maintains the closest ear to client management teams and therefore is the key to business opportunity. While specialization may be more lucrative in the short term than maintaining a general advisory role, the more highly specialized the practice, the more dependent it will become on the GP's referral. Just like the GP in the medical profession, after a decade of change within our profession, the CPA-GP will be the critical position to hold for long-term business opportunity. The CPA-GP will become the business services gatekeeper. And as gatekeepers, one of the most critical skills required to defend this position will be an ability to help organizations facilitate change (which not only has to be a foundation skill for our profession, but is a fundamental component in the skill set of the consulting framework).

The Minimum-Transition Requirement

In order to make the transition to a consulting-focused accounting firm, at a minimum you need to have—

- Management commitment.
- A belief that consulting is *required* to stay in step with the profession.
- An understanding that your maximum return on investment will be earned only when everyone within the firm incorporates a future-focused or advisory mind-set toward the client work they perform.
- The patience to sow consulting service seeds throughout the client base, and harvest those which experience exceptional interest or growth into consulting packages.

While this transition demands a great investment of your firm's time and energy, the rewards far outweigh the costs.

Consulting provides you with a value-adding service delivery mechanism and a marketing platform to ensure your clients can differentiate you from all the others. It forces everyone within the firm to not only analyze where your clients have been, but even more important, where they are going. Consulting creates loyalty because it is apparent that both you and your clients have a common goal—their future. It enhances client satisfaction because your umbrella of services is more encompassing. And what results from all of this is—

- Greater client retention.
- Increased revenues per client.
- A rock-solid foundation positioning you and your firm for the future.

Chapter 3

Why Take the Risk?

Everywhere you go, you can find CPAs frustrated with the business of consulting. And everywhere you turn, another reason why you shouldn't bother formalizing this service is expressed. Here are a few comments that might ring a familiar bell:

- "My small business clients can't afford to pay for consulting. Even though we provide the service, it's just never been profitable. So we try to give a little free advice now and then, and hope we'll be remembered when there is more fat in the consulting budget."
- "Many of our small-business clients occasionally call and ask us a few questions. We don't bother recording the time because it doesn't amount to much."
- "We give away our consulting time throughout the year and adjust our year-end tax fees accordingly."
- "Our clients don't think of us for help in solving business problems. We are their accountants. They have a very narrow view of what we can offer."
- "I have a small firm and I don't have the luxury of being able to offer numerous niche services outside of traditional accounting."
- "Between tax returns, financial statements, and audits, we don't have time to worry about the few extra bucks we can make from consulting. Besides, we make a good living doing exactly what we're doing."

These are just a few remarks we've heard too many times. Unfortunately, there are many reasons why the *implementation of consulting services* and the *realization of increased revenues* has fallen short of expectations. The first and foremost is—CPAs haven't had to deliver consulting services to remain viable or profitable. So if we don't have to, why take the risk? Consulting is not a sure thing, as exemplified by the fact that many firms have already tried, failed and abandoned their consulting expansion. Since success is not automatic, why bother at all? Well, here are a few issues to consider.

Revenue Growth

Traditionally, the typical CPA practice has concentrated on taxes, financial statement preparation, and audit services. Each of these areas has seen revenue stagnation or decline during the past ten years. Since the reduction of tax rates and the diminution of tax shelters during the mid-1980s, the average tax return isn't quite as lengthy or complicated as it once was. This obviously has had a negative impact on gross revenues. If the political rhetoric regarding the implementation of a "flat tax" (or the underlying drive for simplicity) actually becomes law, tax return fees would most likely continue to deteriorate. As for financial statement preparation (or write-up work)—CPAs have been unloading this chore for years due to its low profit margin. Even if you have been shrewd enough to have developed a profitable way to deliver this service, the proliferation of computer hardware and software is moving this function back into the client's office, and for small businesses, into the home.

Further impacting the profitability of tax and financial statement preparation services is the growth of non-CPA providers, such as American Express Tax and Business Services, H&R Block, and thousands of local competitors. Marketing textbooks would describe the current state of our financial marketplace as "mature," which is characterized by elements such as the following:

- Numerous competitors
- Slow to flat growth of the market

- Niche marketers who target narrow, well-defined, under-served segments of the market
- A basically undifferentiated product with stylistic rather than functional nuances
- New business for one firm often the result of lost business from another
- Falling prices
- Shrinking profit margins

Look this up in any textbook. Our profession is not undergoing a unique phenomenon, we are simply experiencing a stage in the well-known model of the product-service life cycle. History gives us insight as to what is likely to happen next. More advertising dollars will be spent attempting to entice the consumer, special offers and promotional pricing (discounting) will be used to attract new business, and marginal competitors will begin dropping out of the marketplace. Consider as evidence American Express's "satisfaction guarantee." If clients are not satisfied with the work, they don't have to pay for it. These kind of marketing nuances are not only to be expected in mature markets, you can count on them continuing and becoming even more dramatic as time goes on. And each time a competitor changes the game, the bar is set just a little higher while simultaneously challenging the industry to react.

If this weren't doom-and-gloom enough, consider the entry of players like IBM, AT&T, EDS, Hewlett-Packard, and many others, which have clearly entered the market on the advice side of our business. If you think these organizations will stop at delivering high-level management assistance, you're kidding yourself. These companies want what you have . . . something you take minimal advantage of . . . called *account control*. Account control gives them easy access to management's ear. You can bet these corporations will push deeper and deeper into your client's organization with services similar to yours until there is no more meat left on the bone. Years of business experience has taught them that it is far more profitable to sell additional complementary products or services (product or service extension) to an existing customer than to find a new one.

Next, let's discuss the viability of audits. The procedures and requirements are constantly becoming more stringent. When you add this to the skyrocketing liability insurance premiums and peer review costs associated with auditing, you'll find that this revenue source has lost much of its appeal too. It is at this point that we hear the argument, "While audits have lost some of their appeal, at least they're not under siege by outsiders, like tax and bookkeeping services. This is one place where CPAs need to make their stand. Assurance services are our only protected area."

We do believe that assurance services, like audits, will continue to be protected. However, what most CPAs fail to see is that the traditional audit is falling out of grace. The information contained in these examinations is not only too old, but too slow in arriving for review. Most of the decisions pertaining to this information have long since been made by the time the reports are available. To make matters worse, electronic transaction flow is evolving in such a way that it makes this reporting seem even more useless.

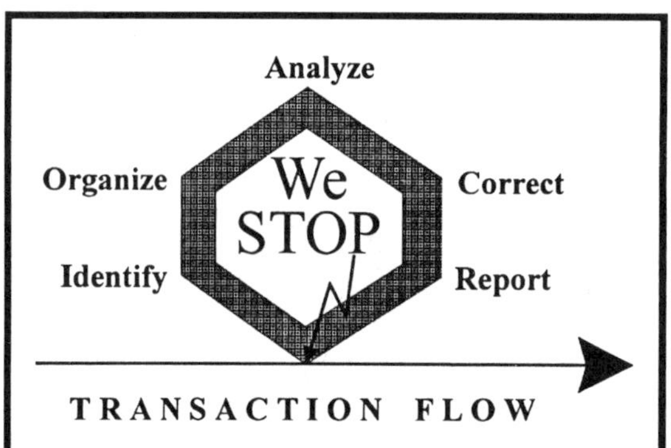

Consider the graphic to the left. Historically, CPAs have had the luxury of stopping transaction flow, then *identifying*, *organizing*, *analyzing*, and *correcting those in error*, and finally, *sharing their findings*. This system of picking a point in time, pretending to be able to stop the world, and then determining the viability of a business has long outlived its usefulness. In today's fast-paced economic climate, information indicating that a company was financially sound six months ago does not provide the due diligence required to know whether to lend or invest in that organization today.

This creates a tremendous need for more timely information. In response to that need, our experience shows that at least 5 percent of the nation's businesses (conservatively) submit summary data on a daily or weekly basis to analysts, investors, banks, and so on. Assuming this trend continues in the future, as more outsiders adopt this method for staying informed about a company's progress, CPAs will have to learn to work with moving, not stagnate, information. This will create an intense demand to be able to validate the reliability of the data-capturing and communicating systems, not the data itself. AICPA's new Assurance Service WebTrust is a great example of this. Unfortunately, the audit as we now know it does not remotely address this dilemma.

That's why it is not surprising that the AICPA's Special Committee on Assurance Services recently proposed that the financial audit will soon be replaced by a broader *information audit*. No one knows exactly when this will sweep the financial marketplace, but those who look to audits for assurance, such as banks, the SEC, and investors, are not satisfied with the out-of-date, narrowly focused, historical review of a company's health.

In a recent edition of *The CPA Letter* (January/February 1996), the Special Committee on Assurance Services stated:

> To seize future opportunities, CPAs must recognize consumers' information needs and the changes in their demands. New services must be designed to meet decision makers' vital needs.
>
> In the future, CPAs will likely find that:
>
> - The power to decide information content will shift from producers of information (such as preparers and auditors) to consumers (managers, investors, creditors and other decision makers).
> - Information technology advances will both enable and drive change in decision makers' needs and the services CPAs provide.
> - There will be many providers of information for decision making. CPAs will have to compete to furnish many new services in a non-regulated, market-driven environment very different from the current market.
>
> To ensure a brighter economic future, CPAs must:
>
> - Capitalize on their strengths to expand their service offerings.
> - Design services that are based on what users need.

What this says to us is that the traditional audit will still be protected, it's just that nobody will be buying that product or service. Keep in mind that the demand for many of our traditional services is not consumer driven; the demand is compliance driven. And when those demanding compliance change their product or service requirements, such as banks requiring an information audit rather than a financial audit, then *overnight*, the viability of some of our traditional services will dissipate.

Given all of this, holding on to traditional accounting as your flagship service seems to be shortsighted. We are not saying for a minute that you should stop performing the services on which our reputation has been built. Traditional services help you keep your current clients and also help bring in new clients. However, we are saying that the future, as well as additional revenue sources, lies in the expansion of our core services.

Account Control

Another reason to plunge your firm into consulting is *protection of your client base.* This is critical to your firm's future survival. Why? Because it is a lot easier, not to mention more profitable, to sell your current clients additional services than it is to attract new clients. As trusted business advisors deliver one service, logical extensions of that service are easily identified, sold, and then delivered (service extension). Our accidental application of marketing theory is one of the main reasons why CPAs have not been devastated by the shrinking fees for tax, financial statement, and audit services—expansion of services horizontally. During the past fifteen years, our profession has been fairly creative in offering new services to existing clients. This has not only increased our average revenue per client, but enhanced loyalty as well. Service extension is most successful when you have account control. Account control occurs when you have easy access to management's ear and management considers you to be a trusted advisor to the organization. Consider this common scenario:

> You are having lunch with a good client and he says to you, "I feel like my company is drifting. While we are certainly

making good money, it seems all we ever have time to do is put out fires that are burning out of control."

You then respond with a really sophisticated marketing statement like, "Several of our clients have felt the strain of exponential growth like yours. What we have done that has really seemed to help is to organize and facilitate a two-day executive retreat. This not only puts the fires into perspective, but brings into full focus the priorities everyone should be working toward."

The client responds, "That sounds like something that we would be interested in. Let me talk to the rest of the team and get back to you."

You then go back to your partners, call them together and comment, "I think we have done this before . . . I wasn't sure, so I sold it anyway. Can we pull this off?"

This is classic *service extension;* because we are trusted advisors of management, we have the opportunity to suggest our involvement and close the deal before anyone considers that they have other alternatives. As mentioned above, service extension occurs more frequently for those who have account control. Unfortunately, the world is full of predators who want the account control that you already have. Many of those predators are other CPA firms. Consider these statistics from AICPA annual reports:

		(shown as a percentage)				
Year	*Total Membership*	*Public*	*Industry*	*Education*	*Government*	*Retired*
1980	161,319	54.1	35.5	2.9	3.3	4.2
1985	231333	51.0	38.8	2.7	3.3	4.2
1990	295,633	44.5	40.4	2.7	3.7	8.7
1995	323,779	40.7	41.7	2.4	4.4	10.8

Clearly, our two growth segments are industry practitioners and retirees. At first glance, it would appear that there should be more opportunity per public practitioner due to the shrinking percentages. However, in raw numbers, there were almost 45,000 more CPAs practicing public accounting in 1995 than fifteen years earlier. The most significant statistic is the approximate 150,000 CPAs working in industry and government, who are performing some or all of the work that was traditionally done by outside CPA firms.

This picture boils down to supply and demand, and our profession has been out-supplying demand for a long time. Consider membership in the AICPA. It grew over 100 percent between 1980 and 1995, which is a significantly faster rate than the growth of our economy. Even in the heydays of the early 1980s, our economic growth was in the single digits. And for the majority of the past fifteen years, our growth index has hovered around the 3 percent mark.

The point is, any time you have supply outgrowing demand, you encounter the "shrinking slice of the pie" syndrome. While the overall economic pie is growing, it is being divided into many more slices, resulting in less economic opportunity per CPA. The best way to combat the impact of this decline is simply to grow the pie. And we have been doing that through service extension, delivering complementary additional services to each client, thereby increasing overall revenues. Account control is why our service extension strategy has been so successful. If we don't protect our client base, thereby losing account control, we will be relegated to delivering only those services that others deem too unprofitable.

Consulting Is a Logical Role for CPAs

Another reason to augment your consulting effort is, *Who is in a better position to offer general business guidance than the CPA?* We regularly examine our clients' financial situations and have a fundamental understanding of their business activities. Logically, the next step is to take a more active role in helping them become more profitable, which inevitably leads to success for the CPA.

The most difficult part of making this transition is shifting your image from the person with the answers to a person who can contribute good ideas. It requires a change in perspective, from one of a purely historical view, to one which considers the past in order to better anticipate the future. How to make this transformation is a major focus in many of the remaining chapters in this book.

The Market Has Changed

Our experience is that today's client is more educated and inquisitive than ever before. This sophistication has created a new breed of clients who are demanding more than a tax return and a balance sheet. They expect more than a financial advisor—they are looking for a business advisor. *If we don't satisfy the need, they'll find someone who will.*

This is best exemplified by the fact that over half of our profession now works outside public accounting. And where you used to only find a CPA controller-type position being filled in a $50-million company, today you are likely to find a CPA controller in most $5-million organizations. If trends continue as they have, by early in the twenty-first century, any company with more than $500,000 in sales will be a candidate for an in-house CPA professional. Therefore, it is our contention that a transition is well underway that positions *the non-public CPA to become the single biggest purchaser of public accounting services.*

What baffles us is how the profession can continue to ignore the significance of this phenomenon. When you look at the typical CPA firm, it holds out its various levels of compliance services as its most significant offering. So tell us . . . *what's wrong with this picture*: Public practitioners continue to sell the same services CPAs always have even though—

- The person in the future that is most likely to hire you is also a CPA.
- You are trying to convince the client to buy services he or she is already performing internally.
- The company is small or financially strong enough not to have an independent compliance requirement.
- Industry professionals are desperately looking for assistance to help them perform their jobs, yet accounting is becoming a smaller and smaller part of that job.
- Management teams are more and more interested in all information, not just financial information.
- Management teams are constantly pushing compliance reporting to the bottom of their priority list.

To put this into a more personal perspective, do you as a public accountant hire an outside CPA firm to help you with your financial statements? Of course not! Typically, when CPA firms hire professional services, they hire people to help—

- Complete projects that require more time than they have available.
- Perform tasks or functions for which they do not have the skills.

This same criteria should be used to determine the kind of services you could and should be offering to our future marketplace, non-public CPAs. We say the following with a deep concern, as the author has heard this comment thousands of times through his experience as a facilitator of industry CPA meetings over the past sixteen years:

> *Public practitioners have consistently diminished in stature as a source for assistance in the eyes of the industry CPA.*

It is generally perceived by our industry counterparts that public practitioners are too narrowly, too historically, and too nontechnologically focused to be a significant value-add in helping them perform their jobs. Quite simply, the market has changed. If we continue to ignore the new paradigm, the most significant purchaser of our services *will stop* looking to us for assistance.

Organizational Opportunities

Consulting work can be more enjoyable, demanding, exciting, and frustrating than traditional compliance work. This intensity often acts as a catalyst to revive and rejuvenate the interest and focus of disenchanted management and staff.

So if you, as a firm, want to attract and retain talented CPAs, you need to be able to offer opportunities and new challenges. Consulting does just that. The additional revenue potential not only provides room for new talent inhouse, but creates management positions as well. This expansion, in turn, secures a retirement funding source. Retirement then creates additional openings.

Why Bother With Consulting?

To answer this question we offer the following:

> *Those who maintain a traditional CPA practice will continue to do well in the short-term, but will struggle in the future. You can expect the public accountants' services and rates to be increasingly challenged by non-CPAs. The demand for services will shift from a historical-focused service, to a future-focused one. The growth of CPAs working in industry will call for a change in service offerings. In order to create differentiation, specialization within our industry will likely flourish, as has already begun. Our competitive edge lies in fine tuning those areas that best utilize our unique training and experience. Consulting is the flagship service that maintains and sharpens that edge.*

Section 2

The Consulting Framework

Chapter 4
Developing Your Self Skills

While it seems an odd place to start, identifying client opportunities begins with a better understanding of ourselves. In order to identify and service the needs of our clients from a consulting perspective, we have to change our role from that of providing answers (acting as an expert) to one of being an information springboard or idea facilitator (acting as an advisor).

This requires the highest degree of communication and persuasion expertise. And in order to maximize both of these, we have to first learn what makes us tick, how we react, when, why, and what messages we send, what makes us defensive, and much more. The more we know about ourselves, the better we can control the messages we send . . . and the more accurately we can interpret the messages we receive. This skill enhancement allows us to become significantly more powerful in our ability to get the client to talk openly with us, to listen and learn what motivates the client, and to be able to persuade the client to take action.

Think back to the consulting framework. By understanding ourselves and how this impacts our ability to communicate and persuade, we can improve six of the seven skills outlined in the consulting framework. Our "ability to learn quickly" is enhanced every time we can take down a self-denigration barrier. In other words, what often gets in the way of our listening is that ever-present feeling that we have to continually prove our worth. This causes us to allocate too much brain power towards finding something impressive to say. Repressing our need to impress makes it easier to stay focused on the client, which in turn enhances our ability to learn.

"Proficiency in asking questions" and "ability to patiently listen and observe" are exponentially advanced by becoming more self-confident. This self-confidence often manifests itself as knowing that we don't have to have all the answers and that we provide value just by listening and helping peoplc formalize their thoughts. As we become better listeners and more aware of the messages we send, our "people skills" dramatically improve.

"Creativity" is directly related to one's comfort in being wrong, which is discussed later in this chapter.

Finally, "competence as a communicator" is the culmination of all of these skills.

While the next couple of chapters are called "soft topics" by many, they deliver relevant and required information. These "soft chapters" have a better chance of immediately impacting your capabilities than any equivalent technical reading you can do. Why? Because CPAs are the greatest analyzer-implementers in the world. However, without better knowledge of yourself, and fine-tuned communication and persuasion expertise, your opportunities to help businesses analyze and implement are significantly reduced.

Treating the Symptoms

Since the beginning of the industrial revolution, businesses have been looking for ways to improve productivity, increase efficiency, accelerate profits, and so on. During the past few decades, many ideas have emerged to promote these efficiencies, including the following:

- Management by objectives
- Situational leadership
- Management by walking around
- One-minute management
- Team-building
- Quality movement
- Empowerment

Each of these has one common thread throughout, improving communications.

These techniques emphasize working together, getting input from each level of workers, and stimulating a friendly, cohesive, nonthreatening, work environment. To facilitate this corporate cultural change, workers at all levels have undergone training to learn more about the communication process and the various techniques which improve information flow. The problem is . . . gaining a better understanding of the technical aspects of communication is helpful, but only treats the symptom. The cause of communication breakdown, in our opinion, is the lack of understanding in each of us about ourselves. This chapter illustrates how your own self-esteem and feelings of worth are often the disease that infects and injures your ability to communicate.

Taking Down the Barriers

The first rule of self-analysis, at least if you want to improve your capabilities, is to shut down your defense systems. By doing so, you allow yourself the opportunity to learn what makes you tick and why. Many people who attempt to analyze themselves, unfortunately, just listen when the discussion revolves around their strengths and then tune out conversations involving their weaknesses. Obviously, this level of denial renders self-analysis useless. Here's the typical reaction to anything that touches an uncomfortable area: (1) *denial,* (2) *defensiveness,* (3) *rationalization,* and (4) *blame.*

Let's plug this series of reactions into a conversation with a CPA over improving his or her communication skills.

Denial

CPA: I have excellent communication skills.

Defensiveness

CPA: Besides, people pay me for my knowledge, not for being a smooth talker.

Rationalization

CPA: Why are you trying to convince me anyway? I'm a top performer in my field, and if this were all that important, I wouldn't have been able to achieve such a high level of success.

Blame

CPA: My professional educational requirements don't even recognize the need for training in soft-skill competencies like communication. How am I suppose to be able to focus on issues like this when I am constantly burdened with technical training? Until the CPA profession starts doing its job and recognizing that skills like this are necessary in the performance of my work, there's nothing I can do. I'm just a victim of the system.

These four comments, unfortunately, are not fabricated just to make a point in this book. They are all too real. Today, without the soft skills, it's getting harder and harder to get yourself in the position of being able to demonstrate your real knowledge. So we ask you to sit back, relax, understand that only you expect yourself to be perfect, and allow some of the ideas in this text to help you improve your communication abilities.

Self-Esteem: The Greatest Obstruction

Self-esteem, in our opinion, is the greatest obstruction to communication today. To emphasize this, consider a CPA asking his client, Bob, the following question:

> *So, tell me . . . what motivated you to invest in the triplex rental unit?*

At a quick glance, the question seems inquisitive, but harmless. The client bought the triplex five years ago, paid $100,000 for the unit, and payments including escrow are $1,100 per month.

In scenario one, let's assume that the real estate market is booming. Therefore, the triplex is now worth $180,000, the rental units average 90 percent occupancy, and the property has a positive cash flow of $500 per month. In this case, Bob's response to his CPA's question might be:

> *Well, I've been around the real estate business for a long time. When you know what you're doing, you can make some great investments. I bought that property because I could see its potential.*

Before we get underway with a discussion of Bob's answer, let's consider scenario number two. In this situation, the real estate market has taken a nose-dive. In Bob's locality, real estate has typically devalued around 35 percent. The triplex is now worth $65,000, the rental units average 60 percent occupancy and the property has a negative cash flow of $500 per month. Under these circumstances, Bob's response might be:

> *I don't really know why I made that investment. I guess I was grabbing for the brass ring and missed. Besides, everyone I know is in the same position I am. And those who aren't, well, they either didn't make enough money to buy in to these kinds of deals, or they're just cowards for being unwilling to take any risks.*

So where are we? A simple question was asked with no inference as to the quality of the decision. Yet the quality of the decision creates a stigma of success or failure that often guides the friendliness or hostility of the response. So using this example, where is the most common bottleneck in communication? It is often dominated by the egos or the self-esteem of those attempting to communicate. Problems occur any time people perceive their self-esteem to be threatened. Once threatened, the barriers go up and the protection systems become armed.

In the second scenario, while Bob's comments started out humble, he was clearly threatened. This was apparent because his response justified his decision, established himself as someone special, and concluded with an attack on those more fortunate. The meaning of what he said was something like this:

> *I know I made a mistake, but so did everyone else. By the way, this mistake could only be made by successful people like me. Otherwise, you couldn't have bought rental prop-*

erty in the first place. And those who are successful like me, but didn't get hurt by the real estate market, well, they're cowards and not worthy of my consideration.

It is understandable why most people become defensive and protective of a poor decision. But why do defense systems engage even when decisions are outstanding?

In the scenario where Bob clearly made an excellent decision, when you analyze his response, a threat was still perceived. Why do we say that? Because Bob made some ego inflating comments. Comments like, "when you know what you're doing" and "because I could see its potential" were not made for the CPA's benefit, but as verbal inflators to Bob's ego to remind himself that he is somebody special. The fact that the inflator statements were stated to the CPA indicates a likelihood that Bob was uncomfortable with himself about something. He might have felt threatened because he was visiting his CPA. He could have been experiencing some self-doubt due to some unrelated event that happened earlier. There are literally millions of reasons why people suffer from self-doubt. However, regardless of the reason, weak egos can quickly disrupt the communication process. Especially when two weak egos collide.

As an example, just think what would have happened if the CPA responded to Bob with similar ego-inflating comments. If Bob was insecure to start with, then he would soon become even more insecure. This insecurity would most likely manifest itself as additional defensive posturing and create even more barriers, impeding the communication process.

While these scenarios are contrived, they were created to make a point: there is a fine line between communication and alienation. Your ability to walk this fine line depends on how well you can manage your own feelings of worth and remain nonthreatening to the person or persons with whom you are communicating.

Communicating With Your Friends

Your most effective communication is usually shared with a friend. Why? Because the fundamental principles of friendship—trust, loyalty, caring, and so on—are all barrier busters. Imagine that your best friend just made the following comment to you:

> *You've been out-of-control from the first day we met! You need to get better organized.*

Your response to this statement, depending on how you feel about yourself at that moment, could be almost anything—from a sarcastic rebuttal to a thoughtful consideration of the comment, from ignoring the statement to having hurt feelings. However, because the criticism was made by your best friend, you are most likely going to consider it in a positive light. Why? Because of the *assumed message*, which varies depending on who made the comment. Consider the following assumed message (in brackets after the spoken comment):

> *You've been out-of-control from the first day we met! You need to get better organized.* [*But even if you don't, I'll still like you and want to continue sharing time with you.*]
> (*or*)
> *You've been out-of-control from the first day we met! You need to get better organized.* [*The only reason I am making this comment is because I know it will improve the quality of your life and I care about that.*]

These assumed messages of unequivocal acceptance and support minimize the chances that protection systems will be armed. That's why you can say almost anything to a friend without having to worry about the consequences. This nonthreatening environment allows everyone's ego to remain in the background, thereby facilitating a free exchange of information.

Consider for a moment the emotional escalation likely to occur when the *out-of-control* statement is made by an acquaintance. First, the assumed message is no longer cradled with feelings of friendship. Because of this, the comment will often be perceived as threatening and foster new meanings. Consider the following:

> *You've been out-of-control from the first day we met! You need to get better organized.* [*Because of your lack of direction, you always waste my time. And until you get your act together, I do not consider you worthy of my respect.*]

While these examples of both positive and negative assumed messages sound extreme, they are not far from the subconscious interpretations people make on a daily basis. Always keep this rule in mind when you are communicating: *9 out of 9.1 times, people will assume the worst possible interpretation of the words spoken!*

As an example, consider that your manager made the *out-of-control* comment. Here's a person who has power over your livelihood, which you can almost guarantee will lead to the worst possible interpretation of the message. This would likely conjure up this mental rebuttal:

> *How do you expect me to get organized when you continually dump more work in my lap? If you were a better manager, you would be able to schedule my workload more effectively.*

The result . . . a boxing match. Blow number one occurred with the *get organized* statement. The counterpunch was: *it's your fault for being a poor manager*. This situation can easily escalate creating long-term communication obstructions. However, all of this can be avoided if the message receiver can keep his or her paranoia in check, hold down the defense mechanisms, and respond as if a friend were giving constructive criticism. The point is, most of the time we let our egos or weak self-esteem guide our responses. When this happens, the barriers restricting the communication process become numerous, difficult to anticipate, and often impossible to overcome.

Self-Esteem: Awareness Goes a Long Way

Clearly, the self-esteem of those involved in a conversation is an obstacle. When you are attempting to communicate with someone, the lower his or her self-esteem, the more your communication has to be filtered to minimize the likelihood of negative unintentional messages. This means that you need to pay special attention to the words and gestures surrounding your conversation so that it is as *non-threatening, supportive, positive,* and *non-confrontive* as possible given the circumstances. Otherwise, a threat is likely to be perceived and the person you are communicating with may go on the attack. And you can be sure that communication is over once a threat is perceived.

Remember, weak egos have a voracious appetite. As long as you are feeding them, they will follow you wherever you want to go. The proper care and feeding of egos includes a number of almost seemingly simple things, such as minimizing the use of the word "I" in your conversation because it automatically focuses on the wrong person. Also, make sure that you allow others to talk about themselves, because by making them the center of attention, they feel special.

If, as the consultant, you attempt to build yourself up during a client interview, you may actually do more harm than good. Consider this example:

Consultant: [*Attempting to impress the prospective client with his expertise*] If you are looking for someone to help you streamline your manufacturing process, I'm your man. I've forgotten more about manufacturing than most people will ever know. It's amazing to me how some people stay in business with the stupid things they do.

Prospective client: [*Thinks to himself*] I've been in manufacturing all of my professional life and I know I've made a bunch of stupid mistakes. If this guy looks around, he'll see some of them. I don't want him laughing at me or telling his friends he can't believe I'm still in business.

[*Says out loud*] I really don't need help with anything. I just agreed to meet with you as a courtesy to a mutual friend of ours.

The prospect feels threatened by the consultant's ego-building comments. As a result, the prospect puts up his defense mechanisms and communication shuts down.

This may sound like a game you shouldn't have to play. But if you want to improve your communications ability, then the consideration and incorporation of these kinds of communication fundamentals must become part of your new daily routine.

On the brighter side, there are rewards. People with low self-esteem are easy to manipulate, control, and direct. It's simple . . . by keeping your ego in check and the spotlight off of yourself and on those around you, egos cease being an obstacle, and they assist you in achieving your desired outcome.

Don't be fooled, however, into thinking that individuals with low self-esteem are all meek, demure wallflowers. On the contrary, low self-esteem is exhibited in many different forms. In fact, very often those you might think of as having very high self-esteem may in actuality have quite the opposite. For example, people who are always dressed to the nines with every hair in place, may in fact have such anxiety about their looks that they are too self-conscious to appear in public in everyday clothes. An even more common occurrence is the person who, in order to cover up for a lack of knowledge or understanding about something, becomes aggressive and overbearing in order to reduce the possibility of being challenged.

So far, we've painted a picture that self-esteem is the single greatest barrier impeding the communication process. But it is not an insurmountable obstacle. The good news is . . . just knowing its impact goes a long way towards overcoming it. In the next chapter, we talk more specifically about the communication process. This information, coupled with an awareness of how our feelings of self-worth create barriers, provides a framework for becoming a better communicator. *It's not easy managing your ego while simultaneously trying to deal with everyone else's. However, in our opinion, personal growth in this area is a necessary part of developing your consulting skills to their fullest potential.*

Failure: A Sign of Real Growth

During communication, as soon as there is a perception that one party is attempting to place blame or fault with another, barriers are hoisted up so fast that information flow is blocked immediately.

Americans seem to have a real problem with the idea of failure. In many corporate cultures, there is such a negative connotation about making mistakes that a considerable amount of manpower is wasted on a daily basis in an attempt to cover up clues that errors ever existed. Often, just fixing a mistake would require far less effort, but that approach won't suffice for many unless all clues to the inexcusable event are also erased. The perpetuation of the idea that failure or mistakes won't be tolerated is not only an incredible waste of productivity and profitability, but a serious detriment to employee morale as well.

How does this attitude toward failure manifest itself? Well, in business, as with life, we are taught by society that to be considered a worthy and good human being, we must "grab for the brass ring." And cliché's like "anything other than first doesn't count" are used to motivate people into obtaining "the right perspective." Unfortunately, comments such as these really damage an individual's ability to learn and grow because the idea of failing is so oppressive that it restricts our willingness to venture into unfamiliar areas. The problem is . . . venturing into unfamiliar areas is how we gain experience and knowledge.

> It's funny, being wise is considered admirable, yet the road to wisdom, which is paved with failure, is avoided at all costs.

A successful businessman was interviewed and asked, "What has made you so successful?" He replied, "Making good decisions!" "How do you make so many good decisions?" the interviewer rebutted. The businessman answered, "My experience." The interviewer questioned, "How did you gain your experience?" He answered, "From bad decisions."

The reality is, growth occurs when we are allowed to make mistakes and learn from them. Why do we say this? Because when you make a good decision, do you spend time reflecting on why it was correct and what made you choose that alternative? Most likely, no! What our egos tell us to do is pat ourselves on the back and reflect on how smart we are. It appears that most of our learning comes from those times when our decision process fails and we attempt to determine why.

So what is the definition of failure? The definitions are as diverse as our world population. To some, it is merely "being caught" doing something wrong. In other words, as long as no one knows about a mistake, it wasn't a mistake.

This at least limits the likelihood of failing. To many, the definition expands to unrealistic heights. It goes back to the idea that "anything other than being first or being the best constitutes failure." What a ridiculous framework to try to work within. Can everyone be first if they work hard enough? The answer is an unequivocal no. Being first shouldn't even be a consideration. We can't control who is first. All we can do is the best we can; achievement within our own limits is the definition of success. Consider the following true story.

> Little Billy trained in martial arts every week. One day, he approached his martial arts Master and asked permission to miss several months of training. He wanted to concentrate on preparing for an upcoming track meet. During this time, Billy trained hard and felt he was ready for the big race.
>
> The starting gun was fired and they were off. Billy ran as fast as he ever had, but finished inches behind the winner. For days after the event, Billy sat in his room, feeling discouraged and beaten.
>
> Not sure how to get Billy motivated again, his mother dragged him to the martial arts studio to see if his instructor could help. When the instructor asked what was wrong, Billy could barely comment through his tears. Once the martial arts Master had heard the whole story, here was his reply:
>
> *Instructor:* Billy, pretend that the boy who won didn't show up because he hurt his leg the day before the race. Because he wouldn't have been there, you would have been the fastest runner. You would have come in first. Would that make you feel better?
>
> *Billy:* Yes!
>
> *Instructor:* [*Grinning as he put his arms around Billy*] Did you train hard and do your best?
>
> *Billy:* [*Nodded yes*]
>
> *Instructor:* Remember this. You do not become a true champion because of someone else's failure. You also are not a loser because of someone else's success. A champion is judged for his or her achievements working within his or her abilities.

Unfortunately, many, much older than little Billy, find themselves falling into this same trap. Why? Because the final outcome becomes more important than the process.

In corporate America, we give more credit to people who stay long hours than those who accomplish a great deal. We bestow rewards on those who merely stay within their known limits rather than on those who try and fail because they attempted to extend their limits. We empower our employees so that they will take action, yet we punish them when their decisions are wrong or inconsistent with our own. We have a system which expects consistent superior quality and performance, but does not allow the personal growth necessary in order to achieve that. It is sad, but most of us, at some time, fall into the "little Billy" trap and judge people by how they finish the race, rather than by the effort they put forth in relation to their capabilities.

Consider this . . . maintaining a positive attitude towards failure is the foundation of success. Here's how it works. As the successful businessman inferred, failure is part of the learning experience. Learning is essential to personal growth. Personal growth is critical to improving one's self-esteem and feelings of worth. Having a strong self-image is the key to effective communication. Quality communication is the cornerstone of building a team. And teamwork is the greatest strategy for prospering in any environment.

As you can tell, we believe that a positive outlook on failure is an essential component of any long-term success strategy. Failure is often the catalyst for major strides in personal growth and learning. And fear of failure immobilizes many to the point of being unwilling to try anything unless success is almost guaranteed. Let's put failure in its proper prospective.

Did you know that Thomas Edison failed literally thousands of times before his first success, the incandescent lamp? How about this one: Walt Disney went bankrupt and had a mental breakdown before he was able to channel his creative energy profitably. Looking at the baseball scene, back when Babe Ruth held the record for home runs, did you know he also held the record for the most strikeouts? Or even more recently, Ricky Henderson has both the record for stolen bases and the number of times put out while trying to steal a base.

Are these people failures? Not in our book. But in order to be successful, you have to cover some uncharted ground. This exploration exponentially increases your chances of falling flat on your face. So think of obstacles as opportunities to excel. If you succeed . . . great. If you fail . . . well, you most likely learned something, probably stretched your personal limits and experienced the growth of trying something new. Keep this in mind. As long as you put forth a commendable effort, you have earned the right to be proud of yourself regardless of the outcome because *failure is a sign of real growth.*

Recapping Some Potentially New Ideas

"Soft" topics like this one often communicate ideas that are easy to agree with, but difficult to implement. Here is a quick recap of some points to ponder.

- We have to change our role from that of providing answers to one of being an information springboard or idea facilitator.
- By understanding ourselves and how this impacts our ability to communicate and persuade, we can improve six of the seven skills outlined in the consulting framework.
- The cause of communication breakdown is the lack of understanding in each of us about ourselves.
- The first rule of self-analysis, at least if you want to improve your capabilities, is to shut down your defense systems. By doing so, you allow yourself the opportunity to learn what makes you tick and why.
- Today, without the soft skills, it is getting harder and harder to get yourself in the position of being able to demonstrate your real knowledge.

- Self-esteem is the greatest obstruction to communication today.
- Problems occur anytime people perceive their self-esteem to be threatened. Once threatened, the barriers go up and the protection systems become armed.
- Always keep your ears tuned to hear "inflator" statements. They indicate a weak ego needing to be pumped up.
- Your most effective communication is usually shared with a friend because the fundamental principles of friendship, such as trust, loyalty, and caring, are all barrier busters.
- Assumed messages of unequivocal acceptance and support minimize the chances that protection systems will be armed.
- When you are attempting to communicate with someone, the lower his or her self-esteem, the more *your* communication has to be heavily filtered.
- Weak egos have a voracious appetite. As long as you are feeding them, they will follow you wherever you want to go.
- As soon as there is a perception that one party is attempting to place blame or fault with another, barriers are hoisted up so fast that information flow is blocked immediately.
- Growth occurs when we are allowed to make mistakes and learn from them.
- Most of us, at some time, fall into the "little Billy" trap and judge people (and ourselves) by how they finish the race, rather than the effort they put forth in relation to their capabilities.

Before You Move On

Before you begin reading the next chapter, spend a few moments working through the *Self-Assessment* exercise on the following page. Identify skills you plan to improve and activities that will facilitate that improvement. This is a personal exercise, one that will help you create a strategy for personal growth.

Self-Assessment Time Line
Relative to Developing My Self Skills

Based on the information covered in this chapter, please take a few moments to assess your weaknesses. Then, using the form below, note any skills you plan to work on as well as a time frame to reassess your progress. In addition, if there are activities or exercises you plan on attempting, jot them down and note your intended completion date. This form is provided solely as a self-improvement tool.

The following are ***Skills** I plan to **Improve:***

______________________________ By when: __________

______________________________ By when: __________

______________________________ By when: __________

______________________________ By when: __________

______________________________ By when: __________

______________________________ By when: __________

______________________________ By when: __________

______________________________ By when: __________

______________________________ By when: __________

______________________________ By when: __________

The following are ***Activities** I plan to **Attempt:***

______________________________ By when: __________

______________________________ By when: __________

______________________________ By when: __________

______________________________ By when: __________

______________________________ By when: __________

______________________________ By when: __________

______________________________ By when: __________

______________________________ By when: __________

Chapter 5

Refining the Most Important Consulting Tool: Communications

Effective communication skills are fundamental to consulting. When you utilize good communication techniques, you gain a better understanding of the client's needs and desires, you become more effective at getting your messages across, and you develop greater persuasive capabilities. Good communication skills equip you with an ability to more accurately interpret both the words spoken and the feelings expressed by your clients.

However, *understanding* doesn't occur just because the message-sender clearly says what he or she means. It only takes place when the message-receiver—

1. *Clearly hears and sees the messages being sent.*
2. *Interprets them in the way they were intended.*

Therefore, communication involves much more than words alone because messages combine both verbal and nonverbal signals. Becoming more aware of these signals is a necessity if you and your organization are going to maximize your proficiency as a consultant.

Yes, we can guess what you are thinking after reading the last chapter and starting this one. We've heard the comments a thousand times: "This is not consulting training, it's sales training." However, this isn't one of those times. Yes, the skills it takes to consult overlap with those required to sell. The difference is that sales training is focused solely on getting in the door and convincing someone to buy. While it is very difficult to consult without getting in the door, and convincing the client to buy your services seems to be an important step in the process, consulting (using our definition) is helping clients better navigate their futures. This transition requires us to move from an expert to an advisory type of service. When it comes to predicting the future, we are *not* experts, but merely knowledgeable members of the decision support team. And in this situation, the skills that are in the highest demand are those that help—

- Identify a game plan.
- Gain consensus.
- Determine the implementation steps.
- Manage the variety of personalities involved.
- Facilitate change.

In many ways, the job of the consultant could be described as that of a "business psychiatrist." We get owners to talk about—

- What's troubling them.
- Where the pain is.
- What they think is causing the problem.
- When the pain is the worst.
- If there has been anything they have done that makes the pain better or worse.
- What they feel comfortable doing about it.

There is no question that our years of experience and expertise working with businesses are essential to this function. However, we feel strongly that CPAs either already have enough technical skills to do a tremendous amount of consulting right now, or can easily fill in the missing blanks with a specialized industry guide or two. In our opinion, and one gaining rapid support by those employing CPAs in industry—

> *CPAs are the premier business problem solvers and project implementers in the country.*

With our detail-focused, system-oriented, procedure-formulating, completion-syndromed, over-achiever approach to problem solving, CPAs are ideal to spearhead an assault against almost any ineffective or inefficient area of a business. That's why businesses around the country are changing the job description of the CPA controller to one that resembles one of chief information officer. This allows our industry counterparts full rights and privileges to deal with every area of the business . . . rather than limiting them to the accounting area.

Just think about the many problems you have helped your clients solve in areas outside the traditional service boundary. What allowed you to be effective working in these uncharted areas was the client's absolute belief in you. Typically, you didn't sell them, influence them, persuade them, or facilitate change using the skills we have been discussing. You told them what to do . . . and they listened attentively to their omnipotent advisor. Well, this is a relationship luxury that you can't count on having with a critical mass of your clients, and one you can't afford to have either.

The Omnipotent Advisor: A Relationship You *Can't Count on Having* as well as *Can't Afford*

Think about it as "substance over form." In this case, we define substance as being some unique combination of technical skills, experience, and expertise. We define form as encompassing persuasiveness, listening skills, communications ability, selling competence, and so on. Our profession's approach has been, if you have enough substance, then to heck with form. Or put another way, if you have enough knowledge, then who cares how you deliver it. For a variety of reasons, with a few of your clients, you and your personnel have been able to build "substance over form" relationships. These clients regularly pick up the phone and bounce ideas off you. They sit down with you several times a year to review issues "that keep them awake at night." You, in turn, deliver the "substance" with virtually no "form" by taking on the undisputed expert role and telling your clients what to do to fix their problems.

However, strategically speaking, how many expert confidantes can your firm truly expect to create and maintain? Certainly, a few of these relationships will naturally evolve with the more experienced members of your organization in specific circumstances. However, these are not relationships you can count on having with the majority of your clients. And even if you could build as many of these relationships as you desired, the risk and cost of this level of expertise, intimacy, and specialization is extraordinarily high. On one hand, it's expensive to train (if even possible) all of your personnel to be skilled enough to tell people what to do and be right. On the other hand, any employees that even come close to achieving this unrealistic level of competency are likely to leave and take your clients with them.

Given that it is difficult (we believe impossible) for any (and certainly not all) of your people to be visionary enough to consistently get away with telling your clients what to do, the liability that goes hand in hand with unquestioned expertise is ridiculous. Unless you are charging about $1,000 a minute, it would be hard to feel good about this approach as a business strategy. Think about it. Which strategy do you think carries more liability exposure: *telling people exactly what to do*, or *teaching someone how to become an advisor or facilitator who can help clients arrive at their own solutions*?

The answer is clear to us. There is no comparison. The approach of developing everyone's advisory or facilitator skills (consulting framework skills) results in a quicker payback, greater profitability, little to no liability, and will slow the growth of splinter firms. The omnipotent advisor is a high-risk, high-cost, low-reward approach to consulting; a relationship too difficult to establish, even more difficult to maintain, and destined to fail.

If This Is So Straightforward, Then Why the Opposition?

Because being the trustworthy, loyal, friendly, courteous, kind, brave, clean, and reverent Scouts that we are, we've been taught to "dance with the one who brung us." This translates to, generally speaking, the success CPA professionals have achieved is based on "providing substantive advice" while acting in the role of expert. Working with clients to *only* help them better organize their strategy, feel better about their approach, fine-tune an idea, identify necessary missing skills, and so on doesn't convert into a valuable service in the minds of most CPAs. These kind of services certainly don't fit the traditional "substantive advice" objective that we have historically endeavored to deliver. Our professionals have made a living providing solutions. However, in the business advisory role *coming up with the solutions is often not nearly as important as asking the client the right questions.*

Our misperceived idea as to "what is valuable" gets us in a great deal of trouble. Reconsider the AOMAR client satisfaction survey results (introduced in chapter 1) indicating that clients are looking for *new ideas*, *customized advice*, *guidance and direction for the future*, and *advice based on perceived opportunities*, just to name a few. In response to this request, the members of our profession have screamed even louder for guides and checklists in order to provide this unique advice and guidance (putting greater onus on the CPA to become an even more specialized "answer person").

As we facilitate CPA firm strategic planning sessions, the demand for more focused skills sets rings louder and clearer than ever. The problem is . . . we've missed the bigger picture. Have we forgotten, or just chosen to ignore, the fact that there have been specialized guides, checklists, and methodologies available for purchase for decades? With this kind of support, why have firms across the country committed to increased specialized training, subscriptions to vertical industry information, and more, with less than stellar results? Because we are still trying to "dance with the one who brung us"—we are seeking the undisputed expert role so that clients will seek us out. Think of the arrogance of this approach. We think that if we spend a couple of months (or even a year) developing an expertise that we will know as much as or more than our clients do about the businesses they have been operating for generations. All the training in the world may not accomplish this.

If we looked for a thousand years, we couldn't find a harder, more costly, less rewarding, riskier way of trying to implement consulting.

This brings us back to where we were at the beginning of this chapter. We feel that the technical skills for consulting currently exist or are easily attainable or supplemented through currently existing books, guides, educational programs, and so on. The part CPAs have trouble with is all the rest. And "all the rest" is what this book is all about. The "soft skills," as they are so often referred to, are fundamental to delivering consulting. The good news is—*with just a little practice, everyone can develop the necessary skills.*

We are not saying that CPAs don't possess these skills. That would be ridiculous. Successful firms are successful because the CPAs have been able to communicate with clients in a way that motivated them to action. However, CPAs are not accustomed to selling and delivering services for which they are not considered to be the experts. It's one thing to talk a client into adopting a tax strategy that has a predictable outcome. Motivating that same client to restructure his or her distribution channels is far more difficult. So, to help you completely develop your consulting framework skills, we wrote this chapter as a primer to the "soft skills."

Communication Foundation

This section is on the psychology behind communication. We discuss four fundamental tips that will enhance the success of your efforts. They are:

1. Make your first impression work for you.
2. Be aware of the nonverbal messages you are sending and receiving.
3. Ask questions.
4. Listen.

Making a Good First Impression

It is scary to think about the dramatic impact the first few seconds make in an introductory meeting. The concept that people can, and often do, judge a book by its cover unfortunately has validity. People have learned to survive in business (and in life) by making quick judgments based on very little information. So in about the time it takes to say *this isn't fair*, you can appease or alienate a potential client without making a sound. This occurs because what we wear, how we look, our size, our demeanor, how we smell, and so on, all send messages. With this in mind, consider the five steps everyone in your organization should incorporate into the first few seconds of every contact:

1. *Look into your client's eyes.*
2. *Smile.*
3. *Verbally acknowledge the person, saying, for example, "Hi, how are you?"*
4. *Say the name aloud. If you don't know it, ask, then say it aloud—everyone likes to hear their own name.*
5. *If at all appropriate, reach out and touch—normally this is a handshake (avoid the wet-noodle and bone-cruncher handshake styles).*

In addition, continually ask yourself the question, *How would I like to be treated?* When this type of attitude becomes standard operating procedure, you can rest assured that your clients will start out with a positive feeling towards your organization. Dr. Karl Krumm, a psychologist friend of ours, put it best when he relayed this comment, "Always keep in mind that everybody needs to feel like they are somebody." So when you start out every encounter focusing on treating the client the way you want to be treated, you send the all-important message that he or she is special to you and your firm.

There are many messages that are sent and received during the first few seconds of an introductory meeting. Becoming aware of them and learning to respond appropriately are of critical importance. Some of these messages are verbal, some nonverbal, which leads us to the next topic.

Interpreting Nonverbal Messages

You can learn as much about what is being said by watching . . . as you can by listening.

Dr. Albert Mehrabian, a noted researcher in the area of nonverbal communication, estimated that more than 90 percent of a person's feelings is communicated nonverbally. Another communication researcher, M.L. Knapp, cited a series of studies that indicated that listeners tend to give more weight to vocal cues (such as inflection, tone, and pitch) than to the words themselves.

Nonverbal messages dramatically affect the meaning of the words we say. *How can we use this information to our advantage?* Well, it isn't as hard as it might seem.

The First Impression

The first step is to recognize the impact of nonverbal messages. The next hurdle is to become accustomed to constantly interpreting these messages, and to become aware of what you do that sends some kind of signal. For instance, how you are groomed, dressed, or smell reflects what you think of yourself, how much money you make, your level of education, and more.

Unfortunately, quick judgments such as these usually are based on stereotypes. Even though stereotyping is a form of discrimination, we all do it in varying degrees. We know . . . not you. Go ahead and tell us that you don't have a clue as to the income, political posture, or hobbies of police officers. Do they belong to the National Rifle Association? Are they typically Democrats or Republicans? Regardless of your answers, if you had any opinion at all, you are guilty of stereotyping. Each stereotype carries with it some combination of expectations and perceptions. These then become the ruler by which all comments and gestures are measured.

For example, many people still have a perception that CPAs sit in ill-lit rooms wearing little green visors and adding up numbers.

It's human nature to subconsciously group people into predetermined categories. So think about how your client is likely to categorize and interpret the nonverbal messages you are sending, like the way you dress, the formality of your office, the car you drive, and so on. The key here is not to change to fit a certain image, but rather, *to be aware of the messages associated with certain careers, possessions, and lifestyles*. This awareness will then allow you to take advantage of the positive impressions and adapt or overcome the negative ones.

For instance, it would not be advisable to drive a Lexus and wear a $600 suit to visit a prospective farm client. As a CPA, you already have to deal with a city image. Adding an expensive foreign car and a high-priced suit to your introduction would be disastrous. However, if you visit that same farmer wearing jeans and boots, you're likely to be less intimidating. If wearing jeans and boots is a deviation too far from your style, then at least take off your coat and loosen your tie.

This same "formality reduction factor" is applicable in a number of other situations too, such as touring a manufacturing plant floor or a construction site. The reason you need to pay attention to this kind of stuff is because you always want to work towards creating an environment that isn't distracting to your client. In other words, your clothing, grooming, introductory first few seconds, and so on, should not demand more attention than what you want to say or do.

A general concept to keep in mind regarding first impression nonverbal messages is that *it is very difficult to sell more than one idea at a time!*

For example, if your job is to better understand what is happening on your client's manufacturing shop floor and you show up in a suit, you are likely to receive heightened resistance. The idea you would likely be selling in this inappropriately formal attire is that you are a "Suit," someone in management trying to con the plant out of necessary equipment, funds, and so on. By dressing more like the workers on the shop floor, you have one less strike against you, and are one step closer to achieving the desired results.

For this same reason, women in business were alerted years ago (through books like John Malloy's *Dress for Success*) to the value of dressing in more conservative clothes. Why? Because a woman wearing a skirt slit half-way up the side was attracting too much attention to her appearance. Considering the concept that it is hard to sell more than one idea at a time, it becomes imperative that we do everything possible to ensure that what we have to say or do is not being diminished by other distractions.

The issues we've just discussed relate to the kind of first impression you make. And that's important. But ongoing body language, both your client's and your own, carries even more weight.

Ongoing Body Language

By constantly monitoring your client's nonverbal cues, you have the opportunity to adjust and fine-tune the communication experience to maximize its effectiveness. Here are some common areas to observe:

- *Tone of voice*
- *Posture*
- *Eye contact*
- *Arm and leg position*
- *Body movement (nodding head or squirming due to restlessness)*
- *Facial expressions*
- *Physical distance between you and your client*

When you are with your clients, pay close attention to eye contact, both yours and theirs. Strong eye contact shows interest, but if it is too strong, it becomes intrusive. On the other hand, if you are continually looking away, then you are sending nonverbal messages that are likely to be interpreted negatively, such as not being confident, or even worse, not being truthful. Obviously, at the same time, your clients are sending back messages through their eye contact as well.

We've worked with thousands of CPAs across the country, and this simple but important area of eye contact is one (of many) that needs some serious work. In exercise after exercise, CPAs exclude people due to sloppy eye contact. Some CPAs just don't want to look at the person they are talking to; they want to look at the floor, the walls, or the ceiling. Others have no problem maintaining eye contact in a one-on-one conversation, but when another party is added, they neglect eye contact with the new member.

Remember, it is up to us to maintain eye contact with everyone in the group, whether that is one person, or many.

Why? Because it's part of the job of a good communicator to manage your eye contact in order to make sure everyone feels included. By doing so, you also let your communication group know you are being confident, honest, and sincere.

However, a more important job is for you to monitor your client's eye contact. If a client won't look at you during your conversation, then there may be a problem. Maybe the client is embarrassed about an activity going on at work, or maybe the terminology you are using is too technical, or maybe he or she is shy. The point is . . .

> *Loss of eye contact is a signal that a problem exists. It's your job to discover what the problem is and then find a way to make it go away.*

Another message to monitor is arm and leg position. If your client's arms and legs are crossed, and he or she is leaning away, this could signal resistance. But then again, maybe your client is just cold. Or how about when the client glances at his or her watch? During a meeting, you always need to keep part of your mind focused on watching such nonverbal cues. It's important to note that gestures usually mean something. When you observe one (or more importantly, a group of them), don't ignore what you've seen—react to it.

We do not profess to be experts in the field of nonverbal communications. Nor do we attempt to dissect every body movement and stamp a meaning on it. However, when two or three messages relay the same thing, it's time to respond. Unfortunately many people ignore this strategic and valuable input and find themselves constantly misinterpreting conversational messages and being misinterpreted as well.

Controlling the Messages You Send

Not only should you monitor the nonverbal messages you and your clients are sending, but you should also *control* your messages. As the need arises, you may specifically manufacture some messages to improve the effectiveness of your communication. Here's an example of what we mean:

> If you are meeting with a client late in the day and you're tired, you might *unintentionally* send messages of disinterest (such as yawning a number of times or lazily sagging in your chair). Think of the message you are sending to the

client: "Thank you for coming in to see me. I'm exhausted and a little distracted, but I'll try to wake up enough to help you. By the way, you get to pay the same rate for my time as if I were fresh and alert." To prevent this misperception, manufacture a quality, caring, attentive nonverbal message by purposefully sitting up and leaning forward in your chair.

By now, you might be thinking: "*Let me see if I understand you correctly. You're saying that I should become manipulative and phony if I want to improve my communication skills. Well, I don't like it . . .and I don't buy it!*"

We suggest you think of manufacturing nonverbal messages as simply utilizing one of the tools available that can expedite better communications. Conscious utilization of nonverbal communication isn't any more contrived than walking up to someone and shaking hands. *Weren't you a little self-conscious and uncomfortable the first couple of times you stuck your hand out*?

The fact is, the controlled mixing of verbal and nonverbal messages is just a good communication technique. In order to communicate proficiently, you have to consciously work on it. With practice, incorporating many of these nuances will start to come naturally. Others will be uncomfortable. But over time, most of the once-contrived techniques (like shaking someone's hand) won't seem contrived at all.

The average communicator can start bridging the gap by consciously tuning in to the nonverbal world. Once you're aware of body language, it becomes easy for you to take advantage of this new information. We all do this now for the more obvious messages. For instance, if you see a dog showing its teeth, you quickly recognize that a close confrontation is not in your best interest. By continuously monitoring the subtle but ever-present nonverbal messages around you, *your ability to understand and be understood will improve dramatically*. Table 5.1 outlines a few basics of nonverbal communications.

Asking Questions

Now that you've made a good first impression and are on the lookout for nonverbal messages, you need to get a better understanding of the client's situation. Good questioning techniques can make a world of difference here.

Table 5.1 Nonverbal Messages

Positive Messages	
Action	*Result*
Make eye contact	One of the most important things to do. Establishes credibility and trust.
Include others in the conversation	Include all people present in the meeting by looking at them, and when appropriate, asking them questions. Otherwise, you are likely to forge an adversarial rather than an advocate relationship with those left out of the conversation.
Lean forward	Demonstrates interest in the topic and the person.
Use, but don't abuse, gestures	Makes the conversation more animated and higher in energy.
Wear clothing appropriate to the area and the occasion	Being a little over-dressed is safer than being under-dressed.
Nod in agreement	Denotes that you are paying attention and depicts a high level of understanding. Don't always assume, however, that someone nodding at you is in agreement with what you are saying.
Smile	A simple act that can quickly change the dynamics of any conversation.
Sit at right angles or next to your prospect at a table	Encourages the perception of equality and "teamwork."
Sit at the head of the table	Conveys that you are in charge or demonstrates authority.
Mimic the other's motions, attitudes, tone of voice	Often done unconsciously by the most persuasive of people because it reinforces the idea that "I'm like you," which is a powerful connection technique.

(continued on next page)

Table 5.1 Nonverbal Messages (continued)

Negative Messages	
Action	*Result*
Excluding people from a conversation	When someone isn't included in a conversation (this pertains to group dialog), such as with occasional eye contact, a reference to them, or questions when appropriate, you may do more than alienate them, you might create a covert enemy.
Leaning away from the client	Gives the impression of disagreement regarding the subject or lack of interest.
Pointing fingers	A threatening or scolding gesture. If you are going to point, use an open whole hand.
Fidgeting or playing with an object, such as a pen	Takes people's attention away from what you're saying.
Sitting across from each other with a desk or table between you in a teamwork situation	The desk is a barrier to building a relationship because it "feels" adversarial or authoritative. However, if this is the message you want to convey, go ahead.
Expressionless face	When you don't convey interest (like trying to smile, keeping your eyes open, nodding when appropriate, and so on), it is easy to disconnect with your clients, leaving them cold to the experience.
Standing tall when others are seated	This is an "I'm in control" move, which can be negative unless you are trying to create formality or assume authority. This technique is powerful in a conversation when you want to change the dialog from an idea-sharing to a take-action mode.
Crossing your arms	This delivers the nonverbal message that you are closed to whatever idea is being discussed or that you don't believe what the other person is saying.

Good questioning techniques lead to a gold mine of knowledge. This knowledge not only incorporates the facts pertaining to a given situation, it includes the perceptions and the emotions that surround it as well. This understanding is necessary because your clients often are not able to articulate what their difficulty is . . . only that something is wrong. They just give you symptoms. Other times, clients will describe some ancillary problem because they are too embarrassed to tell you about the real one. That's why you have to look at the whole picture—the words and the emotions—in order to be able to read between the lines. In other words, you're normally hired for two reasons:

1. *To identify the unhealthy condition*
2. *To help find a cure for it*

Here are some tips that will help you perform a better diagnosis.

Take Notes and Refer to Them Often

A client will often reveal several issues or concerns in a single statement. Written reminders will help you go back and address each one. Also, jot down any off-the-wall comments you hear. These may lead you to the real problems later.

We use a technique called the investigative tree (see the graphic). The theory is that one question often uncovers many issues, and frequently, all of them need to be addressed. However, in a normal conversation, without taking notes, you end up focusing on only the most familiar of the

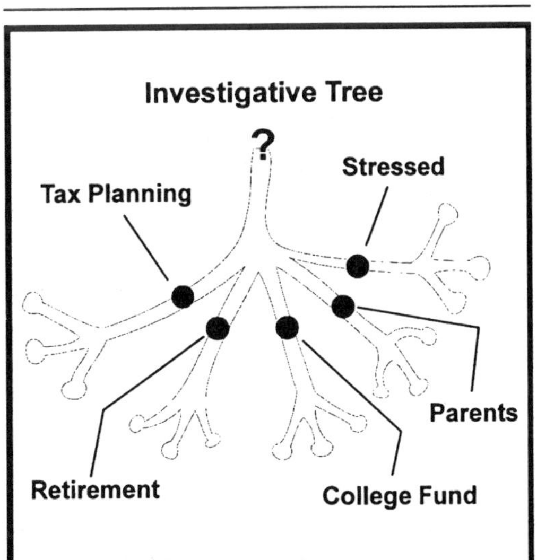

issues. The rest die a quick death. Note the graphic is like an upside-down tree. The root or trunk represents the question, and the branches depict significant responses.

For example, let's assume you ask your client, "So why did you call this meeting?" The client might reply as follows (the italic indicates branches—key words—you might jot down to remind yourself of areas and potential opportunities that require further investigation later):

> Well, I thought it was time I came in to see what I need to provide you so you could *finish my tax return*. You know, it scares me when I think about my taxes, that's why I avoid working on them. It reminds me that I have done such a *poor job planning for my retirement*. It's not that I don't try, but it seems all of my discretionary income is going towards *saving for my kids' college fund*, which looks like it is going to fall short of what I had hoped. By the way, have you heard anything about this new retirement community being built about 15 miles from here? I was thinking that might be *something for my parents to consider* as it is getting harder and harder for them to get around. Now that I sit back and think about all of this . . . it makes sense that I'm such a wreck. *My stress level* has to be off the charts.

While this is exaggerated for the purpose of this text, it's not far from reality. Here's a case where the CPA asked one simple question, and five important issues were raised that require further investigation. Why? Because as advisors, it's important that we understand what is bothering our clients. By always keeping this communication channel open, opportunities for providing assistance will constantly arise.

As a note-taking technique, when you conceptually think about your questions as an upside-down tree, it helps you tune in to responses that would create new branches. When you hear a comment or thought that needs more attention, write down a key word to remind you of the newly created branch and circle it. Continue on your current course of questioning and note-taking, and when you have reached the end of the current branch you are investigating, stop and review your notes. Find one of the circled words jotted down earlier and start a new series of questions until you fully understand that issue as well. By continuously identifying new information branches, you make it much easier to go back later to uncover important ideas or concerns.

The problem of skipping over important information is obvious in so many conversations. Not only do we overlook valuable information because we forget to go back and pursue it later, but we make the reverse mistake as well. This occurs when we string two or three questions together. If you pay close attention to the questions you ask during the next week or so, don't be shocked at how many times you ask more than one question at a time. Since the person you are talking to isn't using our note-taking technique, nine times out of ten, he or she will answer only one of the questions you asked. This is regrettable because often the two or three questions strung together were all significant. In our experience, the questions that are skipped over by the client are then usually overlooked by the questioner as well. Therefore, it's important to use whatever techniques you can to ensure that the questions you ask are answered, and that the issues your clients raise are investigated. This focus increases your chances of helping your clients exponentially.

Ask Open-Ended Questions

Open-ended questions force your clients to do the talking. A question that has become a personal favorite of ours for starting conversations with clients is, "So what's been keeping you awake at night lately?" Another standard is, "What do you see as your biggest challenge in the upcoming six months?" You can easily play off that later with the same question, substituting the word "opportunity" for "challenge." Once you ask one of these open-ended questions, let the clients take you where they want to go. Then, play off each of their answers with more specific questions that help you understand the issues relative to that information branch. This technique stimulates conversation and facilitates a thorough investigation. However, the key is to use open-ended questions to facilitate topic freedom within the conversation. Then use closed-ended (yes-no, or narrow confirmation-type) questions to verify understanding.

The following example demonstrates how to ask open-ended questions and then play off the client's responses.

CPA: So, what's been keeping you awake at night lately?

Client: I'd have to say lately it seems we spend a lot more time focusing on cash flow. As you know, sales have been steadily increasing, but that has the negative effect of incrementally squeezing our cash supply.

[*Information Branch: Cash Flow Problem*]

[*Information Branch: Steady Increase in Sales*]

CPA: You say your business is growing faster than your cash flow. What do you think is causing you to grow so fast?

Client: Well, we've introduced a new product and our customers have been very excited about it.

[*Information Branch: New Product*]

CPA: Tell me about your product.

Client: It's a portable power tool which allows one repair person to do work that, until now, took two.

CPA: Who uses it?

Client: Anyone who performs field repairs on heavy equipment.

CPA: How big is the marketplace?

Client: Our calculation is that there are at least 12,000 workers who could use our product.

CPA: Are you planning to market only in Texas?

Client: Today, yes. But we hope to include California and New York before the end of the year. If that turns out okay, then we'll expand throughout the rest of the states. We also have our eye on Europe.

[*Information Branch: Marketing Expansion*]

CPA: How many of these tools do you need to sell in order to pay the bills . . . given the first year's planned expansion?

Client: Right now, about 600. But we need to add more manufacturing capacity within the next few years. And with the combination of these facilities and our new sales offices, our overhead will drive that break-even number to about 1,800 within the next eighteen months.

[*Information Branch: Manufacturing Capacity*]

CPA: What are your sales now?

Client: So far, we are halfway through the year and our sales and backlog total 500.

CPA: Does this sales volume stress your cash flow?

Client: Well, I guess the answer is yes since it currently is out-of-control. We can easily meet our payables and payroll for the next couple of months . . . but after that, we'll need more money.

CPA: How much additional money do you need in order to handle your anticipated growth over the next twelve months?

Client: Our management team feels we need to double our lending limit. It currently is $200,000.

[*Information Branch: Increased Lending Limit*]

This conversation can continue easily for hours. The abbreviated scenario is used to illustrate questioning built around the words *who, what, where, when, why* and *how*. The CPA follows the client's lead with a combination of open and closed questions to facilitate understanding.

During this conversation, several issues were identified. First, in the near term, the client needs help planning for adequate cash flow around growing sales. This is complicated even further by planned new product expansion into new markets. In addition, demand is expected to stress the plant's capacity within a few years. All of this equates to a complex set of issues that will require lending limit adjustments and more. In this example, the consultant has barely scratched the surface regarding questions left to ask in order to fully understand each information branch. But this example makes it easy to see how a question about cash flow can lead to a number of other concerns, just by following the client's lead.

When You Are Unsure of the Next Question to Ask, Take a Few Moments to Think

Silence is a powerful tool in communication. Using it demonstrates confidence and intensifies the moment. An excellent technique to gain thinking time is to look at your notepad and look for the information branches we discussed earlier. Whether you are actually reading your notes or not is irrelevant. But since your client assumes that you are, it is easy to gain a few uninterrupted moments to gather your thoughts.

USING THE GLOBAL FUNCTIONS AS YOUR QUESTIONING CHECKLIST

There is one more technique that will help in your investigation. Remember throughout the information-gathering process that you are not trying to find one hot button, you are trying to identify all of them (within reason). Often, the first concern identified is not the primary one, it's just the most comfortable one to talk about.

For example, years ago, a new client called us and said he was having trouble managing the growth of his business. After we qualified him over the phone to verify that he was ready to hire someone to help him, we set up a meeting at his office. For the first hour or so, we talked about information he needed that he was not getting. He told us about the inadequacies of his accounting system. He introduced us to his sales department personnel and made it clear they were falling short of expectation. After all of this, with continued diligence in our questioning, he finally revealed the reason he called us. He was turning over his entire ten-employee staff about once a year.

This embarrassed him and was something he was not initially willing to talk about. After about fifteen minutes more of venting frustration, we were hired on the spot to find out why he was experiencing such ridiculous turnover. Before we concluded the meeting, he pre-warned us that his management style probably had a lot to do with it. After a week of interviews, observations, and investigation, we met with him and summarized the results of our findings—his employees thought he was a jerk. We addressed that particular problem by hiring a vice president with thick skin and good people skills. The employees interacted with the VP, and the owner limited his jerk reactions to the privacy of the VP's office.

The moral of this story is that, most of the time, there are a variety of open issues that need to be addressed. Some won't surface immediately because the client is uncomfortable talking about them. Others won't surface in the beginning because the client will attempt to confine his or her concerns to areas in which he or she feels you have expertise. And most clients view our skills as far more narrow than they really are. Therefore, we need to be prepared to bring out issues in a multitude of areas. That's why we came up with using *global functions* as a springboard for our investigation. Remember from chapter 1 that these areas include the following:

- Planning
- Products or services
- Personnel issues and employee benefits
- Operational efficiency
- Profitability
- Marketing
- Technology
- Financing
- Information management

So what do the global functions have to do with the investigative process? Simple. Use these functional areas as a checklist in the investigative process. While this next statement sounds bad, it's human nature, not client intelligence that we are referring to.

Clients rarely remember all of their problems.

A natural response to this statement is, "So if my clients can't remember their problems, how am I supposed to uncover them?" Well, maybe a clearer way to say this is, clients rarely remember all of their problems without prompting. This is why the global functions become so important. During the investigative process, you need to page through in your mind each of these functional areas and where applicable, ask more questions. Here's why.

> In numerous consulting workshops, we add an uncontrolled element to our role-play scenarios: we involved real clients. While this is becoming a common occurrence, recently we added an extra step to the process. Several days before the workshop, we asked each client to list ten areas of their business that "kept them awake at night." In addition, we requested that they consider all aspects of their business, not just the accounting area. Finally, each role-play (real) client was to send us a copy of their list the day before the workshop, with the items prioritized from 1 to 10, with 1 being the most critical issue to resolve.
>
> The day of the workshop, the role-play clients arrived at their designated times with their copy of the *problem list* in hand. We asked each of these people to relax and act as naturally as possible given the "fish bowl" in which this exercise was conducted. Our only request was that they put the list away once the meeting began. Remember, these clients made up the list, they then prioritized it, faxed it to us, and then reviewed it before starting the exercise.
>
> In our role-play scenarios, two groups performed the same tasks without being able to observe the other. The client was then asked to provide feedback on the success of each consulting group. Given all of this, you would expect the role-play clients (there were several) to be organized, thorough, and provide each role-play group with the same information. At least *we* did! We were wrong! Very wrong. The information divulged was different for each group because the clients were responding to the questions being asked. *Remember, the one asking the questions, the listener, is controlling the conversation.* So, not only were the answers different for each group, so were the priorities. And guess what—no group ever uncovered even the top five of the ten pre-defined priorities.

Just to show you how much our questioning and listening skills need to be improved, here is one situation that really hit home with all of us. One consulting group asked one of the smaller business owners if he had any financial projections to share regarding his business. The business owner responded, "No," that he had never done any projections regarding his business.

At this time in the conversation, the consultants were trying to gather information about anticipated volume. The odd thing was that the client had brought with him the performance history and projections of one of his similar sized competitors, which he wanted to emulate. We knew he had brought that with him so after the exercise, we asked him why he didn't share those numbers with the consultants. The owner replied, "I forgot. Their question was addressed at me providing my company's projection, which I didn't have. And I was so caught up in all the things we were talking about, it skipped my mind."

This is just one example of many. Here were a series of clients who were organized and prepared, and yet the information uncovered by the consultants differed dramatically. For example, with one interviewer, the client might say that the company's biggest problem is in collecting their receivables. With the next interviewer, the priority might be identified as ineffective automation in sending out statements and delinquency notices. Yet, with a third interviewer, the real issue causing chaos would be identified as the lack of accountability. While all of these statements are likely to be true because all of them are interconnected, making sure you understand the real problem is hard because the client will follow your lead when responding to your line of questions. This latest change in our role-play scenarios with real clients using a priority list has continued in numerous workshops. The results are consistent: clients rarely remember all of their problems, and even if they did, the priorities would change depending on who was interviewing them.

By using open-ended questions and following the client's lead, you will uncover a vast amount of information. However, the client is likely to have forgotten a few important issues. And some issues identified might be part of other much broader problems that haven't been uncovered. So it's a good idea to visit the global function list throughout the investigation in order to maximize your understanding of all of your client's concerns. Here are just a few of the questions that should come to mind:

1. *Planning:*
    - Does the client have a plan?
    - When was it last updated?
    - Does the plan drive the organization or does the organization drive the plan?
    - Does the plan respond to changing market demand?
2. *Products or services:*
    - Are the products or services growing or declining in demand?
    - What products or services are on the horizon?
    - How are the products or services continually enhanced to respond to market changes?
    - Are the products or services in the right mix for the customer base?
    - What mechanism does the client use to get product or service feedback?
3. *Personnel issues and employee benefits:*
    - Does the client have high turnover?
    - Do the people seem motivated?
    - Do they take care of the customers in a quality manner?
    - Is the operation open to litigation due to inconsistent policies?
    - Do the employees know what is expected of them?
    - Do people work as a team, or is there constant infighting?
4. *Operational efficiency:*
    - Does the operation flow smoothly?
    - Do steps, paperwork, functions overlap to the point that duplication of effort is common?
    - Are there needless steps, paperwork, functions being performed?

5. *Operational profitability:*
   - Is the product mix optimum?
   - Are the products priced in a way that leverages the organization's ability (quantity, quality, speed)? Is the gross margin in line with industry?
   - Is the profit margin in line with industry?
   - Are adequate funds, motivational commission systems, and customer contact procedures in place to support the sales volume required?
6. *Marketing:*
   - Is marketing haphazardly handled or adequately planned?
   - What is the client's market share?
   - What is their targeted market share?
   - Has the marketplace been segmented in order to determine the lowest cost and most effective contact strategy?
   - Has the customer been clearly identified by the client?
   - What motivates that customer to buy?
   - How often does the marketing plan facilitate contact with the most likely customers?
7. *Technology:*
   - Is there technology that can economically be used to streamline a function or process?
   - Do the people know how to use the technology that is available to them?
8. *Financing:*
   - Does the client have enough funds to adequately support R&D?
   - Has the client set up credit lines or established lending or investment relationships to support the strategic plan?
   - Does the client have the right kind of resources (both talent and capital) to fulfill the expectations of the company's plan?

9. *Information management:*
   - Does the client's information system provide timely, relevant, concise and accurate information?
   - Is there adequate communication within the organization?
   - Is the company information protected through daily backup and off-site storage?
   - Is there a disaster recovery plan in place?
   - Does the reporting system deliver the right information to the right people?
   - Do we report everything, or just on the exceptions we expect people to react to?

Questions like these lead the client into thinking about each area of his or her business, which then converts into uncovering more opportunities.

Avoiding the Impulse to Announce Quick Solutions

There is one major hurdle most CPAs have trouble overcoming during the implementation of expanded questioning techniques; we call it *premature speculation*. In other words, as soon as a client starts telling us his or her concerns, we start the stop watch. We begin running a race that nobody else knows or cares about. The objective of the race, which only other CPAs seem to be aware of, is to tell our clients how to solve their problems. As soon as we can speculate what the problem is, we change into our "answer-person" super-hero outfit and solve the life dilemmas of our clients.

All too often, because of our history as technicians, CPAs want to provide quick answers. This may be because we have trained our clients to expect solutions to complex problems in a minimal amount of time. But we need to recognize that the only reason our profession has been able to live up to this expectation is because traditional accounting is repetitive and well-defined by rules. Consulting is just the opposite.

One of the first rules a consultant must get used to is . . . *there are very few rules* . . . if any at all. Second, solutions rarely are all right, all wrong, all black, or all white. They usually present themselves in various shades of gray. To arrive at the best alternative, you have to factor in more than the expected benefits. You also have to consider the disadvantages of each option and the likelihood that the personnel assigned can and will properly implement the solution.

If the solution with the greatest reward is too complicated for company personnel to carry out, then a seemingly less attractive alternative may be the right choice. Following this same logic, if management does not believe in—or is not committed to—a particular solution, then reconsider the other alternatives. Remember, your objective is to help find a solution that works, not just find a solution.

When you consider that a consultant has to identify the client's problem, understand the pros and cons of possible alternatives, analyze the commitment and experience of the personnel involved, and plan on how to overcome any anticipated hurdles, why would anyone feel compelled to provide instant solutions? *We don't know why, but we do know that most CPAs are guilty of this.*

Maybe CPAs have an overwhelming urge to demonstrate competence. Unfortunately, premature responses, more often than not, produce exactly the opposite results. Consider the interplay between the client and CPA in our previous example. Many interviewers would have stopped the questioning process as soon as they had a nibble on their line. In our scenario, as soon as cash flow was identified as a concern, the typical modus operandi would be for the CPA to deliver a twenty-minute monologue on how to control cash. Another soap box oratory that could quickly follow would be one of slowing expansion.

The problem is . . . we too quickly jump to conclusions as to what is really bothering our clients. In the conversation above, while cash flow may have been the first issue to be identified, maybe the client has a more immediate desire to deal with the less than adequate lending limit. However, we haven't asked enough questions to really find out yet. A discussion on cash flow or slowing expansion may be reasonable, but at a later time. It's just that we need to be much more patient during the questioning phase of our work. And if you want to introduce a possible solution, rather than just pressing your monologue button, consider converting possible solutions into questions. Consider the following:

CPA: Have you thought about reducing some of your fixed cost by establishing distributorships rather than sales offices?

Client: Well, we've never used distributors. We've always set up our own offices. Do you think using distributors would help us manage our cash-flow crisis?

CPA: A lot of companies have found that to be the case. So, we should take a closer look at this possibility and outline its pros and cons. I'll make a note of that and we'll get back to it later. Now, what factors are motivating you to grow at such a fast pace?

Client: The demand is there. But more important, we bought the exclusive right to manufacture and sell this product. That right is contingent on our having a presence in at least three states within three years. Also, we need to sell 10,000 total units within five years. If we jump both hurdles, we will have satisfied the terms of the contract and will retain the exclusive rights to this product for the remainder of its patent life.

This sample dialogue reveals two questioning techniques. First, if a direct question is asked, give a short answer (tabling further discussion until later often works well). Then, resume the questioning. This technique allows you to return your focus to the task at hand—the investigation process. By doing a thorough job here, it's easy to understand your client and his or her business. The second technique is, when a thought comes to mind that appears to be a solution, make a note, wait for the appropriate time, and present it as a question. If the client likes the idea, you'll look good. If the client already has considered the idea and rejected it, you still look good for asking a logical and relevant question.

Always keep this in mind: the object of this investigative phase is to gather as much information as possible. You have the greatest opportunity to succeed in this quest when you're asking questions, not when you are giving answers. Why? First, your revelation may seem ridiculous in light of some aspect of your client's situation that has yet to be revealed. Second, most of the time, your client will wrestle with a problem for several hours or days before coming to you. When you spit out an answer after ten minutes of conversation, in a way, you are saying to the client, "Hey . . . thanks for coming in. However, your problem is so simple and trivial I don't have to give it a second thought. But don't worry, most of my clients are as stupid as you are." Give your clients the respect they deserve. Make sure you truly understand what's been keeping them awake at night before you give your opinions.

Once we feel we have accumulated enough facts, especially if the problem is complex, we give ourselves time to think. We like to allow ourselves at least one night's sleep on the information before proposing alternatives. No one will object to your asking for this time. If the problem were simple, you would never have been called in to solve it in the first place. Once some time has passed and you have had a chance to review the information again, don't be surprised if many new or improved ideas come to mind.

This leads us to our last communication foundation element. While improving your ability to ask questions is critical to consulting, this enhanced skill won't have any impact if you don't put significant emphasis on this final communication component.

Your Job Isn't to Have Answers

As a consultant, the client pays you for a variety of reasons; to talk to you, to bounce ideas off of you, to get your perspective, to help identify a problem, to help solve a problem, etc. But considering all of this, it is still not your job to profess instant solutions.

We know we are repeating ourselves, but as tax accountants, our job is to have answers. We are the undisputed experts. However, when it comes to running someone's business, we are merely trying to fill the role of being valued advisors. And as that advisor, our first job is to ask questions. Our second job is to listen to whatever the client says regarding those questions. Third and fourth, respectively, we are to ask even more questions and listen even more attentively to the client's responses. At such time that our contact has told us all he or she wants to share, then we move to the fifth step in the consulting process, and ask questions of other key people in the organization. This leads us to our sixth step, to listen some more.

It may appear we are toying with you, but not as much as you think. We have made a living for almost two decades billing for consulting services that are based on the premise that our clients not only know what their problems are, but how to fix them as well. For example, once a client identifies a problem, our firm members have learned to respond (almost instinctively now) with questions such as:

- What has worked in the past?
- What should work, but seems to be less effective than anticipated?
- What does your competition do that seems to work?
- What have you thought about doing?
- What do you see as being your biggest downside risk if you stay your present course?

Based on the client's response to these and similar questions, an incredible number of times, two or three good ideas will emerge that can immediately improve their situation. This kind of approach allows us to focus our job around helping our clients articulate, organize, and prioritize their primary objectives. Then, we assist them in identifying, cost justifying, managing, and implementing whatever solutions they choose. Do we suggest ideas? Do we provide answers to many questions? The answers to both questions is, "Absolutely." However, that input comes as a natural part of our involvement, with equally valuable ideas and comments being shared by other members of the management team. Most of the time, we contribute more than other group participants. But this is not because we are authorities, but rather because we take the time to capitalize on the knowledge workers surrounding us. Often, this is done on almost a covert basis. For example, if poor accountability regarding the budget appears to be the problem, we would ask questions that lead our clients to that conclusion. We might start with the remark, "Tell me a little bit about the budgetary process." Then we might follow with, "What happens if a manager ends the year 20 percent over budget?" If the client responds, "Nothing," then we ask, "Do you think that's an appropriate reaction in light of the corporate objective?" The point is, we try to leverage the client's knowledge first. After we have exhausted that resource, we provide whatever information we know, or request time to contemplate the information presented, and then attempt to identify the next step in the process.

We also believe that one of the best sources for identifying and fixing problems is to talk with the $6-per-hour workers. Since we are outsiders, through one-on-one interviews, surveys, facilitated discussions, and so on, we commonly get to hear, see, and review information many of the management team members are not privy to. There are a variety of reasons for this. One is that many managers don't make themselves very approachable. Another reason for communication breakdown is the manager-employee relationship. Employees are much more likely to criticize processes and management policy with an outsider, especially if they want change to occur. If the areas in question are sensitive or the criticism is likely to be about powerful players in the organization, then you might have to put in an extra layer of anonymity protection, with vehicles such as questionnaires, if you want to get the real scoop. Why does this work so well with a consultant and not with management? Because the outsider does not pose the same threat to employees' jobs as speaking directly to management. A third reason managers don't obtain this critical information is many don't pay attention to their workers. There is a status misconception you will find in a multitude of organizations that goes something like this: A $60,000-a-year worker is at least three times smarter, with at least three times better ideas, than a $20,000-a-year worker.

Well, this just isn't true. The $20,000-a-year worker most likely won't have the same level of education and knowledge or understanding of the business, and won't have the confidence, communication skills, or opportunity to package ideas as well to sell to top management. But make no mistake about it, there are plenty of untapped, valuable ideas waiting to be discovered if you just take the time to listen to this resource.

Keep in mind that it is common for management to identify problems, and reasons for those problems, that are different from those identified by their employees. Sometimes, management is responding more to the symptoms that the actual causes. The actual workers, the people coping with the day-to-day problems, are typically your best source for good solutions. Think of it this way. If you assume that the people working in the trenches have the right solutions, then it often becomes our job to find out how to make their ideas work. It's like finding a diamond in the rough . . . there are plenty of idea gems buried within the workforce that you have to cut, mold, and polish into workable solutions. This leads us, once again, to the conclusion that *it's not as much our job to have the answers as it is to know how to find or uncover them.*

Listening Is Critical If You Want to Be Effective

The last, but certainly not least, of our communication foundation tips is to listen. If you don't listen, you can't successfully consult. Listening also is the most difficult of these tips to consistently implement. Why? Because it's normally not the focus of anyone's agenda; *people spend almost all of their time either talking or preparing to talk.* For example, why do you think most people can't remember someone's name once they've been introduced? It's simple: we're so busy thinking about what we're going to say, we don't think about what is being said. To be a good listener, you have to be intent on listening.

We've tested this point for years with thousands of CPAs. For example, after spending fifteen minutes discussing the importance of listening, I mention that each participant of the workshop will have to stand up and give a three-minute talk on a recent family event. Following this statement, I will make a comment about a personal family experience in which the names of my wife, daughter, and two dogs are stated. There have been only one or two times when anyone has remembered all four names. Most of the time, it takes all the participants working together to get three of the four names! The reason—as soon as everyone was notified of their upcoming speaking event, *all listening stopped*. Their minds were focused on identifying what they were going to say.

The exercise described above is only one example of several. Even more regularly, we conduct a listening skills exercise that reveals the same behavior—that people love to talk and hate to listen.

In this experience, participants are typically broken into groups of three: a listener, a talker, and an observer. The observer's job is to make a mark every five seconds on the sheet we provide for a period of five minutes. The mark is charged to whoever is talking at the five-second interval. Given that, before the clock starts, I make it clear that the objective is for the listeners to spend as much time as possible listening. I also instruct the talkers not to take on a deposition style of responding to the listener's questions . . . that I want them to answer as if they are an interested party to the conversation. I do ask, though, that the talkers stay self-aware enough to ensure they don't ramble on and on to a single question. What we are looking for is two things. First, can the listener ask the kind of questions that stimulate conversation. Second, can the listener stay tuned into the talker's responses well enough to continue the conversation.

Based on the results from thousands of participants, we find three common traits. Participants have a tendency to—

1. Ask closed-ended questions (rather than open-ended ones) which restrict rather than extend conversations.
2. Listen for the purpose of identifying areas in which they have expertise rather than just listening to learn.

3. Change the role from being the listener to the talker as soon as a problem area is uncovered in which the CPA feels competent.

The listeners in our exercises, with the sole objective of spending time listening, still average talking 50 percent or more of the time, often up to 70 percent. After this exercise, it is common for the listeners to sigh a sigh of relief, commenting that they have just experienced the longest five minutes of their lives. Think of it this way . . . if we talk more than 50 percent of the time when we focus all of our energy on listening, just think how much we talk when we are in our normal conversation mode. We have concluded that many professionals don't need a client in the room to perform their monologues. They just need someone available long enough to identify which monologue to launch.

So now that we've reported the idea that nobody likes to listen, notice the hardship that's created in our questioning technique example. Every question, except for the opening one, came from the client's previous answer. *So by listening to your client, you not only gain insight into problem areas, but you receive clues for your next question.* Even when the topics go beyond your current background, by using our approach, it's rarely noticeable. It allows you to identify your client's areas of concern without requiring a great deal of specialized knowledge. And we find great solace in the fact that what we don't know today we can find out through research, education, or supplement through association, tomorrow.

Playing off your client's responses works well because you condition yourself to ask questions and listen, rather than talk. Therefore, you minimize the opportunity of exposing your weak areas. *Rarely will you stumble from asking questions, but falling is easy when you're talking.* Other ways of saying this—

- *It's better to remain silent and be thought a fool than to speak and remove all doubt.*
- *It's much harder to ask a dumb question than it is to give a dumb answer.*

Getting the client to talk, staying focused, learning to ask open-ended questions, taking notes, stealing think time, and listening are very basic ideas. However, just because they're basic doesn't mean they're not important. Quite frankly, the basics seem to be the first techniques we forget. Make sure you and your staff revisit these concepts regularly. And don't stop there either. Form role-play groups with other members of your firm to refine these concepts and skills. Hire an outside consultant to come in and work with your people to develop more confidence and expertise in this area. Sit down with one of your closest clients and play the game "Can I uncover your top five concerns?" (we have an exercise at the end of chapter 7 which could be used for in-firm role-plays or with a close client). All of this is overwhelming to some. But even if you are comfortable with the concepts, you need to allow yourself a comfortable nonthreatening forum to improve your skills. If you make this commitment, your firm's ability to deliver value-added consulting services will increase exponentially. Take it upon yourself to put together a program to help each member of your firm find the consultant buried inside.

Before You Move On

We have included two role-play exercises to give you an idea as to where your communication weaknesses are. The first one is a good warm-up exercise in that it is the least threatening. The *Listening Exercise* is meant to highlight whether you tend to talk . . . or get others to talk. Obviously, the more you can get your clients to talk, the greater chance you have to find out what might be bothering them. The second exercise, the *Musical Chair Listening Exercise*, is done one person at a time in front of your role-play group. Read the rules carefully. Feel free to modify them to suit your organization. The purpose of this exercise is to bring attention to the fact that we miss a significant number of opportunities to uncover areas for which clients have concerns. There are several other issues that this exercise uncovers that hamper the consulting investigation, including missing nonverbal messages, sending negative nonverbal messages, eliminating discussion by asking too many closed-ended questions, and asking two or three questions at a time.

Finally, and potentially the most important exercise of all, is one of self-assessment. Just as in the last chapter, you are asked to identify skills you plan to improve and activities that will facilitate that improvement. Once again, this is a personal exercise. It's easy to skip this step, but don't. Right after you have read each chapter is the best time to decide which ideas and techniques you want to incorporate into your personal consulting toolkit.

Listening Exercise

This is a listening exercise designed for three or four people. It is simple to do. Get a couple of volunteers from your office and sit down in a room together to try this. One will take on the role of Listener, another of Talker, the remaining one or two will act as Observers. The exercise starts with the Listener asking the first question. From there, the Listener, by listening to the responses of the Talker, is to keep the Talker talking. Theoretically, the Listener should have minimal time recorded by the end of this exercise. To do this, the Listener has to ask open-ended questions, note branches in conversations, and pay close attention to the Talker. Note: Talker, answer the Listener's questions and stop talking. While you are not trying to make it difficult for the Listener, you are also not supposed to listen to the first question and then talk for five minutes straight. After the exercise is complete, rotate so that everyone can role-play every role.

One of the observers is to act as a timekeeper. The other observer, if there is one, is to watch for nonverbal clues. This sheet is for the timekeeper. Here's how it works. In five-second intervals, sequentially place the abbreviation (Abbv) of the person talking in the next available space below. Common abbreviations might be L (for the person on your left) and R (for the person on your right), 1 and 2, the first initial of each person's name, or whatever is easier for the Observer to remember. At the end of the five-minute exercise, tally up who was doing all of the talking.

If there is a second observer, the sheet following this is for you to take notes as to nonverbal cues you noticed during the exercise. List both positive and negative attributes that you noticed, and at the end of the exercise, share your findings with the rest of the group.

Listening Exercise Timer Sheet

Listener Name: ______________________________ Abbv: ______

*Talker Name:*______________________________ Abbv: ______

____	____	____	____	____	____	____	____
____	____	____	____	____	____	____	____
____	____	____	____	____	____	____	____
____	____	____	____	____	____	____	____
____	____	____	____	____	____	____	____
____	____	____	____	____	____	____	____
____	____	____	____	____	____	____	____
____	____	____	____	____	____	____	____
____	____	____	____	____	____	____	____
____	____	____	____	____	____	____	____
____	____	____	____	____	____	____	____
____	____	____	____	____	____	____	____
____	____	____	____	____	____	____	____
____	____	____	____	____	____	____	____
____	____	____	____	____	____	____	____
____	____	____	____	____	____	____	____
____	____	____	____	____	____	____	____
____	____	____	____	____	____	____	____
____	____	____	____	____	____	____	____
____	____	____	____	____	____	____	____
____	____	____	____	____	____	____	____

Total time: Listener: __________ *# times 5 or* > *marks in a row:* _____

Talker: __________ *# times 5 or* > *marks in a row:* _____

Listening Exercise Observer Sheet

Listener Name: ______________________________

Talker Name: ______________________________

Note the nonverbal cues delivered by both the Listener and the Talker. Comment about their style, how they use gestures, what they do with their hands, how they position their bodies, eye contact, confidence in voice, whether they included everyone in the conversation, and anything else you see that conveys nonverbal messages.

Listener: ______________________________

Talker: ______________________________

Musical Chair Listening Exercise

Rules of the Game:

The objective is for the consultant to keep the client talking using investigative questioning techniques for a total of ten minutes. The exercise is played with three people: a consultant, client 1, and client 2. Client 1 is the primary decision maker for the consultant, however, client 2 is considered by client 1 to be a valuable confidant.

The rotation of the game is: the new player becomes the consultant, last round's consultant becomes the current round's client 1, and last round's client 1 becomes the current round's client 2. With each round, a new consultant is brought into the game and everyone else in the game rotates to a new position.

A *round* is over either (1) when the clock counts down from ten minutes to zero, or (2) when the consultant earns his or her third strike.

There are five ways for the consultant to earn a strike:

1. Any time an area of potential opportunity is introduced, the consultant is to yell "branch." If the consultant does not yell "branch," a strike is earned.
2. If the consultant asks more than one question at a time without correcting himself or herself, a strike is earned.
3. Anytime either client sends a nonverbal message that *could be meaningful* to the conversation, the consultant is to yell "message." If the consultant misses it, a strike is earned.
4. If a closed-ended question is asked without the consultant yelling "closed" before the question is completed, a strike is earned.
5. If the consultant doesn't make eye contact with client 2 for at least five full seconds every sixty seconds, a strike is earned. Client 2 is to watch for this and declare the strike as client 1 has the lead in this exercise and is likely to receive all the attention.

Musical Chair Observer Sheet

Consultant: ______________________

Notes: ______________________

Consultant: ______________________

Notes: ______________________

Consultant: ______________________

Notes: ______________________

Self-Assessment Time Line Relative to Developing My Listening Skills

The following are ***Skills*** *I plan to* ***Improve:***

________________________ By when: __________

________________________ By when: __________

________________________ By when: __________

________________________ By when: __________

________________________ By when: __________

________________________ By when: __________

________________________ By when: __________

________________________ By when: __________

________________________ By when: __________

________________________ By when: __________

________________________ By when: __________

The following are ***Activities*** *I plan to* ***Attempt:***

________________________ By when: __________

________________________ By when: __________

________________________ By when: __________

________________________ By when: __________

________________________ By when: __________

________________________ By when: __________

________________________ By when: __________

________________________ By when: __________

________________________ By when: __________

________________________ By when: __________

________________________ By when: __________

Chapter 6
Delivering Value-Adding Services

Preparing to *deliver value-adding consulting services* starts with taking a closer look at each of the words in this phrase.

Delivering is more than just offering or performing services; it includes the ability to provide:

The right product or service,
at the right price,
in the right quantity,
of the right quality,
at the right time,
in the right manner or fashion,
and at the right place for a particular situation.

The words *value-adding* represent a perspective. Delivering value-adding services means more than obtaining results. It encompasses the balancing of:

The benefits achieved
against
The costs to obtain them.

Value also denotes that a transition is in order. This transition is for consulting CPAs to move from primarily dealing with their clients' pasts to concentrating on ways of enhancing their futures. Because the future is not bound by rules or laws (as opposed to tax preparation, audits, financial statements, and so on), our recommendations are often merely educated guesses. Since solutions are rarely clearly right or wrong, good communication skills become essential to the consulting process.

Good communication, future-focused services and the proper balancing of costs versus benefits is the foundation to providing value to your client. But keep in mind that value is a judgment that only the client can bestow.

The term *service* is a reminder that much of consulting is intangible and relationship-sensitive. A major portion of the product consultants provide relies on their ability to perpetuate a problem-resolution environment.

Cash, Capacity, and Capability

Helping companies come up with implementable solutions is not an "at any cost" proposition. Therefore, we have to consider the resources of the client in determining how to deliver the services requested.

There are two basic resources we, as CPAs and consultants, have to offer. The first is knowledge, which has been gained through years of education and experience in dealing with business, accounting, and tax matters. The second is manpower; it is common for CPA firms to supply the necessary management skills and labor force to complete a project. Historically, these resources have been packaged as one service. But for consulting purposes, they need to be thought of, sold, and delivered separately. Why? Because, in order to be effective and efficient, consulting services need to be delivered in a manner commensurate with the client's resources. Simply stated:

Offer the services in increments the client can afford.

The larger the client, the more likely it can afford to retain consultants for advice, vision, and labor. Conversely, the smaller the client, the less likely it can pay for this bundle of services. Interestingly enough, Fortune 1000-sized businesses often provide their own advice and vision and outsource the labor. This has become a huge marketplace for large accounting firms, especially for the four largest firms. Middle market sized operations will just as likely be in need of the advice and vision as the labor side of the consulting service, depending on the project. And finally, small organizations will have a constant demand for advice, vision, and labor, but will rarely be able to afford the labor. Therefore, advice and vision are the focus for these organizations.

A question often asked us about this time is, "How large is a small business?" In our opinion, the key does not lie in the words large or small, nor in the number of employees or sales dollars. Rather it lies in the resources the business has available. Every company is made up of some combination of cash, capacity, and capability. When cash is the most limited resource within a company (for instance, if paying a consulting firm $2,000 in a month would be a significant financial burden), then we approach our work as if the business were small.

For these clients to gain the greatest impact from their consulting dollar, we unbundle each of our services and make a clear distinction between the costs for *advice, direction and vision,* and *human resources required to complete the work.*

By unbundling services, the small business can opt to supply its own consultant labor force. This person or group of people (usually part of or all of the management team) then work under the direction of the consultant CPA. Since the management team rarely receives additional compensation for performing extra assignments, this option allows the company to save a significant amount of money.

The idea of unbundling services is simple and hardly seems worthy of so much attention. But the problem is . . . it is almost second nature for CPAs to package solutions that contain both expertise and manpower. While this combination is easier to manage, control and complete, it is a luxury many small businesses can't afford.

The tradition of the CPA performing all of the work has evolved from years of practical real world experience. Why? Because CPA firms first focused on large SEC-regulated companies. As time passed, that support has filtered down into smaller and smaller companies. Now CPAs provide services from the Fortune 100 companies to the start-up mom-and-pop shops. However, many CPAs attempt to use the same methodology for delivering services to all sizes of businesses. The problem is . . . *the one-approach-fits-all method just doesn't work.*

For years, the philosophy behind consulting has been, "If the client wanted to do it themselves, they wouldn't have hired us." This is a fairly realistic perspective for a business that has more *cash* than *capacity* or *capability*. However, cash usually is *the most limited* resource of the small business. With this in mind, the philosophy behind small business consulting should be:

> The client has done everything they know how to do. They have hired the consultant to help them identify what needs to be done next, direct and train them as to how to do it, and orchestrate the completion of various projects.

The bottom line is . . . time-consuming, tedious, repetitive tasks have to be delegated to the client when performing certain small business consultations or engagements. This change in approach is difficult because old habits have to be broken—habits like providing both the brain work and the grunt work.

Consider this: Small business owners are the designated fire fighters, managers, salespeople, janitors, bookkeepers, and everything else. Unfortunately, this day-to-day involvement keeps them focused on the present. Since many small businesses can't afford the overhead, at least on a daily basis, of a visionary person (like a CEO or CFO), a void in the company's perspective is created. That's where consultants are needed most: to fill that void by helping the client with the brain work of planning, organizing, growing, and becoming more profitable.

Ultimately, the difference between delivering mediocre versus superior services lies in the consultant's ability to quickly and correctly identify the proper level of service (brain versus grunt work) for each client. Here's the process that we follow:

1. Identify projects: Determine the various services or areas for which the client has asked for assistance.
2. Break each project into tasks: Itemize the specific tasks required to complete the job. Sequence these tasks in the order in which they should be completed. Then identify any possible scheduling conflicts (yours or your client's). Find the skill level required for each specific

task. In other words, identify which areas require your expertise and identify which tasks can be delegated (preferably to your client, or if that is impractical, to a less experienced member of your firm). Next, consider the time required to complete each task.

3. Match client resources against task requirements. Your client has some level of capability, capacity, and cash. Evaluate each area for strengths and weaknesses.

This does not have to be a formal process. With small projects, this is a very quick mind exercise that you most likely go through, at least subconsciously, right now. The larger the project, the more important it is to inject formality in this process. The following example illustrates this three-step process:

> Todd, a new client, has spent two years writing a software program in his spare time. He feels his package has a great deal of revenue potential so he wants to market it. Unfortunately, Todd has very little money. He comes to you for suggestions on financing. Additionally, he would like to open an office, but is afraid he may not have the negotiating skills required to obtain a competitive lease. Finally, he says that he may need some help automating his financial information.

Your first step, as discussed previously, is to *identify the projects:*

1. Financing
2. Office space and negotiating the lease
3. Setting up books

Next, *break each project into tasks* and itemize the requirements. Continuing with our example, let's take a look at Todd's situation.

1. *Financing.* In order to obtain a loan, specific information needs to be provided to the lender. Although this can be time-consuming, the critical skills are (a) determining what information should be prepared, and (b) massaging that information into a marketable format.

Assembling most of the documentation does not demand a high level of expertise. The tasks might include the following:

- Identify the required loan documentation.
- Prepare a draft of each item required by the loan document.
- Massage the documentation to maximize its presentation.
- Present the loan package.

2. *Office space and negotiating the lease.* The actual negotiation of a lease generally is not time-consuming. However, the expertise required is high because the negotiator must be able to recognize a fair offer when it comes to monthly charges, utilities, common area maintenance, taxes, insurance, finish-out allowances, and so on. The tasks associated with this phase might include the following:

    - Identify two or three acceptable locations.
    - List the pros and cons of each space.
    - Prioritize the locations.
    - Compare financial commitment.
    - Negotiate the lease.

3. *Setting up books.* Setting up a small company's books requires a high level of skill due to the demand for accounting expertise and computer knowledge. Both types of expertise are required since Todd plans to automate this function. The time necessary to perform this task also is high. So, in this example, the task breakdown might include the following:

    - Verify that an automated system is warranted and feasible.
    - Identify the best accounting software alternatives.
    - Investigate which package is the best fit.
    - Install the application.
    - Create a chart of accounts.

- Design reports.
- Start entering financial information.

After the project is analyzed and the tasks identified, the next step is to review the client resources and match them to the requirements. Continuing with Todd's situation, we will look at the resources of *cash, capacity,* and *capability*.

1. *Cash.* Since this is Todd's tightest commodity, most of the detail work has to be done by him in order to minimize the cash requirement.
2. *Capacity.* Because Todd quit his previous job to focus on his software company, for the most part, all of his time is available. Todd's capacity, or time available to take on more work, is his most abundant resource.
3. *Capability.* Todd's skill levels need to be analyzed in relation to each of the three projects identified at the start:
    a. *Financing.* With a little guidance, Todd has the ability to put together a draft of most of the loan documentation. However, the cash-flow statements and breakeven analysis are going to require some extra coaching.
    b. *Office space.* Todd knows where he would like to locate and can pull together an analysis of his top candidates. However, he does not feel prepared to adequately haggle over the lease particulars.
    c. *Automated books.* Todd, as a programmer, has an abundance of computer skills that will aid him in automating his accounting. Like many programmers, he has a good understanding of accounting, but will need some occasional technical guidance.

The Balancing Act

Having reviewed Todd's resources, it is time to match them against the task requirements. Since Todd has more capacity and capability than cash, the approach is clear:

To limit his cash outflow yet achieve his objectives, Todd must do most of the leg work!

This makes the consultant's role more difficult because he or she is just performing the brain work: *planning, task identification,* and *project orchestration*. For instance, here's how we might approach this project.

1. *Financing*:
   a. Create a "To Do" list for Todd of the required loan documentation.
   b. Instruct Todd to prepare rough drafts of the assigned documentation.
   c. Once the drafts are delivered back to us, look them over for errors and suggest improvements. In this phase, the focus is to improve the overall marketability of the package—to verify that the package emphasizes the strengths of the information.

      For example, make sure Todd's many contacts and good standing in the local software market are highlighted. Check his projections for feasibility and thoroughness. Look over the projected income and expenses to verify that the anticipated profits are ample to repay the requested note. Help Todd with the presentation of his documents—in other words, assist him in preparing a loan proposal that can sell his ideas.
   d. Finally, since Todd does not feel secure with his presentation skills, accompany him to the meeting, and aid him in *selling* his loan package to the bank.
2. *Office space and negotiating the lease*:
   a. Ask Todd to select three places in which he would like to locate.
   b. Once these sites have been identified, have Todd create a list of the pros and cons of each space.
   c. Review his choices with him, guiding him by pointing out the relative importance of each item on his list. After getting an idea of Todd's needs and desires in office space, it's time to choose the preferred location.
   d. Schedule a few hours to meet with the landlord to negotiate a lease.

By having Todd do all the leg work, you minimize your involvement, making your services affordable. But most important, you can offer your expertise where it is most beneficial: negotiating and finalizing Todd's new lease.

3. *Setting up books:*

Since Todd is a programmer, he is familiar with software. However, he doesn't know much about accounting software for personal computers.

a. Give Todd a list of several systems that will accommodate him. Then refer him to a local software or computer store to find more information on each. Advise him to call if any questions arise during his investigation.
b. Advise Todd to choose the package with which he is most comfortable.
c. Next, instruct Todd to install the software, establishing the default chart of accounts and financial statements.
d. Tell Todd to print whatever information he creates. Meet with him to review it. Suggest additions, deletions, and changes to the information presented.
e. Advise Todd to make the corrections that result from your meeting with him.
f. Look over the corrected information. Finally, identify the monthly information necessary to prepare the financial statements and define procedures for accomplishing this task.

How Do You Find the Right Balance?

Obviously, the example above represents a simple situation. However, the general principle is always the same:

> Find the appropriate balance between *the requirements of a project* and *the resources of the client*: whether the resources are in the form of cash, capacity or capability.

In Todd's case, the total project is estimated to take about 70 hours. If the consultant performs all of the work, at $150 per hour, the charge would be around $10,500 (which is out of line with Todd's financial position). However, if you take on the role of *planner-project manager-delegator*, the consultant's involvement is reduced to only about 20 hours, or about $3,000. This approach not only saves Todd a great deal of money, but allows him to learn more about his business along the way.

It is your job to help your client find the right balance for each project. In each of your planning meetings, always be candid and set the proper level of expectation. *Remind your client that the level of your involvement is under his or her control, and that the more time you spend on the project, the more it will cost. Conversely, the more work the client will do, the less you have to do, which in turn saves the client money.* Whenever possible, provide your client with estimate ranges for the various levels of service. By doing this, you give your client the tools necessary to logically manage your efforts.

As your client's situation changes, so will your involvement. As a client grows and becomes more profitable, management skills may be more in demand than cash. Therefore, additional services (capability/capacity) may be appropriate. And that's great ... as long as the services provided are in line with the budget available.

A Simple Format

We offer this simple, four-point consulting format to help you maximize your effectiveness and minimize the consulting dollars:

1. *Meet with your clients and assign them tasks ... or homework.*
2. *From time to time, assist them when they call for additional direction.*
3. *At designated regular intervals, meet with your clients and review their homework.*
4. *Conclude each meeting with a new list of assignments.*

By keeping this in mind, you will find yourself delegating more and more work. And that is the first step towards providing *valued services* to the small business.

What If the Client Doesn't Want to Do the Leg Work?

Let's consider, for a moment, that your client has little money and no inclination to provide the time or skills to keep the consulting bill within reason. What should you do? This is the easiest answer in the book: *don't take the job*. Too many CPAs get burned this way. Knowing when to walk away is the key to both your profitability and your sanity. Given this situation, it's time to draw your unreasonable client a map as to how to get to one of your competitors' offices.

The End Result

By looking at each project and balancing each task's requirement with the resources available, a consultant can—

- *Deliver value-adding services.*
- *Make a significant contribution to the client's prosperity.*
- *Maintain high billing rates.*

The challenge in delivering these small business consulting services lies in *the CPA's ability to change from the doer role to that of project leader or coordinator.*

Your focus needs to be on working to improve your project management and task identification skills. The ability to quickly reduce a large project into bite-size pieces is paramount if you want to step up to the small business challenge.

Even though this strategy can be demanding and, at times, stressful, we feel consulting is still the most exciting and rewarding job in accounting. You're involved, you're contributing and you're making a difference in your clients' future. Remember though . . . *anyone can provide consulting, but few can provide real value*. And that's our constant challenge.

Estimating the Project: Pricing

Upon initial glance, this might seem to be a topic that should be covered later in this text. However, it's important that we cover it now. Why? Because we need to be comfortable with pricing in order to effectively deal with the questions that arise during the selling process. This book is organized so that each chapter builds on the skills and techniques discussed in the previous ones. But before we get started, please take out a blank sheet of paper and respond to this situation:

> You have a bookkeeping client for whom you prepare monthly financial statements. She pays you $250 a month. She recently commented that she would like to bring this function in-house. Your client is willing to use the same software you use in-house to do her monthly processing. What will you charge her to make this transition?

Now that you have written down your estimate, it's time to continue reading. We will ask you to redo this exercise at the end of this chapter in order to see if our approach impacts the estimate you have just completed.

One technique that maximizes your ability to get a commitment is *phasing.* Phasing is nothing more than breaking projects into bite-sized pieces. Each phase should have a logical completion point, one at which a client gains additional insight as to the probable benefits to be gained. Projects under this approach are typically estimated by phase, and while a general idea as to the total cost has been identified, the more tightly controlled budget is at the phase level. The client understands that each phase creates a management decision point—an opportunity for the client to stop the project, continue the project as planned, restructure the project, re-assign personnel, or make some other change in course.

When our firm uses the *phasing* approach, our first phase is almost always the "We need to get a first-hand look at what's really going on" phase, which is best described as *information-gathering.* Typical techniques include—

- Interviewing key personnel.
- Observing operations, technology, and so on.
- Conducting a survey (often the survey gathers information from many more than the key personnel that would normally be interviewed).

- Reviewing documentation, including financial, organizational, procedural, and legal information.
- Completing a simple organizational flowchart which illustrates the business processes.

The first phase usually includes the preparation of a general project plan, with a detailed description as to what should happen or be expected in the next phase. While that sounds easy, determining what you are going to do in each phase (even if it's just the next phase) can be a mind-numbing time-consuming process. A great place to start is to review the approach, timetable, and outputs from other projects you have completed. If your project is a totally new experience, don't get caught up in detailing the entire job; just lay out the objectives from a broad perspective, and only create a detailed plan for the next phase. At the completion of each phase, only lay out the next phase in detail. Why? Because even a project with which you are intimately familiar always has surprises that create problems or delays. Trying to identify every step along a road you may not travel is usually a waste of time. In other words, when the project is an unknown, we rarely plan in detail beyond the next immediate objective because we are so unsure of what we are likely to encounter. And by the way, we make this known to our clients. The clients not only understand, but they get a better understanding of how we work while we simultaneously gain more project freedom and flexibility.

For example, let's assume one of our clients wants our firm to help with their marketing program. As stated above, the first phase is the "let's get a first-hand look at what's really going on." While we would outline generally what is entailed in a marketing plan, going much further than that doesn't make much sense until we know how their organization works, the strengths and weaknesses of their products or services, as well as what's been done in the past. It would be a waste of time to detail much of a marketing plan early on because so much of it could easily be rewritten by the results and findings of each phase, especially phase I. With this in mind, some guidelines to follow when using the phasing approach are:

- Generate a project timetable or time-frame.
- Break the project into reportable phases.
- Make sure each phase has a logical completion, one from which the client obtains new information as to the benefits that should be attainable.
- Hold each phase to less than $5,000 ($2,000 to $3,000 is even better).
- Plan an oral presentation of the progress and findings at the end of each phase (and build that into your pricing).
- Utilize the client's personnel wherever possible, to manage the phases and total project cost.
- Identify the tasks required in detail for the next phase.
- Eliminate phases in four- to eight-hour blocks of time. If this is a very small project, two-hour blocks would be appropriate. Don't try to estimate price down to the half hour; there are too many surprises.

Pricing Factors

When it comes to pricing a phase or a project, there are several factors that drive price up or down. Consider each of the following (as well as combinations of them) before quoting any prices to a client regarding a potential consulting engagement.

Time Frame. When will the project start and when does it have to be completed? The narrower the time frame, the higher the rate. The longer the time frame, the more flexible the rate. When a client calls you and demands your availability the day after tomorrow, and you have to make arrangements to accommodate that demand, then it makes sense that your time should be billed at premium rates. If a project calls for you to complete it in record time, or under tight deadlines, once again, the price for your work should go up.

Client Work. Is the client contributing personnel, or is your firm supplying all of the labor? Logically, the more work your personnel are expected to perform, the higher the project price tag, but the more leverage you have. Therefore, your personnel hourly rate flexibility is likely to increase. The more work the client is willing to perform, the lower the project price tag and the less flexibility you should allow your rate structure. Why? Because when you are leveraging the use of your client's personnel, your work is going to be confined primarily to high level project planning, orchestrating, managing, coordinating, etc., which is premium rate work.

Documentation. What are the documentation requirements? The more documentation required (especially if numerous memos must be entered into the file due to the liability exposure of the project) the more you have to charge. Documentation typically comes down to two elements: quantity and quality. If you are responsible for maintaining both, factor in additional dollars to cover your administrative burden. Whenever possible, we try to offload the burden of meeting documentation to the client because rarely can we bill as much time as the effort requires. This way, our involvement is limited to the review and editing of the information; an effort that takes considerably less time which converts to a bill that is palatable to the client.

Experience. What is your experience performing this type of project? If the work you are being asked to do stretches your fifteen-plus years of experience, then the project price or your rate should go up. If you have little experience in a particular area, or the work could easily be done by less experienced personnel, then your standard rate or a competitive price would be more in order.

Work Schedule. Who controls the work schedule? If you can come and go as you please, filling in gaps of availability in your schedule, then the client should receive a competitive or lower rate. When the client regularly demands your appearance based on their schedule and timetable, then your rate should go up.

Politics. This is one of the most common billing factors that is overlooked. Is the project one that will involve more than normal company politics? This is also a factor that is constantly underrated. Company politics burden the consultant's work in every company. However, some companies are far worse than others. Be careful when taking on family business engagements, for example. It's easy to think you can just get in and do your job. But what you quickly find out is that you have to spend an inordinate amount of time sitting between powerful fighting factions within the organization. These fighting factions often feel that updating each other is a waste of money. So you are caught in the middle arguing over higher than normal fees because the reality of the job is . . . you have to keep everyone informed in many complex projects. Obviously, the more political the project, the higher the price. An easy rule of thumb is . . . the more departments (or in a family business, the more executive level family members) that are involved in a project, the more political that project will be.

Retainer. Is a replenishable retainer part of the fee arrangement? This is simply a financial consideration. Certainly, it makes sense that if you are holding a client's money and applying your charges against that money, that client is more likely to deserve some concession, be it price or otherwise.

Number of Hours Committed. What is the magnitude of time or fees this project will consume? Generally speaking, the more hours the project involves, the better break on fees the client should expect. This is not a new concept . . . it's simply volume buying. The shorter the project, the higher the rate.

While the following is a theoretical statement, we make it to relay a point. When you sit and talk with a client, during the first few hours, they are getting access to an encyclopedia of knowledge gained from years of experience at the "hard-knocks institute" for next to nothing. After the discussion has rambled on for forty or fifty hours, these same clients are mostly accessing day-to-day capabilities which include your logic, gut instinct, business savvy and implementation skills. The point is that your hourly fee for the first few hours should be thousands of dollars per hour, and after ten to twenty hours, your rate should approximate your standard rate. When your project takes you in the hundreds of hours, then a discounted rate is more fair for the value provided because by this time, many of the issues you are dealing with you are figuring out as you go. So in theory, the more work you do for a client, the less significant the leverage they access to for their fee. So it makes sense that the greater the number of days your client commits to, the more consideration should be given to discounting hourly fees. This theory also makes you think twice about how little you charge (or conversely, what a deal you're giving) those clients that pick your brain for a few hours every few months. Doubling your rate might be more in order for them.

How and When to Use Price Adjustments

An analogy we use in our firm is to compare ourselves to a hotel. Whether the hotel is fully occupied or almost empty, the overhead it takes to run our operation doesn't vary that much. However, when you reserve a room early, you get access to discounted rates. When you demand a room at the last minute while a convention is in town, you'll likely get the worst room for the highest price. When you guarantee to stay a certain number of nights a year, depending on the magnitude of that commitment, deep discounts are given with greater access to quality rooms. We have some of the same dynamics at work in our profession. Yet as we travel the country, so many firms pretend that each person has a rate appropriate for every hour of their time. This is certainly true if there is always a queue of work waiting that requires the same effort and experience; this is no different than a hotel that is always fully occupied with a waiting list to get in. However, in most firms, this level of consistent activity only occurs during tax time or during a few large audits. This is why we have changed our pricing structure to look towards the above factors to determine how much to deviate from standard pricing (both up and down), or which rate is appropriate for the project at hand.

As you consider this more complex rate adjustment system, consider this hardly discussed fact: *underestimation of our value is what we do best.*

The best way we know to ensure that your compensation is fair for both your firm and your client is to price each phase or project only after considering the factors identified above first individually, then as a group. How they interact with each other plays a big role too.

For example, if we are hired to complete a project under a tight deadline with quality documentation in a highly political environment, then we would likely estimate the project at our standard hourly fees and then double that amount. If the project is very competitive and our overall fees are not as negotiable, then we take a counter approach. We look at each of the criteria and determine a way to contractually limit their impact. For example, to limit documentation exposure in a strategic planning engagement, we would demand as part of our proposal that someone from the client's office write up the notes from the planning sessions and forward them to us for review and editing. As a safeguard against a highly political environment, we would demand a refillable retainer as part of the contract. If the deadline was very tight, we would specify the exact expected outputs and implement a formal change-order process to ensure the communication of the impact of project modifications. It boils down to this: Consideration and incorporation of pricing factors and phasing are keys to profitably pricing engagements.

Commissions and Contingent Fees: Where Do They Fit In?

Commissions and contingent fees are here to stay. Now part of the present, commissions and contingent fees will be more and more a part of the future. Let's consider when and how these can be used to your benefit.

First, we'd like to paraphrase a *Journal of Accountancy* (November 1990) article:

> If you are engaged to perform an attest function for a client (that is, audits, compilations, reviews), then you can't charge your client a commission during the period of engagement unless it is by a ruling of the court. However, if you are not engaged to perform the attest function, thereby obviating the opportunity of an independence issue arising,

you can charge commissions and/or contingent fees. However, disclosure is required.

Some state boards of public accountancy have added a little more bite to the disclosure mentioned in the AICPA article. For example, we interpret the Texas State Board of Public Accountancy, in section 501.13 (Payment and Commissions) under *Rules of Professional Conduct*, this way:

> Any time commissions are to be paid, a written disclosure specific as to source and amount must be acknowledged by the client before any party becomes contractually bound.

Charging commissions and contingent fees for non-attest projects is an issue that has been violently opposed for years. The rules as they are today came about because the AICPA settled with the Federal Trade Commission in order to protect the attest function. A strong case was made that licensing restrictions regarding commissions would be restraint of trade for CPAs. Because of this, we believe that the potential of future restrictions regarding this topic are infinitesimal. Each CPA needs to consider ways to incorporate or compete with the effects of these relaxed restrictions. Your latitude in this area varies from state to state. However, by ignoring the changes occurring in this area, you may find yourself at a serious competitive disadvantage.

Ways to make charging a commission or contingent fee advantageous include *charging a percentage of—*

- Funds raised in a financing scenario.
- A negotiated lease or note reduction.
- Sales or excise tax overpayment discovered.
- Increased profits for some specific period of time after a marketing consulting engagement, to name a few.

The point is . . . the possibilities are limited only by your resourcefulness. Commissions and contingent fees boil down to a risk-versus-reward decision. If you are willing to gamble that your efforts will produce the desired outcome, then you can leverage your income by charging a results-oriented fee. This leverage occurs because people often are willing to share a greater percentage of their gain than they will pay in up-front costs that have no guarantee of positive results.

BEFORE YOU MOVE ON

Earlier, you were asked to take out a blank sheet of paper and respond to the following situation:

> You have a bookkeeping client for whom you prepare monthly financial statements. She pays you $250 a month. She recently commented that she would like to bring this function in-house. Your client is willing to use the same software you use in-house to do her monthly processing. What will you charge her to make this transition?

As we mentioned, it's now time to redo this exercise. We have included an *Engagement Pricing Form* on the following page to facilitate this process. This time, think about whether there should be a short investigative Phase I. In other words, is installing your general ledger system really the right solution? What about training on either the hardware or software? If you included training in your estimate, was it a fixed cost? What happens if it takes more time to train than anticipated? Did you assume that you did all the set-up (like installing Windows, the new accounting software, etc.) or did you have the client install everything but your data-files? Did you provide your client with a total fixed fee for the project or did you identify the phases required and only provide an estimate for each one. Did you allow yourself a large enough margin of error in your estimate? While there is no right answer, the ideas discussed in this chapter may have given you a few extra tools and a little more leeway the next time you are asked to price a service.

Typically, this exercise reveals one of two things, or both. First, we normally estimate price too conservatively, missing important project steps or phases as well as underestimating the time to complete each one. Second, we tend to estimate projects in too exacting of a manner. An estimate is just that . . . an estimate. The original number you identified at the beginning of the estimating section of this chapter should have been rounded up to the nearest $250 or $500, for example. We often see numbers like $935 or $2,150, as compared to $1,000 or $2,500. The difference comes in client perception. A number like $935, much more so than a number like $1,000, will lead your client to an expectation that you know exactly what his or her particular project will cost, a fact we rarely know.

We have included another form as well at the end of this chapter. You guessed it, a self-assessment exercise. You know the drill. This is a personal exercise, one that is easy to skip over. But as we have stated each time, it's an important process that will help you identify the changes you want to incorporate into your consulting capabilities.

Take time now to fill out the *Engagement Pricing Form* and then compare this price estimate to the one you completed earlier. Finally, complete the *Self-Assessment* form.

Engagement Pricing Form

Client: ______________________________

Project: ______________________________

Current Phase Name: ______________________________

Task	*Hours*	*Rate*	*Total*

Total For This Phase:

Remaining Phases: Name	*Approx. Hrs.*	*Dollar Est.*

Total Project Estimate:

Self-Assessment Time Line
Delivering Value-Adding Services

Based on the materials covered in this chapter, please take a few moments and assess your weaknesses. Note of any skills you plan to work on as well as a time-frame to re-assess your progress. In addition, if there are activities or exercises you plan on attempting, jot them down and note your intended completion date. This form is provided solely as a self-improvement tool.

The following are ***Skills** I plan to **Improve:***

________________________ By when: __________

________________________ By when: __________

________________________ By when: __________

________________________ By when: __________

________________________ By when: __________

________________________ By when: __________

________________________ By when: __________

________________________ By when: __________

________________________ By when: __________

The following are ***Activities** I plan to **Attempt:***

________________________ By when: __________

________________________ By when: __________

________________________ By when: __________

________________________ By when: __________

________________________ By when: __________

________________________ By when: __________

________________________ By when: __________

Chapter 7
The Structure of the Calls

Now that we have covered why consulting is important to implement, tips on how to improve your communication skills and some ideas and techniques that should help you price, organize, and deliver consulting services, it's time to do something with all of this. This takes us to a variety of calls: the discovery call, the sales call, and the consulting call. The structure of all three have a great deal in common. All of them have an *investigation phase* and a *closing phase*. Within each of these phases, there is significant similarity in the methodology. However, each call type has a different objective, therefore the structure varies to accommodate that difference. Before we get into detail about each, take a moment and review this outline of all three calls.

When you look at each call type in table 7.1, notice the similarity. A question that could easily come to mind is, "How can the steps be so similar yet be effective with call objectives so different?" Well, at a conceptual level, all three call types come from the same methodology—the sales call. But in practice, since the implementation is different, we have incorporated some unique wording in the processes to denote their nuances. Each call type requires the consultant to (1) uncover relevant information, and (2) do something with that information.

Uncovering Relevant Information

To be effective in the investigation phase of the calls, your investigative skills will be seriously challenged. For ex-

Table 7.1 Structure of the Calls

Discovery Call	*Sales Call*	*Consulting Call*
	Investigation Phase	
• The introduction • Becoming acquainted with the business • Qualifying the prospect	• The opening • Information gathering	• Relating • Discovery and interviewing
	Closing Phase	
• Abbreviated sales pitch	• The sales pitch	• Reviewing findings and identifying suggestions
• Identifying the next step	• Our approach	• Presenting the action plan
• Seeking agreement	• The summary	• Persuading and facilitating
	• The close	• Supporting
	Objective	
• Qualify, qualify, and qualify!	• Close, close, and close!	• Solve, solve, and solve!

ample, with the *discovery call*, before you commit a great deal of your time, you need to uncover—

- When the project is expected to get underway or be completed.
- Who will be involved in making the final hiring decision.
- What the budget is for this project.
- How high this project's priority is to the organization.

The answers to these questions will *qualify* the prospect or client and help you identify the appropriate next step. If the next step is a *sales call*, then once again, your investigative skills will be taken to task. In the sales call, you are trying to determine what will motivate the prospect or client to buy your services. Therefore, your mission is to uncover—

- Information that identifies the client's concerns.
- Whether these are concerns for which you can provide assistance.

- What creates enough urgency for the client to hire your organization.
- The expected benefits that your involvement will bring.
- Whether those benefits are worthy of the expected price to obtain them.

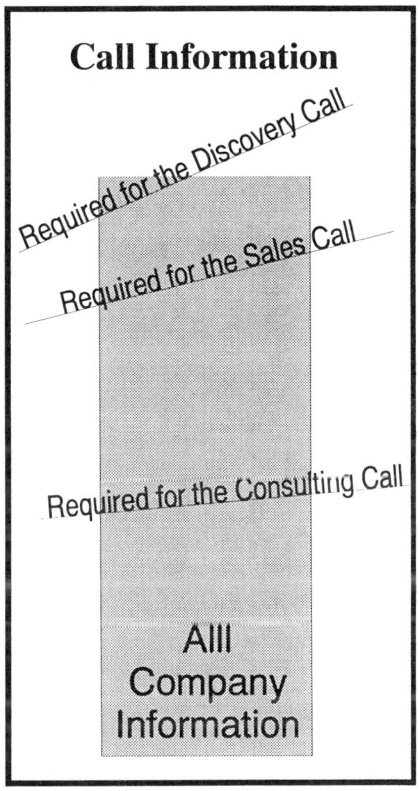

When you find the answers to these questions, your chances of closing new consulting opportunities have exponentially improved. If you don't know the answers, then most likely you will attempt to "close on air," which has a high failure rate (more on this later). As for our final call, the *consulting call*, our focus is to dig deeper and obtain enough detailed information about the client's concerns that possible solutions can be determined. The difference is "cut-off." Consider the call information graphic to the right. The shaded box represents *all the information available* about a particular business. The cut-off point for each call type is where the line intersects with the box. Note that in order to achieve the desired outcomes for each call type, a different level of understanding about the company should be uncovered during the process. As you can see, the discovery call requires the least amount of depth regarding company specific information. On the other hand, the consulting call requires the greatest amount of company knowledge.

In the discovery call, we just need to ask a few basic questions in order to differentiate a "tire kicker" (someone more interested in looking than actually buying) from a legitimate prospect. Then, we try to understand the urgency and budget of the project so the most effective course of action can be taken to close the sale (assuming it is a sale worthy of closing). With the discovery call, the cut-off is very high (little company information needs to be uncovered) because *the focus is on qualifying the buyer, not understanding the business.* With the sales call, our understanding of the company has to go a lot deeper in order to identify the business concerns and anticipated impact of our involvement. We are trying to find ways to help the organization that deliver savings or profit opportunities far greater than the cost of our participation. But the call type requiring the greatest understanding of the business by far is the consulting call. With this call, we need to get a broad enough understanding of each problem so that we can determine—

- The causes of the problem.
- The conditions that exaggerate or diminish it.
- What has been tried in the past to correct it.
- What some of the probable fixes are at this time.
- The skill level required to implement the suggested solutions.
- The potential cost and benefit of each solution.

Too often, CPAs ignore the lines in the call information graphic. For example, during the information-gathering stage of the sales call, rather than getting the last bit of information needed to wrap up and close the business, CPAs often prematurely jump directly into the discovery and interviewing stage of the consulting call. This not only blows the effectiveness of the sales call, but puts the CPA in the position of giving away free consulting advice. Why do we do this? We're not sure. But our guess is that as CPAs, our training and our professional ethics tell us that we can't take on any work unless we have the skills to do it. Therefore, during the sales call, we actually try to gather enough information so that we can determine the specific approach we would use to solve the problem, in order to verify that we meet the skills test.

The problems is, half (to sometimes all) the work of a consultant is determining a logical approach to solving the problem. We are reminded of an experience that happened about eight years ago when a large hospital asked our firm to bid on a contract to provide business advice and administrative support to each new doctor setting up an office in its about-to-open branch hospital. This was a big project, especially for our new firm, which was just created after spinning off from another one. We were primarily competing against three of the "Big Six" firms. We were included because of the exposure through our weekly newspaper column and a couple of very visible projects.

We put together a lengthy proposal, which we rarely do (see our criteria for preparing proposals later in chapter 10). An exhibit in this proposal was a two-page outline of all of the steps we would take to assist each new doctor. After the hospital administrator reviewed all of the proposals, our firm and one other were selected as finalists. Both firms were asked to prepare an extended proposal providing even greater detail as to our planned approaches. Our firm responded by stating that we were not going to update our proposal, but that we would be delighted to perform the request for a fee. However, our competition provided the enhanced proposal. To our knowledge, no firm has ever been hired by the hospital to help the doctors in the way that our proposal was addressing. Why? Because the hospital decided it could do much of the work internally. The point is, what we do best—and our most unique work product—is how we approach the work (the plan). After you have given away the plan, people with far less skill can implement it.

> *That's why it is so important to differentiate between information you are gathering and delivering in order to close a sale versus that needed to determine what you would do to improve the situation.*

The single biggest problem CPAs have in the implementation of the various *calls* is losing sight of what we are trying to accomplish during the *investigation phase* of each call type. There is a critical distinction we always need to keep in mind. In the *discovery call*, all we are trying to determine is what kind or level of attention the prospect or client needs now, from immediate personal attention to just sending information in the mail. With the *sales call*, we are asking questions in order to identify problems or concerns that carry a sense of urgency, and to find expected results that will justify the fees we would charge for our involvement. The investigation we perform in a *consulting call* is to dig deeper into the problem areas in order to arrive at a plan of attack. The "plan of attack" is definitely, unquestionably, a "for fee" function. As noted earlier, once the hospital obtained excruciatingly detailed blueprints for helping the doctors, it decided it didn't need any of us. So, while the concept of the investigation process is similar in all three call types, in reality, they are not structured to uncover the same information.

One last note: don't worry about failing the professional ethics test of not having the right skills. These are skills you already have, even if some fine-tuning may be in order. For example, you may not be able to install a network, but you are more than capable of identifying processes that are ripe for automation. Being able to identify, manage, and facilitate necessary change within your clients' organizations is the most important skill you bring to the table. Once you have identified the issues that need further investigation or to be addressed, the client (with your assistance) can hire the necessary specialists. And if you possess a required specialized skill or two, that's icing on the cake.

With this explanation and distinction behind us, let's first take a closer look at the discovery call.

The Structured Discovery Call

Let's start out by reviewing our call outline.

1. *Investigation phase:*
    - The introduction
    - Becoming aquainted with the business
    - Qualifying the prospect

2. *Closing phase:*
   - Abbreviated sales pitch
   - Identifying the next step
   - Seeking agreement

Next, let's review our call objective. It is to *qualify, qualify, and qualify*. The discovery call is typically made via a phone call. Why? Because you are typically responding to a request for information, a referral from a client, a telemarketing lead, or another type of blind inquiry. The phone call is your best approach because it allows you, without committing a significant amount of your time, to determine the interest level of the inquiry, if there is work to be done, if it's the kind of work that would be profitable, and whether you can perform the work given the project's timetable, to name a few. These are typically lukewarm calls (instead of cold calls) because they are invited; however, you have little to no idea where they might lead. You might find a $50,000 fee-per-year opportunity, or someone who is trying to gather information for a term paper in school. That's why the discovery call's objective is to qualify the prospect or client to see what the best course of action is. Before we look at this call type in detail, note that we will be referring to the contact person as a prospect. Why? Because this is the process for determining whether there is any opportunity or desire to convert this person or business from being a prospect (a potential client) to becoming an actual client. Without further adieu, here are the stages of the discovery call.

Discovery Call—Introduction

The introduction in the discovery call is very brief, usually just a sentence or two. Here's an example of a telephone scripted open we would use:

> Hello, my name is Steve Winters and I am a CPA with Winters, Winters and Reeb. I am calling in response to your request for <u>more information regarding our planning services.</u> Is now a good time for you?

The underlined portion of this script has a variety of inserts depending on your organization's promotional approach. Some firms offer a free tax review, a free hour of consulting, a free information packet (a do-it-yourself type of document or book), a free first phase of a project, or other offers in order to entice the prospect to respond. In addition, this script works equally well on almost any lukewarm telephone solicitation, such as responding to a client referral lead.

If thc prospect doesn't have time to talk now, immediately respond by asking when would be a good time and volunteering to call back then. Assuming that now is a good time to proceed, you can move on to the next step.

Discovery Call—Becoming Acquainted With the Business

It is at this point in your script that you need to identify a question or two that will facilitate a discussion of the background of the person and the company you are calling upon. You are just trying to solicit a brief introduction so you will have a general feel for the size of the business, the industry it is in, the number of employees, and so on. A comment like "Before we get started, could you tell me a little about your business (yourself)?" is one of our default questions. A question that could follow this one might be, "Can you tell me what caught your interest in <u>our mailing</u> (the underlined portion could also be substituted with phrases such as <u>our telemarketing call</u>, <u>your conversation with our client</u>, and so on) enough to request <u>more information</u> (<u>a return call</u>, <u>a tax return review</u>, and so on)?" Only a couple of questions are required at this stage.

Discovery Call—Qualifying the Prospect

Once you have a view of the business from about 30,000 feet, it's time to move on to the most important part of this call—qualification. "Qualifying" prospects is simply asking them a series of questions to find out whether they are really in the market for a specific service, who is going to make the decision, when, and why. People who don't take this step seriously find themselves wasting an inordinate amount of time and giving away a bundle of free advice. They fall prey to the infamous "tire kickers," who love to talk to you and barrage you with questions for the sole purpose of uncovering your approach to solving their various problems with no intent to hire you. How do you smoke these people out? You can eliminate about 95 percent of them by qualifying them using the following questions and techniques.

Time Frame. The first issue to address is time frame. Ask the potential client, "What is your time frame for getting this project underway?" or "When do you want this [some service] to be completed?" It's amazing what people say when you ask them direct questions. With just one or two direct questions, you'll find many "tire kickers" confessing right then and there that they are just looking for information. Once a date or period is identified, you have taken a giant step in starting to determine how to best allocate your time regarding this prospect. Often, the caller states that the project time frame is still months away, but that his or her organization is in the information-gathering stage. This is exactly the kind of data you are trying to uncover, because instead of setting up a face-to-face appointment, a more appropriate strategy might be to send information about your firm and references and set up a meeting a little closer to the decision date. Why? Because you want to make your sales pitch as close to the decision-making time as possible. There's a general rule in selling:

> *Whoever is the last to impress has the greatest chance of success.*

If you show up and make a great impression three months too early, by the time the client narrows the field, you can easily be left out because others are more firmly etched in the client's mind. It's the old adage, "out of sight, out of mind." However, with larger engagements, the strategy is a little different due to the longer selling cycle. So while being visible close to the decision point is critical regardless of engagement size, with very large engagements, getting in early plays an important role too. For example, arriving on the scene early for a $50,000 or greater project can provide you with an incredible advantage. This occurs because you might get the chance to mold the requirements of the proposal process to best suit your organization. The closer the skills sets required to do the project match those of your firm, the more likely you are to be awarded the project.

Therefore, understanding the decision time frame is a strategic piece of information. You want to maintain your visibility throughout the process by staying in touch with the potential client, with the vast majority of your face-to-face energy expended near the time the decision is to be made.

Decision Maker. The next critical piece of information to collect is who the decision maker is. This is a tough question to ask and most versions of the question cause more harm than good. For this reason, we ask you to memorize these words: *"Besides yourself, is there anyone else who will be involved in making the final decision?"* This question assumes the person you are talking to is a decision maker. One of the base rules of communication is:

Never challenge someone's status or independence.

This is a concept we included in our communication framework based on the book *You Just Don't Understand*, by Debra Tannen, Ph.D. According to Dr. Tannen's book, and our experience as well, any time you challenge someone's status or independence, you are likely to threaten that person. And if you do, you have an uphill battle to either get good information or close the business.

That is, if you ask the question, "Are you the one who's going to make the final decision?" you've created a high-risk, low-reward situation. What happens when the person is the only decision maker? You'll hear a confident and potentially arrogant reply, "Yes!" So, you were lucky . . . you dodged a bullet. Since this person is the only decision maker, he or she is not as likely to take offense at the wording of the inquiry. But what happens if the person you are speaking with is *not* the only decision maker, or worse yet, not a decision maker at all? You have put the inquirer in the position of having to admit that he or she is unimportant and just a pawn in the information-gathering process. In this situation, you have not gained an ally. You may have embarrassed someone that could help you get the job.

By asking the question the way we suggest, regardless of the inquirer's position in this process, no one has to lose face. The interesting part of this is that by including someone as a decision maker with the expectation that more people are likely to be involved as well, callers seem to readily admit their position without feeling exposed.

Given all of this, why is it so important to know who is making the decision? Because the worst position you can get yourself into is selling your services through someone. We are not saying that you don't have to appease and provide support to the decision gatekeepers. But from the beginning of the sales or consulting process, you have to set your sights on being face-to-face with the people who call the shots. Otherwise, you will spend an inordinate amount of time convincing the wrong person to do business with you. You can rest assured that 9 times out of 9.1, if you can't get at least minimal visibility with the decision makers, you might as well be throwing money out the window, because the odds of your selling efforts turning into revenue are virtually none.

Budget. The next question to ask pertains to the project's budget. This is not a sensitive question to ask, even though you may not get an answer. "How much have you budgeted for this project?" or "What did you plan on spending?" are acceptable alternatives. You need to know this information in order to assess reasonability. If the client won't divulge the budget, then suggest some broad price ranges in order to level-set their expectations. For example, make a comment like, "The past few strategic planning meetings we have facilitated, depending on the nuances each client has requested, ranged from $7,000 to $10,000." What you are trying to avoid is a client saying all the right things, and clearly ready to go, but with an unrealistic expectation of fees. If you don't qualify on price, it is easy to find yourself expending a great deal of effort only to find out that the client expects a $10,000 service delivered for a $1,000 fee. We have a philosophy at our firm that is appropriate to reiterate here:

> When a potential client expects far more than can be delivered for a price far less than is reasonable, this is the kind of prospect that needs a map detailing the directions to your fiercest competitor.

Priority. Once a prospect acknowledges a price range that is within the realm of reasonableness, the last question we ask concerns priority. Simply stated it's, "What's the priority of this project to your organization?"

Here, we are trying to determine whether this is the president's pet project, was mandated by the board, is an identified component within the strategic plan, or is just one of many projects going on simultaneously. The higher the priority, the more urgency it has, and the more likely the client is focused on getting the project completed. And the investigation being conducted by the client is often to find skill sets, not justification. The lower the priority, the more important justification may become in our efforts. In other words, the client may have little commitment to the project, but is testing for feasibility. Under this circumstance, it may be up to you to create a sense of urgency and identify lost opportunity or over-expended costs in the scenario where no action is taken. Logically, the lower the priority, the greater the possibility that the project will be canceled or postponed. Of the four questions, this one doesn't have to be asked. The answer can often be determined by the general tone and nonverbal messages of the conversation. As a rule, however, the larger the company, the more important it is to ask rather than just interpret. Why? Because large companies implement numerous projects simultaneously and assign priorities to them. As well, large companies are the most likely to shift courses instantly and literally walk away mid-project. Therefore, it's important to know your project's priority in these circumstances up front.

Going back to our telephone script, here's a summary of the questions you might ask in this stage of the call:

1. *Time frame:* "What is your time frame for getting this project underway?" or "When do you want this [some service] to be completed?"
2. *Decision maker:* "Besides yourself, is there anyone else who will be involved in making the final decision?"
3. *Budget:* "How much have you budgeted for this project?" or "What did you plan on spending?"
4. *Priority:* "What's the priority of this project to your organization?"

Once you have asked, and the client has satisfactorily answered, all four of these questions, you have performed the essential time-saving, tire-kicker-avoiding job of qualifying. Does it always work? No, but almost always. And typically, based on the answers to these questions, a selling strategy will unfold. You may have to drop everything in order to respond, or you might create a plan to stay in touch with the client over the next few months so that when the urgency increases, you are in position to step in and take on the business. The main thing is that by qualifying your prospects every time, you avoid the free exchange of billable time for wasted time.

Discovery Call—Sales Pitch

This is the first stage of the closing phase of the discovery call. By this time, you have spent five to ten minutes finding out about the business and qualifying the prospect. You have already expended the bulk of your time commitment and you are only a few minutes from finishing this call. Before you tell the prospect what you think the next course of action should be, you need to provide a brief introduction to your firm's capabilities.

The question to answer during this exercise is, *Why is your firm special?* This is done by reviewing the firm's credentials, describing its various services, identifying individuals' diverse levels of experience, and conveying a sense of compassion and caring for the welfare of the client. There are a million ways to approach this part of the call. But to ensure that you don't ramble at a point you need to appear the most confident, jot some notes down as to points you want to make. An example of something we might say would be:

> Our firm is made up of three CPAs, one programmer-analyst, and three administrative people. Because of our small size, when you hire us, you work with the partners. You are not immediately transferred to a person with just a few years of experience. We have a mission statement at our firm that's short, but gets to the heart of why we think our clients do business with us. Our mission is, "Turning

> Vision Into Reality." We work as closely as you want us to in order to help you identify and implement your plan for success. We want to be more than your CPA firm, we want to be one of the reasons for your future success.

While this may sound hokey, it's the way we feel. And interestingly enough, it's the way many small businesses want their advisor organizations to feel. So we use it to our advantage. Sculpt any narrative you are comfortable with that will allow you to quickly and succinctly share with your prospect why you are the firm of choice. Let me remind you, however, that if you have determined that this prospect is not worth pursuing, you might want to skip this stage altogether. You don't want anyone holding on tight as you are trying to kick him or her away because your sales pitch about the firm was too good. Anyway, as soon as you've said your piece, it's time to identify the next step.

Discovery Call—Identifying the Next Step

Usually, the discovery call ends up with one of the following outcomes, listed from highest to lowest qualified:

- A face-to-face appointment at their office.
- A face-to-face appointment at your office.
- Sending additional information, including your business card and a note that states that you will be calling on a specific date if you haven't heard from them.
- A call-back note to your files when a prospect is found to be worthy of more of your time, but is not ready to meet with you yet, and there is no information appropriate to send. This is one of the main justifications for a general brochure about your firm because you can put something about your organization in the prospect's hands, even though it really doesn't address any specific issues.
- Sending additional information, including your business card and a note asking the prospect to call if he or she ever needs anything.

- Referral to another organization more appropriate for his or her needs.
- Referral to a competitor because you want this prospect to waste someone else's time, preferably someone who is constantly getting in your way with good business opportunities.

Based on the information you gained during the investigation phase (the introduction, becoming aquainted with the business, and qualifying the prospect), it should be clear at this time what course of action you want to suggest. But before we go on, we want to remind you of a fact that so many consultants ignore. Remember:

> *A waste of time is a waste of time, regardless of how you package or document it.*

Just because you have some time to spare or you felt too pushy to ask the questions identified above, you are not doing yourself or your business a favor by staying busy with people who are not interested in buying anything from you. Even if you are very sophisticated in your use of communication and persuasion techniques and "can sell ice to Eskimos," don't expend significant energy on prospects without promise. You most undoubtedly have plenty of clients to court additional services from. And if not, go home and relax, play golf, or do something fun. The point is, don't set up face-to-face calls with clearly unqualified prospects. Your return on your time invested will only look good if "busy" is the only criteria.

Discovery Call—Seeking Agreement

The last stage of the closing phase of the discovery call is seeking agreement. After you have suggested one of the above alternatives (or any other alternative you create), ask the prospect if he or she agrees with your approach. This is often as simple as, "Is this OK with you?" If it is not, find out why. If it is, all that is left to do is follow through. If this is just a note to your calendar and an information drop, that's easy. However, if the next step is to meet face-to-face in a sales call situation, that can be a lot harder. So we've included our 1-2-3 approach to making that sales process work in your favor.

The Sales Process

There is a common misconception that learning how to make a sales call is an exercise reserved for salespeople. This is disturbing because:

Everybody sells . . . regardless of job titles or duties.

From the executives to the cleaning crew, those who develop the art of persuasion always seem to lead the pack. But before we start dissecting the structure behind selling, consider this important matter:

Once a prospect is qualified, selling opportunities should be conducted face-to-face whenever possible, so avoid selling over the phone.

Here are a few reasons why:

- Some of the issues being discussed may be complicated. These can be difficult to communicate over the phone. With face-to-face selling, you can utilize aids such as sample documents, pictures, marker boards, and flip charts to clarify the material being presented.
- When your initial meeting is by phone, it's rarely billable. Even if you are hired to perform a consulting project via a phone conversation, often a free introductory meeting is still scheduled. When your initial meeting is face-to-face, not only can you save time, but depending on the content of the meeting, it may be partially billable.
- Since the client hasn't hired you yet, there is still a great deal of marketing to do. It is difficult to establish the kind of rapport required to close a deal via the phone. Also, you have little control over your selling environment when using the telephone. Therefore, face-to-face communication gives you an edge. You not only

have greater control over the environment, but you can utilize visual tools in your marketing strategy.

- It is much easier to motivate clients into making a commitment when you are sitting across a table from them.

FEATURE, BENEFIT, RESULT

Okay . . . the stage is set. The prospect is in your office requesting assistance (or you are in his or hers), but has yet to engage anyone to perform any work. Before we start selling, there's another issue to consider. *Let's make sure we remember what we are really selling. The feature, benefit, result technique will help you stay focused.*

Most people sell features and a few sell both features and benefits. However, only the silver-tongued salesperson incorporates results into the sales pitch.

> Assume you are attempting to sell a burglar alarm system. The feature is the physical electronic components. The benefit is a warning sound, which will occur should an intruder break the electronic barrier. But the result, and what the customer is looking to buy, is greater protection for the family. *People buy perceived results.*

Let's take this example a little closer to home. A new client comes to you seeking tax assistance. The feature is the tax return. This is the physical product you sell. The benefit is that the client can meet the information filing requirements imposed by the government. The anticipated result is two-fold: first, that the Internal Revenue Service will be satisfied and leave your client alone and second, that you will have found most (if not all) the money he or she is entitled to. For the most part, we believe clients are buying *peace of mind* when they hire CPAs to prepare their tax returns. If you don't believe this, ask yourself this question:

> *If you could legally and enforceably write your clients a letter that released them from all future tax liability regarding a particular year, would they care whether a tax return was filed?*

We believe the answer is, "no." What motivates people to action (creates a sense of urgency) is an expectation of results. Therefore, we need to incorporate results-oriented thinking into our sales kit by utilizing the *feature, benefit, result* technique. This is best accomplished by taking our client' requests and breaking them down into features, benefits, and expected results in order to make sure we spend more time selling what the clients really want to buy.

The Structured Sales Call

It's time to begin pulling all of these tips and techniques together. These tools are most effective when incorporated into a logically organized selling strategy. Everyone approaches this a little differently, and that's fine. However, we offer the following outline of our sales call as an alternative for you to consider:

1. *Investigation phase*
   - The opening
   - Information gathering
2. *Closing phase*
   - The sales pitch
   - Our approach
   - The summary
   - The close

Our version of the sales call has two phases or six steps. As you can see, it is very similar to the discovery call. Just as with the discovery call, most of the time and effort is spent in the investigation phase, or the first two steps, of this process. Why? Because if you don't gather the right kind of information up-front, all the sales skills in the world won't help much during the closing phase.

The Sales Call—Opening

The first few minutes of selling are political, not technical. The objectives are simple—introductions and rapport building.

Introductions. This step of the opening stage of the sales call not only includes introducing yourself and your staff (if present in the meeting), but making sure you know the client's name(s) and correct spelling(s). Commit these to memory. A technique we use is to immediately use (and at least two or three more times in the first ten minutes of the meeting) any participant's name in the conversation like, "Well Joe, how did you find out about our firm?"

Additionally, during this step we need to find out about the client's background, the company, and his or her authority within the company. This information is critical in order to gauge the kind of questions to ask later.

Finally, it is crucial to review and consider the "first impression" issues introduced in chapter 5 in order to start this step of the call as positively as possible. Note that it is premature for you to begin selling the skills of your firm at this time. The objective of the introductions step of the opening is to move through the formality of meeting each other so you can begin to build rapport.

Little things can make a big difference:

- *Be careful about seating arrangements.* If you sit next to a client at a table for a meeting, it might be too awkward to make eye contact. Always think about being able to make good eye contract with all those present. Also, don't trap the client. If two or more from your firm are making the sales call, avoid sitting on each side of the client. If you do, you may make the client feel trapped, and it's impossible for the client to maintain eye contact with both of you. There are a number of other issues regarding seating, such as the formality created by putting a barrier or distance between you and the client, or positioning yourselves so that you can easily use a flip chart or marker board.
- *Phrase introductions carefully.* Introduce yourself as a business consultant as well as a CPA to avoid being pigeonholed as a "tax guy." If someone else uses tax terminology to introduce you, say, "While it's true that I have substantial expertise in tax and accounting, I also consult with businesses on a variety of issues, such as . . . (the blank can be filled in by whatever suits you—loan assistance, operational planning, marketing, tech-

nology implementation, and so on). Continue by stating something like, "These are areas where I have in the past been able to really add extra value to my client relationships." The point is, don't set yourself up as someone who just delivers a product. You also can and do deliver advice; make sure your client understands that distinction.

This entire step only takes three or four minutes typically, but they are important minutes not to waste.

Rapport Building. Building rapport is the second part of the opening stage of the sales call. Rapport is most easily established when the client does the majority of the talking. To make sure this happens, ask open-ended questions, questions that require a response other than yes or no. For example, "Tell me about yourself," or "What do you do in your spare time?" The objective here is to make some personal connection with your client, which then allows him or her to become more comfortable with you. Two strategic facts of life are—

1. *People do business with people they like.*
2. *People like people who listen.*

So let your potential clients talk about themselves and their interests. This quickly accelerates the rapport-building process since almost everyone would rather talk than listen. Why? Once again, because *listening* is hard work.

> *To talk is human, to listen is divine. In the selling environment, listening is your job.*

The rapport-building step might take as little as a few minutes or as long as half an hour. But you're in control; you're asking the questions. When you feel the time is right, change the tone and get down to business. Some say that once you have identified three common interests with your client or prospect, you have sufficiently covered the rapport-building phase. But rest assured, when the client is ready, he or she will give you a sign. It might be obvious, such as the client starting to discuss his or her situation, or subtle, nonverbal signals such as watch-glancing, chair-squirming, or eye-wandering. There are many clues to monitor. When you encounter several messages denoting impatience or disinterest, get down to business. Otherwise, you will lose the client.

Sales Call—Information Gathering

At this point, you've decided that it's time to get down to business. This can best be accomplished by asking a transitional, open-ended question like: "What prompted you to call and set up this meeting?" or "What's been keeping you awake at night?" or, if this is a continuation of the discovery call, "In our conversation last week, you mentioned. . . ." There are many acceptable variations. The two major ingredients are casual tone (not negative or accusatory) and phrasing that allows the client to answer easily. Normally, CPAs will say something like, "What's your problem?" or "How can I help you?" Both of these questions often lead down a road you don't want to go.

The question "What's your problem?" is negative because it keys on the word *problem*. It also assumes that the client has identified the problem. In reality, the client may just have a feeling that the company is inefficient in the way it is currently invoicing and collecting from its customers. The client may have come to you to kick around a few ideas in order to determine whether or not there is a problem to discuss.

An even bigger issue regarding the question, "What's your problem?" is that it is a status-attacking question. Remember, *good consultants don't challenge status (at least at this time)!* One commonly construed underlying message of the above question is, "Tell me, you lowly ignorant business subhuman, what wisdom can the great one bestow on you today?" In consulting, you want to avoid the role of "the omnipotent one." Rather, you want to be thought of as someone to kick around ideas with, or someone to talk to about issues to determine whether action should be taken. The question, "What is your problem?" does not reflect a role of equality, but one of expert and follower or manager and employee.

The second question, "How can I help you?," seems innocent enough. But it assumes that the client not only knows what the problem is, but that he or she is familiar enough with your firm to request a service you offer. In a way, this is a very limiting question. Why? Because most clients see their CPA in a very narrow light. That light shines based on whatever specific services you perform for that client. While your firm might be outstanding in the strategic planning arena, if the only work you do for that particular client is the audit, you are likely to be categorized as the auditor. So when you ask the question, "How can I help you?," you might as well be saying, "Do you need any audit services today?" Don't allow your client to narrow the subject matter to his or her interpretation of what you can and can't do.

We know this sounds like nit-picking. However, this points out why CPAs so often wind up exactly where they don't want to be. Our ability to deliver needed services to our clients is rarely limited by our capabilities. It is almost always one of misunderstanding, miscommunications, or misinterpretation. Stated more succinctly, CPAs lose business because they are often careless with words.

In the world according to GAAP, we have been technicians for too long.

Successful consulting requires a good balance between political and technical skills. For example, we recently performed some internal control work for a manufacturing client. The real issue was that the department heads for manufacturing and accounting were at odds with each other. Our role was to implement a solution acceptable to both sides. This project was 20 percent technical and 80 percent political. There were plenty of acceptable solutions; the problem was getting agreement on one. In this case, communication skills were far more important to the success of the project than technical expertise. As a matter of fact, the client company had several people more experienced technically than we could supply. However, after two years of attempting the project internally and getting nowhere, they hired our firm and the project was completed in less than a year. Communication skills often play as large a role (and many times, a larger role) in consulting as technical skills.

After the Transition Question. Once the discussion is focused on the business concern, continue your role as

Sherlock Holmes (renowned for uncovering the obscure) and investigate further. At this stage of the sales call, your job is to unveil issues, concerns, opportunities, and so on, many of which are far from being volunteered, in order to find out how to motivate someone to buy your services. The objective of the information-gathering phase of the sales call is to gain knowledge about the client's situation and identify his or her hot buttons.

To gain the necessary knowledge, your investigation needs to—

- Uncover your client's concerns.
- Identify what your client expects to gain, protect, or reduce by addressing these concerns.
- Quantify the value of resolving each concern.
- Estimate (roughly) the cost associated with fixing each problem area, including your fees.
- Weigh the expected gain, the likelihood of achieving that gain, and the cost of implementing the needed changes against each other to ensure the end justifies the effort.
- Determine whether you have, or have access to, the required resources, including both time and skill, to manage or perform the detailed work relative to this project.

The information required to satisfy issues such as these can best be gathered by utilizing questioning techniques like those found throughout earlier chapters. Also, pay special attention during this stage to taking notes and using the investigative tree note-taking technique found in chapter 5. Be careful not to sound like you are interrogating the client. You are attempting to gather information, not put the client on the spot. And finally, do whatever it takes to *avoid the desire to*—

- Jump to conclusions.
- Give premature solutions to problems you have just identified.
- Tell clients what to do (phrase your ideas as questions).

In addition to obtaining general knowledge about the client and his or her situation, another important aspect of this stage is to identify your client's hot buttons. Hot buttons are the key to persuasive selling. Hot buttons are issues or needs that push your client into action because there is a sense of urgency about them. These buttons are rarely obvious. The problem is, if you haven't discovered the hot buttons, and quantified the value of resolving them, when it comes time to close, you will be closing on air. If you try to close on air, the client will not be motivated to buy.

Closing on air means that you are trying to persuade the client to commit to doing business with you when there is no tangible reason to do so. With traditional services, there are built-in client motivators. Therefore, our role is to convince our clients that we can do the work, not that it is necessary to do it. For example, in the tax business, we have built-in hot buttons. The clients have to file their tax returns by a certain date. As these dates draw near, people will automatically be motivated into action in order to avoid penalties, interest, and exposure to the Internal Revenue Service. People also are typically externally motivated regarding audits and financial statements, especially if an outside source (such as a lender) is demanding them. In these cases, the clients come to us boiling over with anxiety, focused on meeting their deadlines.

With consulting, rarely are there dates that create this sense of urgency. Even when dates exist, they often are internally generated (which means they are subject to change). Therefore, during the investigation phase of a sales call, you not only have to pinpoint the ideas or concerns that are keeping your client awake at night, but you have to quantify the expected results of addressing them. Otherwise, the client may walk away from a meeting with you knowing that a problem exists, but thinking that it's just one of those irritants that's not worth the cost of resolving.

Case Example. Let's say Mike wants your help in selecting an accounting system for his small business. He spends several hours outlining the requirements for this new system. While Mike has done a good job, you know through experience that even if you found a system that satisfied every wish on his list, he would likely be unhappy. This dissatisfaction would occur because the price would be beyond reason, the system would require that he change the way he has always done business, or it wouldn't perform many of the "not listed" but assumed functions.

Therefore, you feel a work-flow analysis should be done in order to identify what and how paper travels through the company, the information outputs that are required, and the bottlenecks that cause the organization problems. You know this preliminary step will cost from $5,000 to $10,000, and will be in addition to the research he is requesting that you do. Mike has already commented that he is concerned about money so you know he is going to resist this idea.

In order to sell the work-flow study, you are going to have to find a hot button to push.

During your investigation, Mike told you about several friends who spent hundreds of thousands of dollars on computers that proved to be marginally effective. He also commented that his greatest fear was making the same mistake. For that reason alone, he has never made the transition into the world of automation. However, when asked why he has decided that now is the time to automate his accounting, Mike replied, "Because my inability to adequately manage my inventory, invoicing and accounts receivable is not only putting the company in a major cash bind, but causing me to lose customers because of too many out-of-stock conditions."

Well, if you ever wanted a hot button to slap you in the face, there you have it. By the way, if most CPAs actually quantified their clients' hot buttons to the degree we demonstrate in this scenario, our closing ratios would be excellent. But even in this case, there is still more work to do.

So far, Mike has said he is scared of spending a couple hundred thousand dollars acquiring a marginally effective system. He has also told you that, by not doing something, he is losing business. *The logical next question, and we can tell you this after monitoring hundreds of role play scenarios, is rarely asked.* The next question should be: "So how much revenue do you feel you are losing each year due to stock-outs?" He replies, "Half a million in sales." Then ask, "If you had the automated accounting system you identified earlier up and running, how much of that stock-out revenue loss could be avoided?" Mike states confidently, "At least 75 percent of those stock-outs wouldn't happen with a better inventory system." Finally you ask, "What would you say your average gross margin is on the items that are typically out-of-stock?" "My average gross margin is 35 percent on almost everything we sell," is his reply.

Even with all of this great information, you also need to *quantify* what Mike thinks is the downside of purchasing a marginally effective system. Maybe you should say something like: "You stated earlier that you have several friends who spent hundreds of thousands of dollars on marginally effective computers and that your greatest fear is making the same mistake. What do you feel a mistake like this will cost you?" Let's assume that he replies, "I'm concerned that I'll spend $200,000 and still have the same problems I have today."

In this case, he has just quantified the risk of failure to find the right system at $200,000 plus valuable employee time. There are a lot of questions you can ask to quantify the value of doing or not doing something. And those questions vary based on whatever the client said last.

Before you end this phase of the sales call, you want to make sure you have identified all the issues Mike is concerned about. As discussed in chapter 5, when this time occurs, visit the *global functions* checklist. Consider this continued exchange with Mike:

Consultant: Mike, so far you've identified cash shortages and inventory stock-outs as critical issues costing you money. Are there any other areas of the business that you're apprehensive about at this time?

Mike: No, if I can get a system that will help me better manage my inventory, everything else will fall in line.

Consultant: Well, if you don't mind, I would like to review several functional areas of business that our clients constantly struggle to improve.

Mike: Go ahead.

Consultant: First, are you getting the kind of information you feel you need on a daily basis to run this business?

Mike: Yes, except for inventory of course.

Consultant: How about your people. Do you feel you have motivated personnel?

Mike: Yes. I try to treat and pay everyone fairly. Most of my people think they should earn more, and I don't blame them. I think I should earn more too. However, I am wondering if I should put my salespeople on commission. Right now, because there are so many service issues the salespeople have to deal with, they are all paid a salary.

Consultant: A number of our clients have struggled with that same issue and we have some ideas to share. However, I would like to ask a few more questions in this area first. Do you feel your company is at much risk due to the expanded laws regarding sexual harassment and discrimination based on regulations like the Americans with Disabilities Act?

Note several things in this example. First, we have begun the process of reviewing the global functions (information management was touched on, followed by personnel) to broaden our understanding about the problems the client's business is facing. While we try to get clients to volunteer this information with questions like, "What do you see as your biggest opportunity (or hurdle) in the coming six months?" for many reasons, they might not think about many areas for which we could provide valuable assistance. Therefore, we can fall back to the global functions checklist to assist in our efforts.

Also notice an important characteristic about the questioning above. Many CPAs, when the idea of salary versus commission was introduced, would have focused intense attention on this topic. While we are admitting that more questions can be asked, during the sales cycle, you want to keep the conversation on a high level. Keep your questions on a *quantification* level. For example, asking a question like, "What do you feel you would gain by putting your salespeople on a commission system?" might be appropriate. This might lead to more justification for getting you involved. However, if you have plenty of justification already, you might set this issue aside as something that should be discussed in more detail later.

The key is to keep from succumbing to the temptation to dive in and solve problems. Once you have quantified an issue, or found out it can't be quantified easily, the investigation needs to quickly revert back to high-level questioning. And in this case, once personnel was covered, another global function should be introduced. Remember the graphic at the beginning of this chapter. Selling requires much more high-level investigative questioning than consulting. If you are not diligent about maintaining that high-level perspective, you will find yourself to be the most popular overworked, underpaid consultant around.

We're not trying to tell you what questions to ask. Rather, we are reminding you that you need to gather the kind of information that allows your client to better understand the magnitude of the decision he or she is about to make.

Considering the scenario above, by quantifying the risk of making a hasty judgment regarding which new accounting system to implement, you begin to build a wall of reasoning that adds support to your involvement. For example, Mike has said that he doesn't want to do what his friends have done and virtually throw away several hundred thousand dollars. On the other hand, he feels he is walking away from over $130,000 a year in lost profits due to his mismanagement of inventory ($500,000 in lost revenue times a 75 percent recapture ratio if a good inventory system were implemented times a 35 percent gross margin). By asking the right questions, Mike is allowed to convince himself (which is the most persuasive way) that it is time to take action. While his fear of buying the wrong system is costly, his inaction is carrying an even higher price tag.

Now that there is adequate information, later when it is time to ask for the business, your fees of $10,000 to $50,000 (which might have seemed enormous at the start of this conversation) are being fairly compared to the anticipated results. In other words, by spending the money up-front to do adequate investigation as to the needs of the business, you not only significantly reduce Mike's chances of wasting several hundred thousand dollars, but you offer an end to the annual $100,000-plus profit bleeding that is currently occurring.

If we don't quantify the expected results, we can't create the proper perspective regarding our fees or a high enough level of urgency. Or more simply put, without this required information, you will be closing on air, which rarely converts into business opportunity.

The Last Step to Information-Gathering. Once you have asked all of the questions you can think to ask, it's time to briefly summarize what you have learned. Review the issues the client has identified as problems that need to be addressed. Note the emphasis on client. Be careful not to take on the task of establishing the priorities yourself. This sets the stage for the next step of the sales call which will be covered momentarily.

Investigative Questioning Wrap-Up. The difference between selling investigative questioning and consulting investigative questioning is that with selling, all we really want to know is what's bothering our client, what it's worth to him or her to fix it, and how that compares to what we will charge. When you start asking detailed questions as to what kind of commission structure Mike has in mind, what his competitors do, and so on, you are attempting to determine the feasibility and implementation steps of the idea. This is consulting. This is what you need to get paid to do.

Keep in mind that this is the most difficult transition you will be asked to make in this book. However, there is nothing that will provide you more opportunity, more revenue, higher client satisfaction, and greater success with your projects than improving your investigative skills. Improving this process is not only powerful for selling, but essential to being a quality consultant.

The Closing Phase of the Sales Call

Now that we have covered the *investigation phase* of the sales call, it's time to move to the *closing phase*.

Due to the quality of the information you gathered earlier in the sales call (because you were listening, taking notes, qualifying, quantifying, and so on), you are ready to convert this into new business. Remember however, that this is a dynamic process. If you are in one of the later stages of the sales process and new information is uncovered, if necessary, put your investigative hat back on and ask more questions. Based on what we've accomplished thus far, it's time to move to the first stage in the *closing phase,* which is the *sales pitch.*

The Sales Call—Sales Pitch

The intent of this stage is to discuss *who you and your firm are and what you and your firm do.*

Many cover this information in the rapport-building stage. However, we believe that the beginning segment of a sales situation should be conversationally dominated by the clients; let them empty their buckets. In other words, until the clients have had ample time to express their feelings and concerns (emptied their feelings-concerns buckets), we know from experience that it will be hard to get their full attention. Once their buckets are empty, the stage is set. As well, waiting until you discover the issues that need to be addressed allows you to tailor your sales pitch to fit the services that fit the situation. It's time to begin the firm's floor show. This includes—

- *Discussing partner and employee credentials.*
- *Outlining the various services your firm performs.*
- *Distributing firm brochures, newsletters, and other sales information.*
- *Introducing references.*

As we stated in this same stage of the discovery call, the question to answer during this exercise is, *Why is your firm special?* This is done by reviewing the firm's credentials, describing its various services, identifying people's diverse levels of experience, and conveying a sense of compassion and caring for the welfare of the client. This is not accomplished by running down a competitor, but by making sure the client sees the value-add your organization brings.

As noted by one of the bullets above, during this step of the *closing phase*, this is a great time to tell stories that demonstrate how you have helped others in similar circumstances, to mention that your firm has numerous clients in their specific industry, and so on. This is also the time to assure the client that together, you will form the kind of team that can identify and uncover solutions that will be beneficial to the organization. Unlike the discovery call, the sales pitch in the sales call is much more detailed. While this stage would only be a paragraph of words in the discovery call, in the sales call, you want to make sure your client understands why your organization's skills match the requirements he or she has previously outlined. This stage is likely to take anywhere from 5 to 15 minutes.

The Sales Call—Approach

By following the structured sales call, here's about where you should be at this time:

- *Everybody knows everybody*
- *Everybody likes everybody*
- *The client's bucket has been scraped clean*
- *The client is in awe of your firm's capabilities*

The next step is to discuss how you would approach solving the client's problems. Most often, we start by discussing the *cash, capacity, and capability technique*. It always seems to comfort clients when they understand that—

- *We offer various degrees of involvement.*
- *They control our degree of involvement.*

After everyone is comfortable with this concept, we lay out a game plan that could resolve their dilemma. Although we can rarely pinpoint the exact details of our approach at this point, we can speak in general terms (because our earlier investigative process was focused on identifying hot buttons and quantifying them). Remember, this is a sales call, not consulting. This is not the time to lay out the intimate details of the plan, even if you have a good idea what they are. We can't say this enough: Don't give away the plan—that's what consultants are paid to do. In this stage of the closing phase, all you are trying to do is convince the client that you know what you are doing.

For this reason, *phasing* becomes an essential technique. It is logical that we need to do more investigation before we can give the client a more definitive outline of our game plan. Based on the information we have gathered about the company, we can estimate the cost of phase I (usually between $1,000 and $3,500).

If we have performed a similar project for a similar sized company with similar circumstances, we would provide the client with an overall estimate for the project at this time. If we haven't, then we might relay a wide range, quoting a past project or two as a point of reference until we know more. Or more commonly, we tell the client that we can only provide a reasonable estimate after having a better understanding of the business, its people, and the obstacles. We know what you may be thinking, that this strategy would never work with your clients because they demand to know the cost before they will hire you. While it's true that clients do demand a cost estimate, they don't require one. We've been selling services this way for almost two decades with minimal resistance. The key is to make sure that you are not trying to close on air.

During the investigation phase of the sales call, you should identify enough of the client's at-risk money that your client feels that it's worth spending money to get a better understanding of the problem. We remind our clients that if they decide not to proceed with our involvement after we have completed phase I, they can use the information we gather to proceed on their own or with any other firm. This lets them know that we are confident in our work and that the effort has value even if the project is not feasible at this time.

Using our phasing technique, the client can commit to the overall project in general, but only has to specifically commit to one stage within the project. Even though it is incredibly rare when we don't perform all the various stages of a project, the client commits to them one at a time. This creates a type of safety net for the client. If they don't like the way the project is progressing, then at the end of every stage, there is a logical place for us to be dismissed and for someone else to take over.

For example, let's say that a very small client is interested in obtaining financing: Our first step would be to analyze their situation. Let's assume that in this scenario, based on the information we gained during the investigation phase, we estimate that it will take two hours to take a cursory look. If the client's actual situation was similar to what we expected, our second stage might be to help identify the funds required and how they should be spent. This could take another couple of hours. Specifying the information that needs to be prepared for the loan proposal is a likely third step requiring a couple more hours. At this point, we would jointly decide who is going to prepare what.

The point of this is that we lay out a simple approach in multiple stages. We make it clear that our estimates are merely rough guesses and that we charge by the hour. Therefore, unexpected problems, lack of information, unusual complexity, and so on, increase the time requirement. However, the reverse also is true.

A downside to our multiple phase approach is that occasionally a client gets the wrong impression as to the overall cost of a project. So we work hard to ensure that we don't have any misunderstandings in this area. We attempt to—

1. *Establish the appropriate expectations as to the anticipated results.*
2. *Make it clear that the price is for a certain phase only.*
3. *If appropriate, inform the client that our fees are for the services we perform and not for achieving specific results.*

Given the above, we might conclude this way. Assuming the client does most of the detailed preparation of the loan package, by the time we lay out the required documents, look over and critique the loan package, and attend several meetings with bankers, our charge for a loan package like this would typically be around $2,500. If we were comfortable with that as a reasonable price, we would mention it to the client.

We lay out our approach in multiple stages, give some general estimates, and allow ourselves plenty of flexibility. The clients are usually satisfied because they only have to chew their projects—and costs—one bite at a time.

The Sales Call—Summary

By this time, you and the client have covered a great deal of information. Now is the time to bring it all together in preparation for *the close*. In this stage is summarizing the issues, quantifying the reasons for taking action, and reviewing the game plan that has been identified.

Here's where you can pull all of this work together and make the client beg for your involvement. For example, reconsidering Mike's computer dilemma, the summary might sound something like this:

> Mike, you mentioned earlier that you really wanted to avoid making the costly mistake of purchasing an ineffective computer system. You even said you were concerned you could easily throw away $200,000 by making poor decisions. You also told us that you feel you are walking away from at least $130,000 a year in lost profits because of your current inventory control capabilities. Just a few minutes ago, we talked about our firm and how we've developed a great deal of expertise in this area. You even commented that you hold one of the companies we've assisted in high regard as to their effective use of automation.
>
> With this in mind, let me summarize what we see as the financial side of this situation. The last two projects like this we performed for clients similar to your organization ran in the $30,000 to $50,000 range for consulting services. And as we discussed earlier, we will be able to pin this number down much better after we complete phase I of our work. Given all of this, you have a high-side approximate cost of $50,000 to ensure that you don't buy $200,000 of technology trash. You've stated your upside cash flow potential is at least $130,000 a year in additional profits. Over the course of the next three years, you have identified almost $600,000 dollars at risk.

As you may have noticed, not only did the summary recapture the reasons uncovered in the investigation phase as to why action is necessary, but the firm's capabilities and experience were directed towards solving the problem as well. This client should be chomping at the bit to say, *"I'm ready. Please, please! When can you get started?"* This is why the close follows the summary. The close in this situation would be a "no-brainer." All you have to do is finish with something like:

> Mike . . . we know we can help. We are asking you to spend $50,000 with us to protect $600,000. We have availability to get started either next week or the first week of next month. When would be better for you?

This closing sentence has several complexities to it. For that reason, it's time to take a look at the many variations of how the close works.

The Sales Call—Close

It's time to examine the final stage of the sales call. By this time, you have successfully—

- *Gained your client's trust by building rapport.*
- *Gotten down to business by asking a transitional open-ended question.*
- *Investigated the client's problems by listening and questioning.*
- *Fine-tuned the flow of the meeting by using all of your available communication skills—both verbal and non-verbal.*
- *Identified your client's hot buttons.*
- *Quantified the reasons for the client to take action.*
- *Given your sales pitch.*
- *Summarized the key points.*
- *Outlined the approach you will follow to resolve the various concerns.*

Therefore, the close is imminent. The close is a critical part of the sales call because that's when you ask for the business. Until now, you could have made a great deal of mistakes that would have little impact if you finish with a strong close. On the other hand, you could have been flawless up to this point and blow it all here. This is the point at which most people fall on their own swords.

A technique that can dramatically minimize the frequency of this sword falling is called the trial close. Trial closes allow you to identify or further define obstacles hampering the selling process. In other words, if you are looking for a yes answer, why are you still hearing no? For instance, let's say your client has a problem that you wish to solve. But based on a couple of recent negative experiences, you really don't want to accept the client's job unless you can also manage the project. A trial close might be, "Let's assume that by tomorrow afternoon I can put together a plan that addresses this situation. If you like the plan, could we get started next week with me as project manager?"

This trial close conditionally asks for the business. In this case, it also positions you as project manager and establishes a beginning time frame. If the client has no objections, he or she is allowed to accept the proposition conditioned that you can put together an acceptable plan. By asking for the business in a trial close format, this allows you to bring unresolved issues to the surface. For example, the client might respond, "Well, I like the idea of you managing the project, but I'm not sure I can afford that luxury."

This response clearly resolves the project management issue assuming the money can be worked out. Therefore, the trial close has leaped successfully over one hurdle and identified another. The next step is to come to terms on the finances of the project with another trial close, such as, "Well, assuming you and I can come to terms regarding my fees, is next week an acceptable starting time?"

The point is, by properly utilizing the trial close technique, you can identify the hurdles that stand between you and your final objective: approval. This process also is worthwhile because you can obtain commitment before valuable time is spent preparing a proposal or preliminary material.

Once you have jumped the various hurdles (satisfied your client's objections), it's time to ask for the business.

There are several guidelines to follow when attempting to do this:

1. *Don't let your potential clients leave without asking for their business.* People normally avoid making decisions. By forcing the issue face-to-face, you increase the odds of obtaining a positive response. It's much easier for them to refuse you later, over the phone or by letter, than right then in person. This fact has clearly influenced a whole category of product sales that fall under the consumer credit contract provisions. For example, products such as swimming pools, sunrooms, magazines sold door-to-door, and hundreds of other products fall into this category, which requires that several days pass (often three) before the contract is valid (providing ample time for the customer to back out). Why? Because it is hard to turn people down face-to-face.

2. *Before you ask for the business, discuss your rates and how you will bill for the project.* Try to minimize the number of possible put-offs, or buying objections, before you ask for the business. Don't let rates bog you down; cover them up-front in a matter-of-fact way. When your potential clients are forced to ask you for this information, or when you are shy about revealing your fees, the cost of doing business is given more of a spotlight than it deserves.

3. *If you require a retainer, discuss it with confidence.* Be confident when asking for a retainer. Nothing is worse than someone requesting a retainer and then stumbling all over trying to explain why. If the client wants to know why, he or she will ask. After you mention the retainer, expect your client to be silent. This is not a bad sign. It is normal. Everyone seems to require a few moments of silence before deciding to spend money. These quiet seconds are often used to decide some financial specifics, such as whether there is enough money in the checking account, what bills are due this week, and so on. Regardless of why, don't overreact to the silence.

4. *Ask for the project in a way that suggests an affirmative answer.* As we stated above, most people avoid confrontation. They would rather say yes than no. So, phrase your closing question in a manner that takes advantage of human nature. For example, "We could get started next Monday or Thursday. Which would be better for you?"

   By phrasing your question in a positive fashion, there is an implied yes to doing business together. So in order for your client to turn you down, he or she would almost have to argue with you. In contrast, "Would you like to sleep on this decision?" suggests an easy out for the client to postpone making a decision.

5. *When it's time to ask for the business, ask and shut up.* At this point in the marketing game, after you have asked for the business, the old saying goes, *Whoever talks first . . . loses.*

   In other words, *learn how to live with the silence that follows tough questions.* If you say anything, you divert attention away from the question, giving the client an opportunity to change the subject, postpone the decision, or many other less desirable alternatives.

   If your client has a real objection, this silence will give him or her time to formulate a response. Remember that an objection is not fatal; each time you satisfy one, you get another step closer to making the sale.

6. *If the client does postpone the decision, find out what must be done to finalize the deal.* If your client must postpone the decision for good reason, such as needing approval from a higher company official or wanting time to check your references, be sure to agree on the next course of action before your meeting is adjourned. This might entail a "to do" list, scheduling another meeting or identifying who should contact whom and when. If the responsibility of contact falls on your client's shoulders, always give yourself another in, such as, "If I don't hear from you by Friday, can I call you on Monday?"

By following the structure of the sales call, and by paying attention to what may seem to be the minutia of detail surrounding each step within it, your ability to close tough business situations will improve dramatically. The good news is, once you get comfortable with the process, it will become natural very quickly. After you close the business, it's time for you to move on to the consulting call.

THE STRUCTURED CONSULTING CALL

As stated in the beginning of this chapter, the discovery call, the sales call, and the consulting call have a great deal of similarity. Since we have gone into the discovery and sales calls in detail, we want to mainly point out the nuances of the consulting call. The place to start, as we have done with each call type, is to review the structure:

1. *Investigation phase:*
   - Relating
   - Discovery and interviewing
2. *Closing phase:*
   - Reviewing findings and identifing suggestions
   - Presenting the action plan
   - Persuading and facilitating
   - Supporting

Consulting Call—Relating

The first stage in the *investigation phase* is relating with a client. How is this different from the opening (the combination of the introduction and rapport-building) in the sales call? Simple. By this time, you have already sold the client your services, and hopefully, have developed some rapport with the owners or management team. Therefore, while we always have to be concerned about maintaining good impressions (or making a good first impression every day), our beginning of the meeting dialog shifts from making a connection to building on the one we have already established. That's why we refer to this step as relating, which is defined by Webster's as "to establish a meaningful relationship with a person or thing."

There is nothing we need to say about this area; this is nothing new. One of the reasons our profession has thrived over the years is because our professionals know how to build strong client relationships. The foundation of this relationship often rests on our ethics, including trust, honesty, and integrity. It certainly doesn't hurt, however, if you also make a concerted effort to accelerate the relationship-building process by talking about shared hobbies, enjoying some after-work activity together, or showing interest in subjects that you know are of interest to the client.

Consulting Call—Discovery and Interviewing

The second step in the *investigation phase* is discovery and interviewing. Discovery is virtually the same as information-gathering, except that rather than looking to quantify why something should change, you are now looking for ways to facilitate the necessary changes. Interviewing is self-explanatory. While this could be said to be a tool of the discovery process, because so much time is spent utilizing this technique, we included it to differentiate the kind of analytical investigation a consultant performs on his or her own versus the information gathered through formal interviews with key personnel.

All of the tips and techniques discussed throughout the book so far regarding communication skills, questioning techniques, avoiding premature speculation, paraphrasing your ideas as questions, not feeling you have to have answers, and more absolutely apply here. Remember in the sales call section, when we discussed making sure that both you and your client understand the value of hiring you (quantifying the reason for fixing the problem). Well, in the consulting call, you are attempting to solve, solve, and solve. Once again, this does not mean that it is your job to have the answers. It means that it is your job, with heavy involvement from the client, to arrive at alternatives and help evaluate them. For example, in a recent workshop, a real client participated in the role-play scenarios. Here's an excerpt from that dialog that supports our position:

Consultant: Tell me a little bit about your business.

Client: I'm the president of a restaurant chain. We have seven successful company-owned locations, and have franchised four more.

[*Later in the conversation*]

Consultant: Why the mix between wholly-owned restaurants and franchised ones?

Client: Years ago, all of our locations were wholly-owned. But as you know, the cost of expansion is high. There is not only the cash flow requirement to fund new locations, but you need to know the area in order to select good locations, you need to find management that you can count on and trust, and a number of other issues. The bottom line is we saw franchising as being an excellent alternative in that it looked to be very lucrative, provided us with more buying power (which would be good for both the franchisees and our own locations), and allowed us to grow much more rapidly with significantly less risk.

Consultant: How is the franchising going?

Client: Not nearly as well as we had hoped!

Consultant: Why?

Client: I don't know. We've sold four locations, and they seem quite happy. But we need to do more to support them on an ongoing basis, especially if we want them to remain happy.

Consultant: Like what?

Client: More products, better marketing, lower costs . . . you know . . . anything to help them attract more customers and make more money. Since we take a cut of the gross revenue, it's in both of our best interests for us to help them grow.

Consultant: What's stopping you from making all of that happen?

Client: Time! I just don't have enough time to get all the things I should be doing done.

Consultant: Is there someone you can delegate more work to?

Client: No. Everyone here is already so busy. Besides, the kind of person I need to help me would cost us about $50,000 per year. I'm just not ready to spend that kind of money.

Consultant: I'm just curious. If you had this $50,000-per-year person working for you, how much *of your time* do you think you could realistically free up?

Client: Probably about half, easily more than a third.

Consultant: If you spent that freed-up time selling new franchises, conservatively, how many could you sell in a year?

Client: Maybe five, but conservatively, three or four.

Consultant: How much revenue in franchise fees would you expect from each of those newly established franchises in a 12-month period?

Client: In the first 12 months, probably around $50,000 each.

Consultant: Are there any other benefits that you would enjoy by having, let's say, three new franchised locations?

Client: Definitely. As I said earlier, with each location, we gain greater buying power, which makes every location more money, including company-owned restaurants, and spreads the cost of promotional and advertising pieces because there are more operations sharing the cost burden.

Consultant: What do you think that would be worth to you?

Client: I don't know, but it would be in the thousands of dollars.

Consultant: So, you feel that you could conservatively add three new franchised restaurants per year netting you an average of $50,000 each, and that you would gain thousands of dollars in savings per year through greater buying power if you had more time you could devote to this area?

Client: [*Long pause*]. It seems kind of silly that I've hesitated hiring someone to help me, doesn't it? Your question doesn't even consider the compounding nature of adding three franchises a year, because by the end of the second year, I would have added the equivalent of six $50,000-a-year income streams. I have to admit, putting off $300,000 to $500,000 in revenues or savings just to save $50,000 in payroll cost doesn't make much sense.

This is a perfect example of how consulting heavily utilizes communication and questioning skills, avoids premature speculation, is more powerful when ideas are paraphrased as questions, and requires patience to refrain from too quickly providing clients with answers. This is not to say that the consultant doesn't have to have any knowledge at all. But when you believe that your clients or their employees have the necessary answers, the discovery and interview step of the consulting call becomes a fun game. You know there is buried treasure in your client's company and that a map exists, even though no one person has the entire map. The object is to successfully piece that map together by combining your expertise with theirs.

It wouldn't surprise us if you were thinking, "Consulting can't be this easy. My clients would never pay for this kind of service . . . and even if they did, they would be mad at me for billing for this!" Well, we certainly can't speak for the world. But we can repeat what thousands of CPAs have said after they have tried this, "I wish I would have starting doing this a long time ago. It's easy, it's profitable, and the client is really happy with the outcome." Anytime clients are involved in our workshops, we ask them if the information discussed in the role-plays is valuable to them. Each time, to the amazement of the participants, the answer is emphatically, "Yes."

While consulting, many of the answers or potential solutions will fall out just as they did in the questioning dialog above. However, many will not. And that's OK. This is to be expected. But for each branch identified on the investigative tree that is not resolved, a go-forward action plan should be established. This is where you apply techniques such as (1) "to-do list" planning, (2) cash, capacity, and capability, (3) phasing and others, to satisfy the needs of your clients in a way that matches the resources of your clients.

Consulting Call—Reviewing Findings and Identifying Suggestions

This is the first step in the closing phase of the consulting call. Review of findings and identification of suggestions is the analytical part of your work. After you have gathered the information you need, you take it back to the office, or to a space in the client's office, and reflect on what you have found. Reflection is an important tool for CPAs. But as we discussed earlier, our desire to provide instant answers gets in the way of utilizing this as often as we should. Usually, after allowing yourself even minimal time to think through the events that transpired and the information gathered, you arrive at some startling revelations. Many times, reflection allows you to envision ideas far better than those you originally pictured. Or even more important, after some thought, you realize that you are operating without some critical information. This realization forces you to take a quick step back into the information-gathering process to collect more information. At this stage, you need to keep bouncing back and forth between gathering information and analyzing it until you feel that you really understand what is going on.

CPAs are uniquely qualified for work like this. We, as a profession, have excellent skills when it comes to looking at business systems, processes, procedures, workflow, and so on, and deriving more efficient and effective ways to meet or exceed organization objectives. Our only drawback here is that we often expect these revelations to come instantaneously. So make sure that you allocate time to this creative process. This not only includes quality think time (several hours of noninterrupted thought), but also a few days to let your brain subconsciously do some work on its own. Obviously, the more complex the project, the more think-time you have to allocate to it. But it's amazing the time-saving, money-generating, cost-reducing ideas that come forth when you give yourself enough flexibility.

Consulting Call—Presenting the Action Plan

This is the reporting step of the consulting call. Large firms do this well. Formal reporting is part of their methodology for managing projects. For smaller projects, which are often done by smaller firms, we change the rules slightly. While the reporting element is still essential, we change the delivery from written to oral reporting. Chapter 9 addresses many of the techniques required to manage meetings and make high quality presentations. At this point, we just want to explain why reporting is so important.

In almost any project, many aspects will work as planned, a few better than plan, and a few (although it sometimes seems like all the important ones) worse than plan. This is just a day in the life of a consultant. We've seen from our own experience, as well as our CPA firm clients, that too often we are faced with enormous challenges and are constantly asked to scale the highest peaks. Upon arrival at the summit (overcoming the continual barrage of hurdles), in total exhaustion we might add, you will inevitably be greeted by the dreaded phrase, "What did you get done today (this week, this month) . . . it seems we haven't made any progress at all." Often in these cases, an unexpected problem arises that you or your team works on furiously for hours, days, and weeks to resolve. Many times, these problems are caused by the client or their personnel, or they are just unexpected problems unique to that particular situation. Instead of being greeted with accolades and gifts for your creativity and genius, you are slashed by the penetrating suggestion that you have underperformed. There are few moments harder to take than these. Why do they happen? How can you avoid them? Client reporting is the answer.

The action plan presentation is your minimum presentation requirement. When you use phasing, this step comes up quite often. But if you have a project with a phase that lasts weeks or more, then you have to incorporate mini-updates along the way too. Our rule:

Martyrs don't live long and prosper
in the field of consulting.

Translated, this means that when you encounter a significant problem (one that requires more time than planned), let your clients know. While you want to let them be aware of what you are up against, you also want to assure them that their problems are in good hands. Why do you go through all of this effort? Because we believe that when we are losing sleep attempting to solve a problem, so should the client. While they have the luxury of leaving the project in your hands, they typically will also try to gain an understanding of how a problem might position them for less desirable alternatives. The good news, and what makes this all worthwhile, is that when you finally identify an implementable solution and share it with the client, he or she is as excited about your accomplishment as you are. This is a hard lesson to learn, and one we didn't take to heart easily. We spent the first 5 years of our consulting lives accomplishing incredible feats with less-than-overwhelmed clients. When we shortened our phases and added this reporting step to the process (and occasionally threw in extra reporting steps along the way), we found greater appreciation for our work, higher client satisfaction, and less friction over fees.

In the consulting call, the action plan presentation step is an excellent way to let your client know where you are and open a dialog about where to go. This is not something that should take days to create. Obviously, the more complex the project, the more formal the oral report. For example, instead of using a typed meeting agenda as you would for most meetings, you might use presentation tools such as Powerpoint™, Freelance™, Astound™, or any other software package that would help you deliver complex materials succinctly and easily. Don't be shy about keeping your client informed. It's funny. CPAs tend to think this is a non-essential and costly step compared to the other work performed. However, the less your client knows about what you are doing day to day, and what you are accomplishing, the less satisfied he or she is likely to be with your work. This is just another case in point where the politics of doing the work can easily be more important than the actual work itself.

Consulting Call—Persuading and Facilitating

A great plan or a superior idea is meaningless if there is no consensus to take action. As a consultant, being able to take on the role of change agent is critical to ensuring forward momentum. Too often, we get bogged down in our analysis and our quest for the right answer. After hours, days and even weeks of deliberation, it is common for our professionals to enter a room of their peers with their statistically valid or highest probability of success approach to choosing an action plan. We weigh the pros and cons of each alternative, assess the risks, and then hold steadfast to the idea that one solution is better than another. Unfortunately, while our analysis is most likely correct, it often contains a fatal flaw. We don't consider the "people factor," which can easily undermine even the best of ideas.

We are not suggesting that CPAs change their deliberate conscientious approach to problem solving. However, once your analysis is done, when you sit down with your client's management team, it's time to peel your pride of ownership from around your suggested alternatives and open your mind to another set of decision-making parameters. The new parameters are simple and straightforward. They are—

- Does the client-management team believe in the alternative?
- Does the client-management team understand the nuances of implementing the alternative?
- Will the management team know, at a gut level, how to respond when the alternative goes awry?
- Will the alternative receive a great deal of resentment or undermining from the rank and file?
- Is the alternative one that fits the style and capabilities of the company's personnel?

Depending on the answers to these questions, the best solution could easily move from last on your list to the number one position. The "people factor" is what makes consulting so difficult. As a consultant, you are not trying the find the perfect solution for you, but one that achieves the greatest results given the environment and personnel that will implement it. And as a consultant, you will not always be there to implement it. So, you have to strive to install systems and procedures that will endure when you are not around.

It is here, at this step, when you have to determine if it is best to motivate, educate, and persuade those around you as to why one option is better than another, or for you to do everything in your power to make an inferior idea work because of the commitment and support that surround it. The persuading and facilitating step does not, by any stretch of the imagination, mean that it is your job to get people to do what *you* want. Rather, it is your job to help your client achieve success by taking action, with the appropriate personnel working as a cohesive team. This often means that your ideas get scrapped and you have to scramble to shore up all the holes that exist in the alternative chosen.

Before we leave this step of the consulting call, we would like to remind you of what we consider to be an important perspective. The day you believe your answers are always the best ones, well, that's the day you need to stop doing this kind of work. People are unpredictable, projects are always unveiling unforeseeable difficulties, the work environment is constantly changing, and the marketplace is perpetually shifting. Given this, how can any one person have the vision to predict the result of an action taken amidst this evolving chaos? Keep in mind that taking on the role of change agent is difficult. It not only requires the skills we cover in this text, but a great deal of business experience combined with uncommon patience and humility.

Consulting Call—Supporting

This is the last step of the consulting call. Doing this well separates a great consultant from a marginal one. After an action plan is identified and agreed upon and tasks have been assigned, there are political issues, conflicts, new priorities, and so on that can quickly throw your client off track.

Let's say your client is ready to implement an expanded marketing plan. A week or two (of a three-month concentrated front-end effort) after the project starts, which was deemed the number one priority by management, a new priority called "our biggest client is unhappy with our product and is threatening to change suppliers" instantly rises to the top of the list.

This kind of scenario is so common it can't be considered an anomaly. Yet, a tremendous amount of work is at stake if the client, as soon as the crisis is averted, doesn't immediately pick back up where he or she left off. If the unhappy client leaves, then implementing the expanded marketing plan in this case even becomes more important. Supporting is the step that keeps you involved and in contact with the client. Supporting occurs in actions such as—

- Occasional phone calls (planned in advance by you using a contact management systems).
- Pre-arranged quarterly update meetings.
- Working on-site while performing other services so you can watch for the anticipated changes.
- Strategic, tactical, and budgetary planning meetings.

Just because your portion of the project is over doesn't mean that you should walk away. When you take on consulting work, you should sell your ongoing involvement as a critical success factor to the client's future. We do. We're not talking about this function consuming a great deal of time, or billing much money for that matter. We are simply referring to the act of providing a watchful eye over the progress of your client in some systematic way. By doing this, when projects get derailed, you can easily and quickly step in to help get them on-track again.

The Number One Failing

All three of the call types discussed in this chapter have some overlap, a great deal of similarity, require the same skill sets, and work in conjunction with each other. For example, before you meet with a referred client, conduct a discovery call. Once the prospect has been qualified, and there seems to be mutual benefit to doing business together, a sales call is the logical next step. And at such time that the prospect accepts your offer to deliver services and becomes a client, a consulting call is in order. Each call type picks up where the previous one left off. As we stated in the beginning of this chapter, the key is cut-off. Often, there is a natural delineation between one call type and another. For instance, you make a phone call and execute the stages of the discovery call. Once qualified, you set up an appointment to make the sales call. Once the client hires you, you set an agenda and timetable to begin the project later (the consulting call).

Sometimes, however, the delineation between these call types is vague. Sometimes they occur one after the other, or even simultaneously, in the same setting. In these cases, you have to create the necessary distinctions. For example, if you find yourself making a sales call before a discovery call was made, then the two call types blend together. Because you are in a selling environment, you should follow the process of the sales call. However, once the opening phase (which includes the introductions and rapport-building) is complete, the discovery call objective of qualification becomes the focus of the information-gathering phase. If the prospect doesn't meet the basic tests of qualification, you quickly cut your losses, stop selling, and find a courteous way out. If the prospect is qualified, then you just continue with the sale process and ask a lot more questions. As you know, at this point, the call objective would shift from one of qualification to quantification.

If the sales call goes well and the client says, "Let's get started right now," then do so. You have to make the clear distinction at this point that you are on-the-clock and beginning the project. There should always be a clear distinction between the sales call and the consulting call. Why? Because one is for free and the other is not! A problem we have within our profession is that we continually merge the sales call with the consulting call. If we can't make the necessary distinctions between them, there is no way our client will be able to. With the consulting call, the objective is to solve. This is significantly different than the sales call's objective of quantification.

The number one failing we see in our work with CPA firms is that all three of these call types are performed simultaneously with no distinction between them. This typically results in a great deal of wasted time, prospects who just won't make the final commitment to specific consulting services and consulting expertise given away. By understanding the differences between each of these, their nuances, and their cut-off, you will not only find yourself generating more consulting work and revenue, you will also find yourself in a better position to satisfy your clients. Why? Because your skill in performing these calls will help them better understand the priorities of their organization, the value of taking action, and the plan to facilitate the necessary changes.

Before You Move On

We have a variety of exercises for you pertaining to this chapter. This is partially the case just because there is so much material here. However, although many of these concepts seem familiar, they will not have their full impact until you experience them first-hand, by participating in a role-play or two.

The Discovery Call Role-Play

The first exercise is a discovery call role-play. The *Role-Play Scenario Sheet* assumes that the CPA firm regularly sends out advertising direct mail pieces that include a return postcard. Potential customers can check any of the following boxes:

- ❑ Yes, I want more information about the various services you offer.
- ❑ Yes, please call me. I would like to talk about ways your firm can help me.
- ❑ Yes, I would like to take advantage of your 30-minute free consulting offer.
- ❑ Yes, I would like to take advantage of your free tax return review.

This sheet identifies a few scenarios for the "potential client" in this role-play.

Here's the way this role-play works:

1. The consultant makes the discovery call in front of the entire group.
2. A speaker phone is utilized in the role-play room so everyone can hear.
3. Those observing use the *Discovery Call Observer's Note Sheet* and record constructive advice to be passed on to the consultant at the end of the call.
4. The "potential client" takes the role-play scenarios list and sets up in some other room in the office. The "potential client" can choose one of the scenarios on the list, or can make up his or her own. Regardless, the scenario has to be identified and written down before the role-play begins.
5. The consultant reviews the *Discovery Call Prompter* (the next form) to help him or her prepare for the call. Feel free to look over the discovery call section of this chapter as a refresher before the call. We recommend using scripts in this type of call not only to build confidence, but because the calls are meant to be short and to the point.

The objective of this exercise is to qualify the "potential client." Although you might have to live up to an advertising obligation, you want to either minimize how much time you waste, or maximize how much opportunity you might uncover. Part of this exercise is for the consultant to correctly identify the "potential client's" situation. For example, if the "potential client" is merely a student looking for information with no business opportunity, the consultant should be able to correctly state that at the end of this exercise. The consultant should also correctly determine whether this "potential client" should be—

1. Referred to someone else so as to not waste any additional time.
2. Sent information and noted in a tickler file to call back because there might be opportunity in the future.

3. Given an appointment at the office in order to live up to the advertising commitment but minimize the time commitment.
4. Given an appointment at the client's office to maximize potential opportunity.

If a free tax return review is the requested service, having the client mail in or fax the return to minimize the time commitment is also an option if it is determined that the client's only desire is free advice. Have everyone in the room cycle through this exercise one at a time until everyone has participated except the "potential client." Then, someone should take the "potential client's" place so that person can also experience this exercise.

Paper Closing Exercise

The next activity is a two-page paper closing exercise appropriately called *Closing Exercise*. A situation is described and you are asked to identify your client's hot buttons, write out a trial close, and, with additional information, propose a closing statement. This exercise is meant to make you think through the sales call process and lay out the most difficult step of all, the close.

Sales Call (Information-Gathering) Exercise

This is an exercise many firms redo often. Why? Because it is focused on identifying consulting opportunities and then quantifying reasons justifying the consultant's involvement. Skill development in this area can quickly increase revenues. The first step is for each person to work through and fill out the *Client's Priority List*. Put yourself in the shoes of a client you know well and follow the instructions from there. After everyone has done this, then divide up into groups of three; one participant is the consultant, another the client, and the third is an observer. Logically, the observer should take notes on the sales call's *Observer's Note Sheet*.

To start the exercise, the client should hand his or her *Client's Priority List* to the observer. At this point, the consultant is given about 20 minutes to uncover all the issues on the *Client's Priority List* by interviewing the client. Once the time expires, the consultant is to identify the issues uncovered, prioritize them, and discuss how they were quantified. This information should be compared against that found on the *Client's Priority List*. Finally, the observer is to share his or her observations about the exercise.

Self-Assessment

This is the last exercise. Each chapter has built on skills found in the previous ones. However, the exercises in this chapter force you to pull them all together. After you have gone through the forms and role-plays, you will find that you are comfortable in some areas, and extremely uncomfortable in others. Analyze this discomfort to determine what developmental areas you should be focusing on.

Role-Play Scenario Sheet

The Structured Discovery Call—Objective: Qualify

- ***Investigation Phase***
  - *The introduction*
  - *Become aquainted with the business*
  - *Qualify the prospect*
- ***Closing Phase***
  - *Abbreviated sales pitch*
  - *Identification of the next step*
  - *Seeking agreement*

Role-Play Scenarios:

- ❑ Wants additional general information because prospect is a pack-rat. Checks all information request boxes because of curiosity. Has no intention of spending money.
- ❑ Wants a free half hour of consulting and the prospect feels a need for help, but has no money.
- ❑ Wants additional information, specific to planning. Has a company that is ripe for a planning engagement.
- ❑ Is a student wanting information for a project.
- ❑ Works for a company now, thinking about starting a business, and would not blink an eye at spending a couple thousand dollars for assistance.
- ❑ Wants a free half hour of consulting, but is just curious. No need exists to prospect's knowledge. Wants as much free advice as possible.
- ❑ Wants additional information, specific to automating a PC-based QuickBooks® level accounting system. The company can easily afford a full-blown accounting system.
- ❑ Doesn't remember sending anything in or talking to anyone, and is too busy to talk.
- ❑ Wants a free half hour of consulting, feels a need for help, and has a business large enough to pay for such assistance.

(continued on next page)

Role-Play Scenario Sheet (continued)

- ❑ Wants free tax review and currently does a 1040EZ.
- ❑ Doesn't remember sending anything in or talking to anyone, but is struggling with several business issues at the current time.
- ❑ Interested, not ready now, call back in six months.
- ❑ Works for a company now, thinking about starting a business, and spending $300 for assistance would be an enormous commitment to make.
- ❑ Wants free tax review, is having some problems with an IRS audit, and spends about $1000 a year on a tax return.

Discovery Call Observer's Note Sheet

Consultant: ______________________________

Client: ______________________________

Write down your observations regarding the consultant's questioning style, use of open-ended questions, or lack thereof. Did the conversation comfortably lead to qualifying the business? Did the client drop clues that the consultant never picked up, or clues the consultant picked up but never followed? Did the consultant make a commitment that was unwarranted given the way the call went? Please note any thoughts you have that might help the consultant in future discovery call situations.

Notes for the Consultant: ______________________________

Discovery Call Prompter

Write down your scripted open.

Write down an open-ended question or two.

Consider now whether the following four areas were addressed during the discovery call:

1. Time Frame

The first issue to address is time frame. Ask the potential client a question such as, "What is your time frame for getting this project underway?" or "When do you want this [some service] to be completed?"

2. Decision Maker

The next critical piece of information to collect is, *who is the decision maker?* This is a tough question to ask and most versions of the question cause more harm than good. For this reason, we ask you to memorize these words: *"Besides yourself, is there anyone else who will be involved in making the final decision?"*

3. Budget

The next question to ask pertains to the project's *budget*. This is not a sensitive question to ask, even though you may not get an answer. "How much have you budgeted for this project?" and "What did you plan on spending?" are acceptable alternatives.

4. Priority

Once the potential client acknowledges a price range that is within the realm of reasonableness, the last question we ask concerns *priority*. Simply stated, "What's the priority of this project to your organization?"

Notes

Closing Exercise

Situation:

You have just completed an information-gathering meeting with your new client. She operates a computer network consulting firm and wants to expand her practice. She currently has five programmer-analyst employees working for her. She wants you to help establish a marketing plan. She has told you that she thinks she has lost over $200,000 worth of projects due to the fact that she has been very haphazard regarding how she markets her business. This loss in project revenue is partially based on inside information about her competitors. While it appears she spends about as much in marketing as her competitors, she consistently does not receive nearly as many inquiries regarding her services.

Your new client also is interested in improving her billing process. She feels it is slow and inefficient, and because of that, she knows of over $20,000 in lost billings from last year that are uncollectable because those projects are complete and considered paid-in-full.

Finally, the owner seems to have excellent skills in attracting and closing new projects. However, she is not so good (by her own admission) regarding day-to-day firm administration. She would like to brainstorm with you about ideas on how to improve firm administration because, if things stay the same, she feels her lead programmer-analyst will get so frustrated he will quit.

Step One: List your new client's hot buttons.

1. ______________________________

____

2. ______________________________

____

3. ______________________________

____

Step Two: Without committing to a price or a cost estimate, write down an example of a trial close.

Step Three: Write down an example of a closing statement based on the following additional facts.

Assume that you are comfortable with the skills required to perform this engagement, that your price estimate to help your new client create a marketing plan is $10,000, that for an additional $2,000 you could review her billing system procedures and be in a position to make recommendations, and that the three-hour brainstorming meeting regarding firm administration would run about $400. Assuming that all three projects have the same priority and she wants to hire someone to help her with all three immediately, what is your closing response?

Sales Call (Information-Gathering) Exercise
Client's Priority List

Put yourself in the shoes of one of your good business clients. For the sake of this exercise, consider that you have a good relationship with your consultant, you call or see him or her two or three times a year, and that you have gladly accepted a lunch or office appointment. Write down the business you are in, where you are meeting, the last time you met, and why you met. Finally, list your current priorities; areas that are of concern for you in the business. In other words, list what is keeping you awake at night. None of these areas has to be financial. After you have listed at least four areas of concern, prioritize them.

- ______________________________ Priority: ______

____

____

- ______________________________ Priority: ______

____

____

- ______________________________ Priority: ______

____

____

- ______________________________ Priority: ______

____

____

- ______________________________ Priority: ______

____

____

- ______________________________ Priority: ______

____

____

Sales Call (Information-Gathering) Exercise Observer's Note Sheet

Make notes regarding the progress of this exercise. As potentially sensitive situations occur, jot down how well or poorly the CPA handled them. Some issues to consider are:

Did the CPA listen carefully to the conversation, or talk too much?

____

____

How well did the CPA make eye contact with all the players, use gestures, have a confident tone of voice, act interested, and so on. Write your thoughts regarding nonverbal messages.

____

____

Did the CPA seem to pick up on subtleties of the client's comments and concerns?

____

____

Did the CPA interrupt the client or start talking before the client completed his or her thoughts?

____

____

Did the CPA miss consulting opportunities (branches)?

____

____

In what area(s) did the CPA seem most comfortable?

____

____

Other comments regarding this exercise.

____

____

Self-Assessment Time Line
Relative to Improving My Call Skills

Based on the materials covered in this chapter, please take a few moments and assess your weaknesses. Then, using the form below, make note of any skills you plan to work on as well as a time frame to re-assess your progress. In addition, if there are activities or exercises you plan on attempting, jot them down and note your intended completion date. This form is provided solely as a self-improvement tool.

The following are ***Skills*** *I plan to* ***Improve:***

______________________________ By when: _________

______________________________ By when: _________

______________________________ By when: _________

______________________________ By when: _________

______________________________ By when: _________

______________________________ By when: _________

______________________________ By when: _________

______________________________ By when: _________

______________________________ By when: _________

The following are ***Activities*** *I plan to* ***Attempt:***

______________________________ By when: _________

______________________________ By when: _________

______________________________ By when: _________

______________________________ By when: _________

______________________________ By when: _________

______________________________ By when: _________

______________________________ By when: _________

Section 3

Identifying and Marketing Your Services

Chapter 8

Two Approaches to Business Consulting

Winters and Associates, a successful CPA firm, decided to offer some new, specialized consulting services. As a logical place to start, these services were marketed to its existing client base. Immediately, there were several hot prospects. Within a couple of months, the consulting projects fully utilized what normally would have been off-season idle time by management and staff. Yet, additional requests were being made. Rather than miss these lucrative opportunities, management hired personnel for the sole purpose of consulting.

Six months later, operating with a beefed-up consulting department, the pent-up demand of the existing client base had been consumed. The consulting requests were starting to come in at a more normal pace. Over the next twelve months, the nonbillable time of the consulting staff was growing and beginning to get out of hand.

Knowing that the firm's financial resources were draining fast, management put together a comprehensive marketing campaign to expand the firm's consulting visibility. This resulted in an even more restricted cash flow because, while there was significant interest due to the expanded marketing effort, new business was slow to materialize. The firm quickly discovered that selling consulting services to new clients was a much harder and slower sell than signing up existing clients. And since Winters and Associates was not financially strong enough to support the ever-increasing idle time of its expanded consulting department, at least for the length of time it would take for demand to catch up with supply, the firm decided to go back to its bread-and-butter services and leave consulting to other CPA firms. Because of this decision, one of the partners took several of the firm's key employees, a good number of the clients, and started a competing firm. The result was disastrous. It took years for Winters and Associates to recover from its consulting fiasco.

This scenario should ring a familiar bell. If you didn't personally go through it, you most likely know someone who did. History reflects that CPA firms have had difficulty implementing consulting and we blame most of the problems on three factors:

1. Confusion between consulting services and consulting packages
2. Delivery of consulting through a one-approach-fits-all strategy
3. Consulting service and consulting package offerings inconsistent with firm objectives

The first factor was covered in chapters 1 and 2. The second factor, delivery of consulting through a *one-approach-fits-all strategy* was discussed in chapter 6. Finally, "consulting service and consulting package (niche service) offerings inconsistent with firm objectives" is the focus of this chapter.

Understand to Whom the Service Is Targeted

Before you offer any new service, you need to understand whom the service is targeted to serve, and why it is important for you to serve that market. This is where the concepts of the fortress and empire come into play. Let's take a closer look at the meanings we've assigned to these terms.

Throughout history, *fortresses* were built in order to protect communities from outside forces. Barriers were created (walls, moats, and so on) to fend off would-be attackers. All the needs of the community were supplied from within the confines of the fortress.

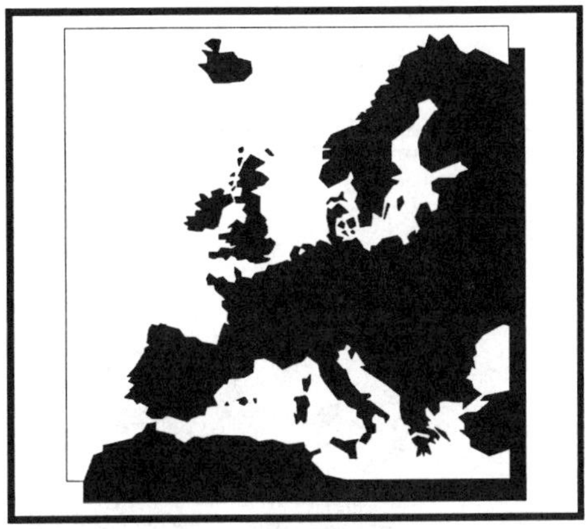

Empires were built by conquering new territories and expanding well beyond original boundaries. The community's needs were supplied through a combination of resources available within the *empire's own fortress* and in the new wealth found amidst the annexed provinces.

With these brief definitions in mind, here's how these terms form the foundation of our service offerings analysis.

Fortress Objective: Client Retention and Service Extension

The fortress has a short-term horizon and is directed at offering consulting packages to a community of existing clients. The goal is—

> *To enhance loyalty and revenues while simultaneously denying opportunities to competitors by building a wall of essential business services around your client base.*

With the fortress, consideration should be given to the short-term needs of the CPA firm's client base, the profitability of delivering a particular service, the CPA firm's in-house talent, and the CPA firm's long-term objectives, in this order.

This approach is a client base protection strategy that simultaneously generates additional revenues. By continually offering client-desired consulting, you eliminate the need for clients to look to your competitors for help. In order to keep your competition at a distance, you build a wall of services that addresses all reasonable consulting opportunities.

For example, let's say one of your major clients requires financing support. The fortress suggests that you find a way to satisfy this need, or your client's cry for help will be heard by competitors. And should one of them respond, all of the other services you provide to that particular client are at risk. By remaining visible and maintaining at least some level of involvement with the client, you minimize the chance of losing account control. Your firm also presents the positive image of being a one-stop-shop, a firm that can cater to all the needs of its community.

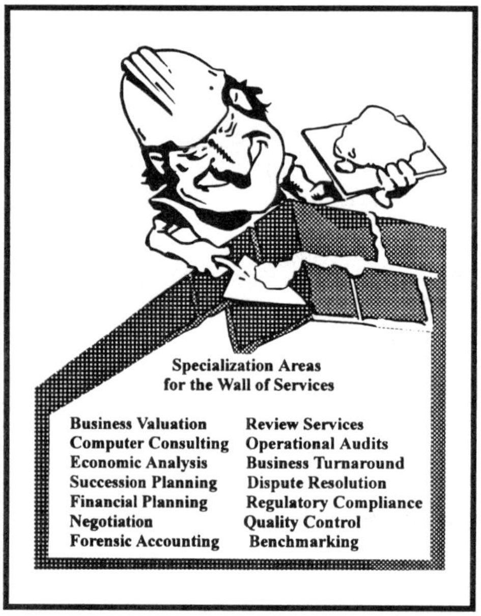

A real plus for the fortress is . . . it typically returns a high profit in minimal time. Why? Because revenues can be generated quickly (you know the clients are ready to buy since they are asking for the services) and the cost of marketing is low (since they are existing clients, the selling cycle is short and inexpensive).

What services should a fortress offer? Well, according to a recent AICPA Management Consulting Section Survey, the consulting packages in the graphic above were considered hot. On the other hand, according to a recent AICPA Information Technology Section Top 15 Technologies list, the following technologies and functions were considered of prime importance to the marketplace:

1. Image processing
2. Security
3. Communications technologies—general
4. Area networks
5. Client/server computing
6. Business process re-engineering
7. Expert systems
8. Telecommuting
9. Electronic data interchange
10. Electronic commerce

11. Workflow technology
12. Collaborative computing & groupware
13. Intelligent agents
14. Mail technology
15. Quick response

Which consulting packages are best for your organization to implement? While picking a service or two from the two lists above would likely work, we think *asking your clients what they need on a regular basis* is probably the safest and most accurate alternative.

Empire Objective: New Client Acquisition

The second alternative, the empire, requires a long-term horizon and is time- and resource-intensive. We call it the empire because its intent is—

> *To select a few niche consulting packages and use them to annex new clients while also supplying them to the community within the fortress.*

This approach, referred to previously as the "swiss cheese" approach, is the one most commonly employed by large firms. The tools used are consulting packages, specialization, or nontraditional services. This might also be called a "niche service" approach. But there's more to this methodology than just offering a few niche services, which is why we gave it the more expansive title of empire. Within the empire strategy, firms market highly specialized consulting packages to attract new clients, while simultaneously supplying these services to their current client base. The great news for large firms is that, based on the critical mass of clients alone, it is easy for demand to outstretch supply.

Large firms often don't have to consider new client acquisition to justify the expense and effort required to deliver these various nontraditional services. On those occasions when the supply for a unique service is undercommitted, they just re-allocate those resources to the delivery of some other consulting package.

However, for the rest of us, the empire approach doesn't work quite so easily. Because of the small size of our client base relative to the largest twenty CPA firms, these unique packaged services will almost always be underutilized when the current client base is the main target. So while you may be able to increase revenues in the short term by delivering these services to your current client base, the empire is much more effective for client acquisition. Think of it this way: With the empire approach, you are making a few highly specialized consulting packages visible in order to create a distinction between your firm and your competitors. Since you have unique skills and experience in these consulting package areas, the empire highlights these strengths to attract new clients.

As you can see from reading just these few paragraphs, randomly offering "consulting packages" in order to make a few extra bucks might prove counterproductive to the long-term positioning and success of your firm. The first step is to determine whether the fortress or empire strategy is right for your organization. Then, based on that decision, many issues as well as what consulting packages to offer should become much clearer by the time you get through the worksheets at the end of this chapter.

Before elaborating more on the specifics of these two approaches, two more definitions need to be reviewed:

1. *Subcontract:* An arrangement with outside sources to provide a CPA firm with temporary staff or expertise. From the client's perspective, the contracting firm (for example, your firm) is in charge of the work. Therefore, as the manager of the project, it's important for the CPA consultant to stay involved and visible to the client. Logically, your firm is also the one held responsible. As the manager of subcontract workers, the CPA firm's role is not only technical, but also admin-

istrative, from project planning through the billing and collection function.

2. *Refer:* To send or direct a client to other sources for assistance without any expectation of further involvement.

Knowing when to subcontract versus when to refer plays a major role in the successful building of either the fortress or the empire. Let's now examine the nuts and bolts of each approach.

Building Your Fortress' Wall of Services

First, identify the *wanted services*—those services your clients want to obtain. The simplest way to do this is to listen. Clients tell you what they want in many ways—by the questions they ask, by sharing interesting comments from friends such as, "Joe tells me his CPA is . . .," and so on. More directly, you can have each member of your staff ask about the client's near-term operational priorities at the end of meetings and phone conversations (*this technique is not only simple and free, but effective*). More formal alternatives to solicit this kind of information include sending out surveys or questionnaires and conducting focus groups.

After gathering the information you need (and by the way, this is an ongoing process), prioritize these wanted services into a sequence of highest to lowest demand based on your clients' responses. Next, consider your competition and increase the priority of those services most likely to receive CPA competitive interference. This process helps you *distinguish the services of greatest interest to both your competition and your client base.*

After you have thought through the services that are in high demand, it's time to identify your *skills inventory*. You accomplish this by reviewing the background and experience of your managers and staff. A good way to begin this phase is to have each member of the firm analyze and list his or her own talents and strengths. Emphasize that this is no time to be modest or shy about abilities (for example, your data entry person may be a closet programmer, more than capable of expanding some of your technology service offerings). Once you have consolidated this information, you are likely to have a broader insight into the skills possessed by your in-house talent.

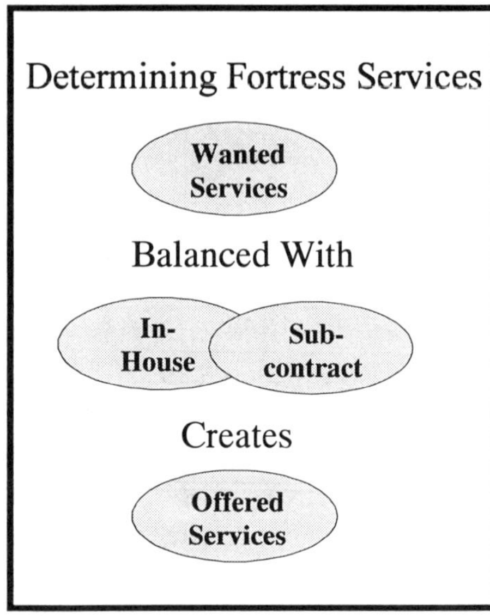

Another resource that you need to consider is that available through subcontracting. Many firms across the country are regularly utilizing subcontractors or outside consultants to help deliver client-demanded services. This is a critical support system for fortress firms because it is highly unlikely that the internal talent alone can satisfy the varied desires of the client base. Therefore, finding reputable firms that are capable of supplying quality contract services is essential. In a way, we are suggesting a strategic alliance with those who can augment your in-house talent. By making such alliances, you—

- Build additional loyalty by becoming more responsive to client needs.
- Provide a training ground for your personnel as they learn from these specialized outsiders.
- Generate additional revenues. First, many times you can mark up the contractor's fees. But even if there is little to no room for mark up, your billings from either including members of your firm on the contractor's team or managing the project can be significant.
- Strengthen your fortress' wall of services and make it more resistant to competition.

Finally, determine which services your firm should offer (offerable services) by balancing wanted services with available in-house and subcontract skills. This process results in identifying the services that—

- *Protect your client base.*
- *Are easy to provide.*
- *Are profitable to deliver.*

The steps just described work well in helping you determine which services you should offer to your fortress community. Still, you have to be ready to deliver client-tailored services as well as the services you formally offer. For example:

> Let's assume that one of your clients is about to begin the painful process of converting inventory and receivables from a manual system to a computerized one. Let's also assume that this is not one of the consulting services or consulting packages that has come out of your service analysis. However, your client has come to you for assistance or has commented that he or she needs assistance.
>
> The first question to ask yourself is . . . "Do we have access (internally or through subcontract) to the skills required to perform this project?" If the answer is *no*, then the AICPA's one-consulting standard precludes you from taking on the work due to the professional competence issue. For the sake of this discussion, let's assume the required skills are available.
>
> The next question is . . . "Is it likely that a competitor (who offers basically the same services we do) will take care of our client if we don't?" If the answer is *no*, then the decision as to whether to pursue this job should be based predominately on its profit potential. Should competitive pressure exist, the client's relative significance to your firm becomes of paramount importance. If the answer is *not substantial*, then once again, the project's overall economic impact determines your level of involvement. But if the client is an important player in your firm's revenue stream, then taking on a marginally profitable, or even unprofitable, job may be warranted to reduce the threat of poaching.

Building the Wall Profitably

Building the fortress' wall of services is likely to require a variety of talents and unique expertise. Few firms have the diversity of in-house talent to pull this off. So with each new opportunity, availability of talent becomes a central issue, raising questions such as—

- *Do we have the in-house talent required for this project?*
- *If we have the talent, is it currently available?*
- *If the in-house talent doesn't exist, is it worth developing?*
- *If the talent is worth developing, should we train existing personnel by contracting with someone already possessing this specialized knowledge, or work out a special on-the-job training arrangement with the client?*
- *Should we just subcontract this work because client demand is likely to be sparse?*

This series of questions brings up an important point to emphasize regarding the fortress: *minimize overhead!* Looking back at our computer implementation example and assuming competitive threat, if the talent is not readily available in-house, then subcontracting is the next best alternative. Why?

> *Because hiring or internally developing unique technical skills is a very low priority in the fortress strategy.*

The reason why is simple. The needs of your clients are constantly shifting. *Responding to these shifting needs is what the fortress is all about.* In other words, some of today's very specialized demanded services are likely to be less important several months or a year from now. For example, expertise in how to implement one of the various peer-to-peer network systems has changed dramatically with the delivery of Windows95™. Since consulting services and consulting packages are exceptionally sensitive to timing, adding overhead in order to meet today's client needs could be the catalyst for disaster tomorrow.

The importance of low overhead cannot be overemphasized. Since you have a narrow primary marketplace (your clients), and since consulting work by nature is nonrepetitive (you don't build a good client-consultant relationship if you have to solve the same problems over and over), the demand for unique consulting services is unpredictable at best. This environment often creates a string of feast-orfamine situations. That's why the success of this approach depends so heavily on a firm's ability to maintain lean-and-mean overhead. Here's another way to think of it: picture your consulting offerings as an accordion. Imagine it expanding and contracting based on current opportunities, client demands, and competitive pressures. The expansion should, for the most part, be supplemented through subcontract arrangements. This allows the contraction to occur without threatening the viability of the firm.

Real World Examples

The fortress is not only a viable alternative, it is also the option best suited for most CPA firms. Why? Because few firms have a large enough client base to support day-in-day-out specific consulting packages, or even more grandiose, a fully staffed consulting department.

For those of you who feel the fortress is more theoretical than practical, we offer these concrete examples.

> Not so long ago, the American automotive industry focused on large cars. Since large luxury cars were the most profitable, building small cars was almost perceived as an inconvenience.
>
> The Japanese auto manufacturers thought differently. Some of them viewed the American hesitation in developing the small car market as an opportunity to expand into the United States. So they did. Once they established an excellent reputation for building quality small cars, they announced luxury small cars. Today, these auto makers are providing all shapes, sizes, and styles of cars and trucks to the American consumer. This expansion has significantly impacted the profitability, and at times the viability, of the big three American automobile manufacturers.

Here was a situation where the American automotive industry overlooked the changing sensibilities and needs of its community. However, if the fortress strategy had been followed, the Japanese would have been denied their easy invasion of the marketplace, and the American automobile manufacturers might have been able to maintain a much greater market share than they enjoy today.

If you think the auto industry experience was a unique and extreme case, consider a more current example, the banking industry. The combination of deregulation, increased regulatory scrutiny, new technology, and marginal long-term interest investment yields has led to a financial battlefield. Over the years, banks, savings and loans, and credit unions have found an increase in their investment, rather than their lending, portfolios. As these institutions try to loosen their lending policies in order to achieve a better financial balance, an ultracompetitive environment has been created. Financial institutions are making cutthroat deals to attract consumers and businesses alike. But what's surprising is that although these organizations contend they are very creative and aggressive, they have lost sight of the needs of the fortress community they serve. Here's an example:

> Financial institutions have traditionally attracted customers with competitive checking and savings alternatives, interest rates, lending policies, and so on. Today, while these services are still important, other new services are gaining in priority. For example, customers want—
>
> - Access to free automated teller machines for both deposits and withdrawals.
> - An ability to apply for loans anytime.
> - Quick turnaround of lending requests.
> - An ability to move money between accounts anytime.
> - An ability to pay bills electronically with a more traditional accounts payable type functionality.
> - Zero balance and disbursement accounts to improve cash management.
> - Concentration accounts that roll excess funds to outstanding loans, lines of credit, or overnight investments.
> - Electronic funds transfer and electronic data interchange to minimize the administrative costs of doing business.
> - Lock boxes with electronic accounts receivables updates.
> - Consumer and business credit card services . . . and much more.

The bottom line is . . . consumers and businesses alike are demanding 24-hour banking. Obviously, providing this list of services requires a strategic focus. However, the marketplace is making its expectations clear. Very soon, many of the financial institutions that are conducting business the same way they always have are going to wake up and find mass movement of their customers to competitors—not because of better rates (because they might be higher), but because of high-priority new services.

Here's how this story translates using our fortress and empire terminology.

> Bank E, using an empire approach, selling a niche service such as concentration accounts that roll excess funds to outstanding loans, lines of credit or overnight investments, will motivate many of Bank F's customers to subscribe to Bank E's new services. It is probable that in order to take advantage of this new service at a reasonable cost Bank E will require Bank F customers to move all of their business to Bank E. Bank F has lost a tremendous business opportunity overnight! Why? Because it lost sight of the fortress it was serving. Had a fortress approach been taken, then Bank F would have spent less time playing musical interest rates, and focused more energy on the *desired services* of its customer base. This would have rendered the empire approach of Bank E less effective and would probably have stopped the mass customer migration.

What we are saying is, those firms that expand into the consulting arena may soon be encroaching on *your* client base. If one of these firms is engaged for a specialized project or two, within a year or so you may find yourself with fewer clients. The fortress approach dictates that if one of these specialized services is required, you are better off subcontracting to potential competitors (or referring them to a noncompetitor) than letting competitors run loose among your clients. This way, you maintain control of the account.

The handwriting is on the wall in big bold letters: PROTECT YOUR CLIENT BASE. Sustaining a wall of services around your clients is the best way to build a fortress that can stand up to the competition.

Building the Empire

What do you do if you don't have a client base to protect? What if your current client base isn't big enough to support your desired lifestyle? Or if the current work you perform isn't challenging enough? Are you looking for a growth vehicle that would allow you to promote and retain your quality personnel? It is these kinds of questions that lead us to our next approach, the empire, which is committed to *client base growth*.

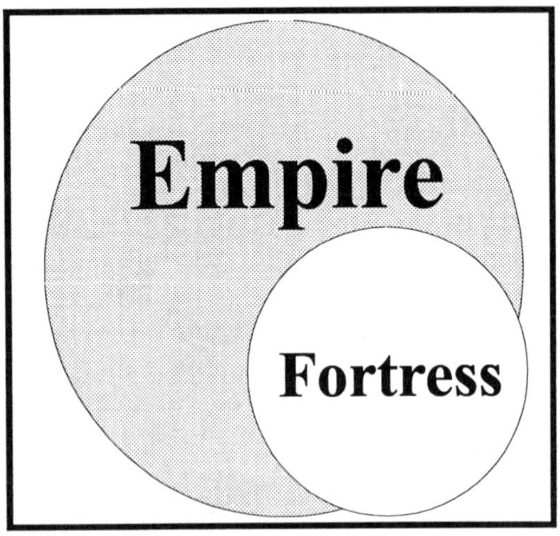

As a starting point, the empire is almost a superset of the fortress. When you think about it, there is some logic to this. Securing your homeland should be an integral part of an expansion program. And as you know from our previous discussion on the fortress, securing your homeland is accomplished by taking care of the consulting needs of your current clients.

The empire focuses on the CPA firm's *strategic plan*, not the current needs of the client base. However, the empire does attempt to take advantage of all business opportunities within the current client base as long as they are consistent with the *long-range plan*. An example of an empire firm's mission statement might be—

> *To build a consulting department that has the skills and reputation to expand and dominate new markets by providing superior services in arbitration, divorce litigation support, and valuation.*

Considering the above mission statement, if a current client needed support in the resolution of a partnership dispute, since arbitration is part of the long-range plan, this project would be aggressively solicited. However, if financing were the demanded service, it would most likely be referred to some other firm. Note: Empire firms should try to refer nonstrategic services to firms that complement their areas of expertise so that their referrals can be reciprocated. Or, they can move one step forward in institutionalizing the arrangement and form strategic alliances with firms that deliver complementary services and expertise.

Why would an empire firm give up a service opportunity just because it wasn't part of the strategic plan? The reason is focus. With the empire, you endeavor to use specialized services (often consulting services) to attract new clients. Since many specialized services (as exemplified by those in the mission statement above—arbitration, divorce litigation support, and valuation) are typically nonrepetitive in nature, the idea is to continuously add clients in order to maintain a steady supply of service delivery opportunities. From day one, the empire's spotlight has to be on penetrating new territories. To encourage potential clients to hire your firm, you must offer super-quality services to the masses. To provide super-quality services, you have to possess unique experience and expertise in a specific field or area. To attain this level of specialization, your firm must choose a few select services, and then continually fine-tune and develop their delivery.

As your list of services becomes more narrow and specialized, the geographical area of your target marketplace will most likely have to expand. In other words, if you need to work with ten clients per year, and only one out of 100 businesses will require your service, then your marketing campaign had better encompass at least 1,000 businesses. If that ratio were one to 1,000, then your exposure would need to be ten times broader.

Creating super-quality service distinction and visibility is costly, both in time and money. Therefore, deciding to implement an empire strategy is not a decision to take lightly. For it to be the right choice, you have to decide on the specialty services that will be the cornerstone of your future practice. We believe that the kind of general practice (GP) consulting we have been preaching about throughout this book should be a big piece of that cornerstone for the vast majority of small to middle-market CPA firms. However, many organizations will develop highly specialized consulting packages and leave the general consulting to the CPA firms that maintain account control. This can be a very lucrative choice, especially in the short term. If supporting a few specialized consulting packages is the choice your empire firm is learning towards, recognize that you are significantly changing the long-term position of your business—from one of being a CPA consulting firm to one of becoming an organization supporting CPA consulting firms. If you can maintain good relationships with the CPA firms you support for an extended period of time, you are likely to find that you have protected yourself by building an extensive client list of your own. This becomes critical to accomplish as time will improve the odds of the two CPA firms (yours and the one who originally put you in contact with the client you support) running into service overlap disputes.

Determining the Most Appropriate Services

With the empire approach, services offered are based primarily on the CPA firm's long-range plan. So, performing some business planning internally is the right place to start.

Note: By having one of your firm's CPA consultants facilitate the internal planning sessions, you will provide an excellent forum for training and confidence-building. If you would rather bring in an outside facilitator, assign one of your CPA consultants to work very closely with the facilitator in order to glean as much information as possible from the experience.

The CPA firm's skills are also a major ingredient to the future services of an empire-focused firm. These can be divided into two categories: current skills and planned skills.

Current skills should be fairly self-explanatory—those skills currently in-house or available through other sources. *Planned skills* are those to be obtained through training or future hiring. Both are viable alternatives. In order to choose the best option for your organization, you need to consider the technical expertise needed as it compares to the aptitudes and interests of the current staff, managers, and partners.

An interim solution to this development process is to establish a good working relationship with subcontractors. This not only allows you to offer super-quality services from the onset, but also to tap the subcontractors as trainers for your consulting staff.

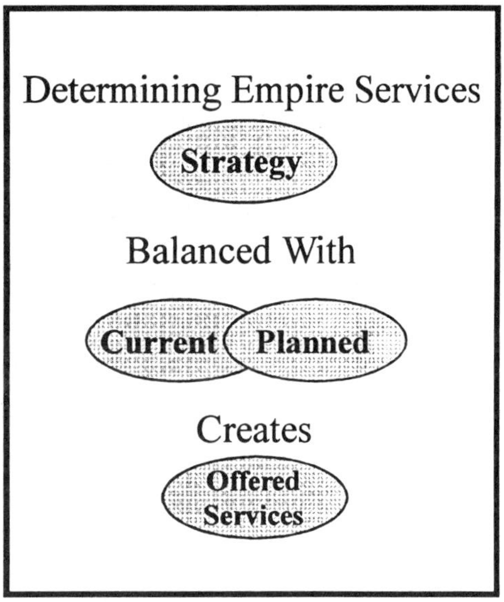

Offered services are the end product of blending a CPA firm's long-range strategy (or plan) and its skills. Another way to put this is, offered services are merely those services identified within the long-range plan that can presently be supported. As additional skills are developed, offered services should be expanded to encompass these changes.

Before any offered services are actually delivered, the central focus turns to the project. Remember, with the empire, you are attempting to deliver a few super-quality services to a larger marketplace. This large target market should contain many opportunities. It is the intent of the empire approach to skim off, or cherry pick, those projects with the highest profit potential.

Managing Risks During the Transition

The empire's expansion philosophy takes a great deal of time and money to implement, especially compared to the fortress. In order to be successful, from the onset you need to sell to both your clients and prospects simultaneously. Why? Because today's prospects will be slow to react to whatever marketing effort you put in place. Experience dictates that it takes about a year to eighteen months before a new target audience builds enough trust and confidence in you to solicit help. This means your current client base will play a critical role in allowing you to bridge this span of time. So, especially in the beginning of this transition, *every consulting opportunity within the current client base that is consistent with the long-range plan must be aggressively pursued.* Some projects inconsistent with the long-range plan also may be undertaken during this initial time frame if excess consulting capacity exists, as long as you don't lose sight of your final objective.

Since your current client base is limited in size, at some point you will have capitalized on all of the lucrative projects matching your current and planned skill set. The trick is to create an effective marketing campaign that produces new clients and service opportunities before you have depleted the excess service demand from your existing clients. This is the risk associated with the empire. If you don't create the necessary stream of new clients fast enough, your firm will have to be financially prepared to carry your consulting department during this transition. The hope is that eventually a transition will actually occur and there will be adequate demand for your select group of super-quality services. For many firms, this transition never occurs, mostly due to haphazard marketing efforts and minimal financial commitment from the beginning.

This is one of the main reasons why the empire is riskier than the fortress. The empire assumes that you are building a long-term niche specialty firm. This requires a higher cost structure, including higher overhead and marketing. Higher overhead will come in the form of subcontractors, staff development, and training costs. During the time that demand for your niche services outstretches supply (especially in the beginning, due to service demand from your current client base), the expenses associated with your empire transition are likely to be immaterial. And once you begin to expand your market and sign up new, lucrative opportunities, your overhead should be very manageable. But, in the interim, if demand declines (which is very predictable) and overhead costs continue to rise or maintain, this strategy will certainly place a great deal of stress on the financial resources of your firm.

The best way to minimize this risk is by understanding that marketing is forever in the empire. *Marketing must be consistent and continuous.* The sooner you start marketing to these vast unconquered territories, the sooner you will reap the rewards. Too often CPAs become overconfident due to the responsiveness of their current clients.

By the time an expansion marketing campaign is finally implemented, it often is too late. The transition period discussed above has exacted too much of a financial toll. The result: the empire crumbles.

The point is ... the empire is for the aggressive, marketing-minded, growth-oriented CPA firms. Firms adopting this approach will, no doubt, face a few fortress-minded CPA firms. Don't be concerned because these firms have to be part of the empire's marketing strategy. The empire firms should position themselves as subcontractors to fortress firms. These two methodologies really work hand-in-hand, especially when empire firms support the idea that the fortress firms maintain control of the account. Therefore, as an empire-*builder*, you should expect to sign agreements that prevent your firm from invading other services which are already provided within the fortress of the contracting firm.

Many lucrative client-requested projects are being ignored today by CPA firms. Delivering a few super-quality services using an empire approach is not only profitable, but the work is fun and challenging as well. And if our prediction is correct, within ten years many successful, prosperous firms will be highly specialized. This means the empire-*builders* will be way ahead of the game and well-positioned for the twenty-first century.

Combining Both Approaches

Some of you may be using both approaches simultaneously. And that's OK. You can build an empire and also protect your fortress at the same time. But problems will arise. Understanding the pitfalls will help you avoid the most common mistakes.

Danger #1: Ineffective Marketing

Remember that when you sell to your empire market, you need to be selling competence, experience, and so on—because the potential clients don't know you. When you sell to the fortress market, you need to sell how you have helped others—so the client, who already trusts and respects you, can relate to the services you have to offer.

Consider a traditional firm newsletter. It is common for newsletters to dedicate 70 percent or more of the available space to technical matters (which your clients often could care less about, since you handle those problems for them). This type of newsletter conveys that you are a quality service provider, but a message such as this isn't necessary to deliver to your clients. Hopefully, they already believe you are a quality service provider. However, demonstrating competence is important if you want to interest people who are unfamiliar with your work. Therefore, when you send out the standard newsletter described above to both your fortress clients (those that already know, like, and trust you) and empire prospects (those that don't know and don't care about you), your marketing effort is compromised and is only marginally effective at motivating either.

For the fortress, 80 percent or more of the newsletter should describe, in non-accounting terms, the many ways you can and have helped your clients. For the empire, 80 percent or more of the newsletter should focus on convincing the audience—prospective clients—that your firm has the background, experience, and specialized knowledge to add value to their organizations. The point is . . . messages that will motivate the fortress marketplace are completely different from those necessary to motivate the empire marketplace. So when you use both strategies in your firm, it is easy to get careless about how you communicate to each group. The net result of trying to optimize your marketing dollar by creating a one-approach-fits-all campaign is wasted money and poor results.

Danger #2: Spreading Yourself Thin

When you utilize both approaches simultaneously you risk dissatisfied clients. This occurs because of limited resources and is more evident the smaller the firm. Let's say for example that a firm has three CPAs. One primarily does tax work, another audit and the third financial statement preparation. When these three services represent 98 percent of those demanded by their clients, everything is fine. But as client demand changes, and as each partner creates new niche areas of expertise, it will become harder for them to maintain command over the traditional services as well. Time will simply be spread too thin. Because so much energy and emphasis has to be given to establishing new niche areas, existing clients are often ignored in an effort to sustain the viability of these services. Clients can easily be lost to a competitive firm reaching out to satisfy unfulfilled needs.

Therefore, the smaller the firm, the more limited the people resources, the more important it is to determine the primary strategy in advance. Is your organization's focus to take care of and grow the services delivered to the existing client base (fortress)? Or, does the firm plan on making it's mark by providing a few super-quality niche services (empire)? It is our contention that during the next ten years, many small firms will choose the empire strategy and become niche service providers to other small and middle-market CPA firms who have committed to maintaining their fortresses. These small firm strategic alliances will basically allow them to operate with most of the same advantages that large firms enjoy today. They can have offices with fortress mentalities, and when appropriate, deliver unique niche expertise (empire) from people who are scattered throughout the country.

Danger #3: Complacency

Competition can change a marketplace overnight. As an example, today you may be comfortable referring all computer work to outside vendors. This approach works as long as your accounting peers don't expand into the technology arena. Once a direct competitor builds strength in one of your weak areas, they can and most likely will use it to infiltrate your client base and eventually take away other work you provide. Even though a middle-of-the-road strategy works now, it may not work for much longer. As a matter of fact, in many markets the competitors have already restructured their priorities, and you may soon feel an abrupt impact as the results of their last year or two's work comes to fruition. Dramatic change in your market may not be eminent, but rest assured, change will occur. Don't be caught off guard.

Danger #4: Forgetting Your Game Plan

If you are building a fortress, then the marketing effort must be focused at your current clients. If you are not directing your marketing efforts where they belong, you're walking on the edge of disaster. You will miss opportunities because, at some point in the future, your clients' requirements will either shift or be satisfied by current efforts. New opportunities for service will arise, and if you are unaware of these new demanded services, you are opening the door to poaching by competitive CPA firms.

If you are expanding your empire, an aggressive, consistent campaign promoting your services needs to extend well beyond the current client-base boundaries. Again, a poorly defined marketing strategy will doom your endeavor to build an empire. And remember, don't allow the initial wave of interest you enjoy early on (typically generated by current clients and referrals from those clients) to lull you to sleep regarding the importance of marketing.

In order to be successful, you need to be able to do either one of the following:

1. Adjust quickly to current client demand (the fortress strategy)
2. Continue to expand into new territories where the market for your super-quality services is untapped (the empire strategy)

Since both strategies require planning and preparation, the earlier your approach is identified, the better. We offer this analogy:

> In sports—whether it be football, basketball, golf, tennis, racing, and so on—those who win the gold follow some kind of game plan. Their strategy may take an offensive or defensive flavor. The objectives, talents, and current conditions determine which tactics they utilize. The players and teams with the best game plans are the ones most often found in the winner's circle.

The same planning and preparation is required when implementing a firm-wide consulting philosophy or niche consulting packages—you need to follow a plan. If you want to posture your firm defensively, then consider the fortress approach. If you view consulting or niche consulting packages as an offensive weapon for expansion, then follow the empire strategy. If you want to adopt both strategies, planning becomes even more essential to prevent sloppy vacillation between the two.

A Summary of the Differences

Table 8.1 recaps the differences between the fortress and the empire as discussed throughout this chapter. We know through experience that it is easy to get confused with this methodology. By the time you fill out all the worksheets in this book, and as you begin to develop your firm's strategy and formalize your marketing plan, you will most likely be re-reading this chapter. Determining what strategy best suits your organization is critical if you want to maximize and protect your scarce personnel and financial resources.

Table 8.1 Comparing the Fortress and Empire Strategies

Fortress	*Empire*
• Aggressively pursues almost every consulting opportunity with existing clients.	• Seeks out only those opportunities consistent with the firm's long-range plan.
• Centered around client-base protection. Leverages client relationships through service extension and referrals.	• Targets client-base growth. Leverages clients assessable through strategic alliances, industry-specific target markets, networking with complementary product or service providers, and so on.
• Defensive approach: Expands by taking care of the changing needs of clients and client referrals.	• Offensive approach: Takes business away from less specialized service providers.
• Requires minimal time and money to implement. Low costs of marketing and commitment to personnel training and overhead.	• Requires a great deal of time and money to implement. Substantial cost of marketing and commitment to personnel training and overhead.

(continued on next page)

Table 8.1 Comparing the Fortress and Empire Strategies (continued)

Fortress	*Empire*
• Low risk—due to minimal time and money required to implement. Also, because firm continually shifts services to meet the needs of client base, the sell cycle is short, and revenue opportunities are plentiful.	• High risk—due to larger overhead and predictable revenue shortfall during the transition from a more traditional accounting firm to a niche specialty firm.
• Services provided change rapidly since they are based on the ever-evolving needs of the client base.*	• Services provided remain fairly consistent over time because they are based on the firm's long-term strategic plan.*
• De-emphasizes past services that are not a priority to the current client base.	• Service offering is not dependent on the demands of the current client base.
• Works with a select group of subcontractors or forms strategic alliances with empire firms, since the fortress emphasizes a wall of services with minimal overhead. Stays involved in the project regardless of who actually performs the detailed work.	• Refers requests that do not fall within the long-term plan to other firms, especially if there is an alliance with a fortress firm. Does *not* stay involved if the services are outside the firm's niche offerings.

*As long as client-demanded services are consistent with the CPA firm's long-range strategy, the variation between these two approaches is strictly in the marketing effort: The *empire* will direct its efforts towards generating new clients, while the *fortress* will attempt to hold on and expand service delivery to the clients it already has.

It's Time to Make the Determination

Consulting and consulting packages are services that are education- and experience-intensive . . . the highest and best use of both. These services are directed at helping our clients solve today's problems and take advantage of tomorrow's opportunities. The challenge is to support our clients in a manner that allows them to more profitably manage their businesses, financial affairs, estates, and so on.

We believe that the future of our profession lies in our ability to expand our offerings into areas that help businesses survive and thrive. We also believe that CPAs are uniquely qualified for this job. Some of our current bread-and-butter compliance work, like tax and bookkeeping, will soon fall prey to a growing service industry of new CPAs and nonlicense holders. Experience will become our most distinguishable and marketable characteristic. And, since consulting and consulting packages require both the theoretical and practical application of knowledge, these non-traditional services are our edge for competing in the twenty-first century. Understanding whether your firm is a fortress, empire, or some combination of both is critical if you want to maximize your firm's potential in the most cost-effective way. By incorporating and utilizing the strategy best suited to your firm's objectives, you will—

- Improve your ability to plan, because each strategy has nuances and market reactions you can anticipate.
- Be better able to respond to your marketplace with appropriate services.
- Be able to send messages that will motivate your clients and prospects to action more consistently.
- Significantly improve your odds for success when launching new services.
- Enhance client satisfaction and loyalty.
- Be able to accomplish all of the above more efficiently and less costly than without the use of this methodology.

BEFORE YOU MOVE ON

We have been working through the exercises at the end of this chapter with firms for at least ten years. They were created to force everyone to think about the skills they possess. As with any organization, it is critical that you take advantage of what you and your staff do well. It is also essential that you leverage what you enjoy doing. Filling out the *Skills Inventory Worksheet* will help you get a better understanding of what you and your people have to offer.

After you finish this exercise, move on to the *Requested Services List*. This form was created so that you would list all the services you have personally heard one of your clients or prospects request in the last twelve months. You can also give a copy of the form to every staff member to complete.

The next form, *Anticipated or Upcoming Requests*, is included so you can jot down those services you think will be important in the next few years, even if they are not in demand now. This becomes your own "services watch list."

Each of these lists should prove helpful as you begin to think through whether your firm should adopt a fortress or empire primary strategy. Once that decision is made these lists should provide assistance in laying out a service delivery strategy—including what services you should offer, what services you should build capability for internally, what services you should develop relationships to deliver, and more. And once these decisions have been made, it will be time to create a marketing plan to ensure your marketplace is aware of what you have to offer, which is the subject of our next chapter.

Skills Inventory Worksheet

Take an inventory of the skills you feel you have to offer. Keep in mind, these are not services, but personal skills you possess. While there may be some similarity, such as tax knowledge logically manifesting itself as a tax service, other skills—speaking skills, being a good communicator, or knowing a foreign language—might not be as directly attributable to a current service offering. If there are others in your firm, have everyone fill out this form. Then merge the lists together to establish a comprehensive list of skills.

1. ______________________________
2. ______________________________
3. ______________________________
4. ______________________________
5. ______________________________
6. ______________________________
7. ______________________________
8. ______________________________
9. ______________________________
10. ______________________________
11. ______________________________
12. ______________________________
13. ______________________________
14. ______________________________
15. ______________________________

Requested Services List

Prepare a list of all the services you have personally heard one of your clients or prospects request in the last twelve months. Remember, this list is based on personal experience only. Once again, feel free to have everyone in your firm fill this out.

Description:

• ____________	• ____________
• ____________	• ____________
• ____________	• ____________
• ____________	• ____________
• ____________	• ____________
• ____________	• ____________
• ____________	• ____________
• ____________	• ____________
• ____________	• ____________
• ____________	• ____________
• ____________	• ____________
• ____________	• ____________
• ____________	• ____________
• ____________	• ____________
• ____________	• ____________
• ____________	• ____________
• ____________	• ____________
• ____________	• ____________
• ____________	• ____________
• ____________	• ____________
• ____________	• ____________
• ____________	• ____________

Anticipated or Upcoming Requests

Prepare a list of all the services you believe will become important to your clients in the next eighteen months to three years, even though they may show little interest at this time. You are completing this list as an exercise to keep you thinking ahead of your clients' needs. Then this becomes your "services watch list."

Description:

- ____________________ • ____________________
- ____________________ • ____________________
- ____________________ • ____________________
- ____________________ • ____________________
- ____________________ • ____________________
- ____________________ • ____________________
- ____________________ • ____________________
- ____________________ • ____________________
- ____________________ • ____________________
- ____________________ • ____________________
- ____________________ • ____________________
- ____________________ • ____________________
- ____________________ • ____________________
- ____________________ • ____________________
- ____________________ • ____________________
- ____________________ • ____________________
- ____________________ • ____________________
- ____________________ • ____________________
- ____________________ • ____________________

Chapter 9
Marketing Your Consulting Practice

People are too busy, too distracted, and generally too focused on their own problems and opportunities to be very observant of all the messages around them. Therefore, if you want to get their attention, you have to develop a marketing strategy that will be delivered with enough frequency that it becomes hard to ignore, rather than hard to catch.

In order to accomplish this, you need to design a marketing program that covers at least a year's horizon; eighteen months is even better. It also should be designed to best utilize your firm's skills and resources. A marketing plan not only manages tools like advertising, but every method and technique your organization uses for (or prohibits you from) obtaining new clients. Consider organizations you and your firm belong to, your network of friends, your compensation plan, the sales and communication training that is provided to everyone in the firm, the internal structure of your organization, and so on. These are but a few of the factors to consider when developing a quality marketing plan.

We are not referring to a three-pound document which takes months to create; we're talking about an informal action plan laying out issues such as the following:

- Actions planned
- How often you plan on making something happen
- Whom you are attempting to reach

- What you are expecting your audience to do in response to each effort
- What each step will cost
- How you will know if what you did was effective

In our profession, the level of commitment required to pull this together is rarely found. Most marketing plans are vaporware. A simple test to determine how your organization feels about marketing is to answer this series of questions:

> *When you conduct your firm's planning sessions, where is marketing on your agenda? Is it after the real issues have been covered, or somewhere towards the top of the agenda? Is marketing considered by the partners to be essential or optional?*

If marketing is not positioned near the top of your agenda, it's in the wrong place. Since today's efforts generate next month's or next year's opportunities, a good marketing plan is imperative if you want to remain successful as a firm, and especially if you want to compete in the consulting marketplace. Otherwise your results will be inconsistent. When you consider that the demand for consulting is erratic to begin with, a sloppy marketing effort will only make matters worse.

Here's one more reason why marketing should be a focal point within your firm.

> *You have to continually attract new clients in order to survive.*

The explanation is simple. Some percentage of your current clients won't request your services next year. Their reasons for leaving will be varied, from moving out of town, to being dissatisfied with your products or services, to no longer requiring outside assistance. Many of their reasons will have nothing to do with you or your firm, they'll just reflect changes in the clients' lives. So attracting new clients is not just a growth issue; it also is necessary in order to maintain the status quo.

If you still are not motivated to concentrate on marketing, reconsider something we pointed out in chapter 3: the "shrinking slice of the pie" syndrome. With the growth of CPAs in public practice in raw numbers being proportionally greater than our economic growth, competition will continue to increase. More competition translates into more firms fighting over the opportunities that exist. *Your marketing plan is your strongest tool to help your clients differentiate your firm from all the rest.*

Developing a Marketing Strategy

The first step to a good marketing strategy is considering your firm's—

- *Products and services.*
- *Customers.*
- *Competition.*
- *Management team.*
- *Financial resources and limitations.*

This analysis is likely to require some research, including focus groups, surveys, interviews, and numerous brainstorming sessions. Otherwise, you will be attempting to select the best approach for selling something that hasn't been identified. What makes this kind of planning confusing is that effective marketing is difficult to identify. What works for one CPA firm may prove to be worthless to another. Think of your organization's marketing plan as a suit of clothes; even though two suits may appear to be the same, altering each one to fit the individual wearing it results in the best fit.

So where do you start if you are not sure how to tailor your suit? From a simplistic viewpoint, any good strategy must focus on—

1. *Understanding the potential clients.*
2. *Identifying their hot buttons.*
3. *Pushing those hot buttons.*

The remaining sections of this chapter will discuss in detail how to accomplish this.

Developing Your Marketing Plan

Putting together a quality marketing plan doesn't have to be expensive. It doesn't have to take an inordinate amount of time either. But make no mistake about it—creating a marketing plan, especially for the first time, is not an effort to take frivolously. There are numerous steps involved. The good news is that once you have gone through the process, the next time around is substantially easier and quicker.

Here are the steps you should take and, generally, the order to take them:

1. *Understand your market.*
2. *Understand what you are selling.*
3. *Determine your objectives.*
4. *Establish a budget.*
5. *Fine-tune your target audience.*
6. *Fine-tune your message.*
7. *Choose the exposure vehicles that are best for your organization.*
8. *Monitor the results.*

Understanding Your Market

As we covered in earlier chapters, our business is changing. CPAs are offering services to smaller and smaller organizations, clients are demanding more for their money, and the needs of the marketplace are moving away from compliance. We are being asked to offer more services that impact our clients' future success rather than just to report on their past performance. While CPAs in public practice tend to know the multitude of services our professionals can deliver, our marketplace does not have this same understanding.

A recent survey conducted by the AICPA regarding its national advertising campaign provided some interesting information. The survey included 500 key decision makers, including CEOs, COOs, CFOs, chairmen, presidents, owners, partners, treasurers, trustees, principals, vice presidents of finance, and controllers. (Although many of these job titles are predominately held by CPAs, no CPAs were included in the survey.) A different set of 500 key decision makers was surveyed both before and after the advertising campaign. Basically it worked like this. Various messages were imbedded in advertisements, including five print, five radio, and one television advertisement. The survey respondents were asked whether they agreed with the message contained in each ad. Some of the most interesting results are shown in table 9.1.

To us, these are startling findings. Even though the people in this survey were not CPAs, they certainly should be aware of a CPA's capabilities. For example, it's shameful that only 47 percent of those surveyed after the ad (Image) campaign felt "CPAs can help individuals and businesses plan for the future." Only 44 percent agreed that "CPAs see more than the numbers, they see opportunities." We can't blame the ad campaign for these results—we need to take a hard look at ourselves. We have done a *horrible* job letting our clients know what we are capable of doing. It would be one thing if only 44 percent agreed that CPAs

Table 9.1 AICPA National Advertising (Image) Campaign

	Agreement With Message	
Ad Message	*Before Campaign*	*After Campaign*
CPAs can provide the financial insight crucial to retirement planning	28%	41%
CPAs see more than the numbers, they see opportunities	33%	44%
CPAs can help screen potential merger and acquisition candidates	25%	36%
CPAs can help individuals and businesses plan for the future	37%	47%
CPAs are a trusted resource for knowledgeable solutions to business and financial planning needs	45%	55%

were the premier provider of automation solutions, but that wasn't the topic. The question was whether they thought CPAs can "see beyond the numbers." And their answer is frightening. Clearly, not only do we not understand our market, but our market doesn't understand us either. And each of us, especially in relation to our own clients, is to blame for this.

So what does our market want? Obviously that varies from area to area, industry to industry. But when you consider some of the examples shared in chapter 1, helping companies find ways to survive and thrive is way up there. Consider the services identified each year by the AICPA's Technology Research Subcommittee (the top 10–50 technologies). This is a list of technologies that organizations around the country are struggling to implement. And there are numerous other places to look. Your best source of information is in your own backyard. Talk to your clients, conduct focus groups, and survey your clients on a regular basis. They are the ones you should care about. They are the ones you should know about. They are the ones that you should understand.

Before we leave this topic, we want to leave you an idea to ponder. It is our belief that *the single largest purchaser of CPA services in the twenty-first century is likely to be the CPA in industry*. Why? Because the jobs of controller, vice president of finance, and so on, more and more, are to manage all operational or informational issues. This change in role redefines these traditionally accounting jobs to only be about 20 to 30 percent accounting. The remaining 70 to 80 percent includes a multitude of other operational responsibilities. Therefore, when you match the expanded scope of services we are suggesting for public CPAs (consulting and consulting packages), it mirrors very well the scope of control that our counterparts in industry are managing. And our counterparts in industry are screaming for assistance. We know this because we conduct classes for controllers around the country, and have done so for more than ten years. We are probably in front of more than 2,000 controllers each year in discussion settings. The opportunities have never been greater for our profession, assuming we take the time to *understand our marketplace*.

Understanding What You Are Selling

We've spent a great deal of time on this subject in earlier chapters. Remember the feature-benefit-result technique? One example used was a burglar alarm: the contacts, horns, and inferred devices are the features; notification that someone has entered your home uninvited is the benefit; protecting your family is the result. And our point was that people buy results. This is one angle.

You need to understand exactly what it is you are selling—whether it's expertise, piece of mind, a long-term relationship, improved odds of success, or a higher level of confidence. Are you selling a product (such as a tax return) or a service (billing purely for your time, however the client determines to use it)? Taking this a step further, specifically, what services do you offer? And more important, what are the logical outcomes a company can expect when buying each of your services?

You know you have accomplished the step of understanding what you sell when you can give a series of pop quizzes to everyone in your organization, asking questions about what it is you do and why people do business with you, and hear similar responses. For example, ask the simple question, "Whom do you work for?" If you get the answer, "I work for a CPA firm," you're not even close to where you need to be. We will cover this in more depth later in this chapter.

Determining Your Objectives

Why are you spending your valuable resources (time and money) marketing? What are you trying to accomplish? Why now? If you are marketing just because you think you should, don't do it. If you are marketing to retain your current clients, make a note of that. If you are trying to build more referrals, make another note. If you force yourself to sit down and answer the few simple questions at the start of this paragraph, you'll be halfway there. After you go through this exercise, let a day or so pass, and then review the questions and your answers again. Don't be surprised if you add another reason or two, or more sharply define the ones you have already written down.

ESTABLISHING A BUDGET

This is something you know how to do in your sleep. We have included a form at the end of this chapter that we use to identify each exposure alternative, when we plan to use it, how many people we are targeting, and what it is going to cost. It's just a simple form we put together to help us look at the combination of alternatives we have selected, so we can make sure we try to get the most from each one as it relates to everything else in the plan. The last item on the form is imperative—determining what results you expect from the exposure campaign. List and quantify your reasonable expectations before you leave this step, such as number of new clients, growth in total revenues, new projects delivering a specific niche specialty, and so on.

Beware of this common costly error regarding the budget:

Spending an entire year's exposure budget on a week-long comprehensive advertising campaign.

This kind of blitz mentality is typically very ineffective. The success of a blitz campaign is based on the premise that you have a product or service that is so unique, so much in demand, that people will beat your door down to obtain it once they know your organization exists. It also assumes that your customers or clients will be so enamored by your product or service that they will remember you forever. This phenomenon virtually never occurs. The normal result of blitz exposure is that it draws significantly more prospects during the blitz period than would a normal advertising effort. The problem is, in order to justify this financial outlay, the blitz would have to generate a year's worth of traffic during the blitz period since minimal funds will be available for marketing after the event is over. The reality usually is that three or four normal exposure efforts will have a greater cumulative impact than the blitz effort.

This is not to say that blitz campaigns are ineffective. Organizations use this kind of exposure method all the time. The key is that the money expended for the blitz effort is still just a small percentage of the overall exposure budget. This way, a great deal of attention is drawn to the product or service in a short period of time, and then that visibility is maintained on a month-in-month-out basis by the normal planned exposure itinerary.

So the trick is to put together an exposure campaign that can be implemented in small increments over a long period of time. Why? Because visibility and exposure need to emulate a dripping water faucet. Even though each drop of water may be insignificant by itself, as these droplets continue, they make an impact. You have to constantly chip away the various distractions surrounding your potential clients. Then, in that fleeting moment when you have their attention, your message must quickly motivate them into action. Consider being able to emulate this dripping water faucet when you allocate money to your marketing budget.

Fine-Tuning Your Target Audience

The first issue is to think through how the fortress and empire strategies apply to your objectives. Here's a quick review of how each can impact your marketing approach.

The Fortress

By choosing the fortress, your target market is your existing client base. Our Fort Worth office follows this strategy. Since it has been operating for many years as a traditional practice, a sizable client base has been established. Therefore, client base protection is a primary focus.

To accomplish this, all marketing efforts are directed towards building client loyalty. One way to do this is to promote a wide range of services. So about eight years ago, we put together a list of services (created during several brainstorming sessions) that became the primary wall of services surrounding our Fort Worth client base. By promoting these services, we subtly remind our clients that we can take care of a wide variety of their needs. This list included these services:

- Negotiation and arbitration of operational, financial, and personnel issues
- Tax planning and minimizing
- Management and leadership training
- Help in obtaining financing
- Acquiring and selling businesses
- Strategic and tactical business, technology, or marketing planning
- Business valuations and litigation support
- Managing audits and reviews
- Accounting, budgeting, and reporting assistance
- Internal controls and procedures advice
- Technology consultation and training
- Profit enhancement or cost reduction analysis
- Cash management assistance
- Prebankruptcy and bankruptcy support

How did we create this list? After completing the *Skills Inventory Worksheet* (found at the end of chapter 8), interviewing a group of our clients, and composing the *Requested Services Worksheet*, we came up with a services offering that we felt fit the needs of our client base.

If a client is in need of a service outside this list, we will either refer them or satisfy their need through the use of subcontractors. The decision as to which way to go is easy to make. If the service desired is performed by a competing CPA firm, then we will most likely perform the work through subcontractors. Remember, the idea behind the fortress is client base protection. We don't want anyone making inroads with our clients that might threaten their loyalty to us. So we only refer when no such threat exists. Note that your services list constantly changes in the fortress approach.

To keep our clients' attention, we have to continually remind them that we are their CPA firm, and that we offer a wide variety of services. The good news is, it's easy to accomplish this with fortress-style marketing. Why? *Be-*

cause we know our clients by name, where they work, where they live, what they do, and so on.

Due to the availability of this information, the cost of communicating the details about various new services is relatively low. By utilizing monthly or quarterly newsletters, workshops, direct mail, or even a firm open house, you can stay in touch (we cover these in more detail later). This regular communication is an essential element of building loyalty.

The primary requirement of a fortress marketing campaign is that you consistently and regularly expose the firm's various services. Response to this campaign is not as important as its visibility. Even when you don't achieve additional direct revenues from the services promoted, the main objective will still have been met. That is—

> You have reminded your clients that you care about them, that you always are looking for new ways to keep them satisfied, and that you provide much more than traditional CPA services.

This constant barrage of information also tells them that *something exciting is always going on at your office.* As a result, they will want to stay in contact with you. By creating these positive and recurring images, *your clients should always think of you first for help.* And that's a critical marketing objective of the fortress.

The Empire

If you select the empire, your target market is much broader than your existing client base. Typically, this approach is selected by firms—

- *With an inadequate number of clients,* such as a recently opened office.
- *Desiring a change in stimulation,* such as a group of CPAs who are tired of performing daily tax work and have decided it would be more rewarding to build a litigation support practice.

In both of these cases, new clients have to be actively solicited. The first question we want to address regarding this subject is, "Are CPAs allowed by our Code of Professional Conduct to actively solicit uninvited prospects?" While the level of flexibility in this area varies from state to state, the AICPA's Code of Professional Conduct, as amended January 14, 1992, states under Rule 501 Acts Discreditable:

> A member shall not commit an act discreditable to the profession.

Rule 502 Advertising and Other Forms of Solicitation states:

> A member in public practice shall not seek to obtain clients by advertising or other forms of solicitation in a manner that is false, misleading, or deceptive. Solicitation by the use of coercion, over-reaching, or harassing conduct is prohibited.

Clearly, this is one area that has undergone significant change in the last fifteen years. It wasn't long ago when a CPA needed to be invited before a personal contact could be made. Today, it's really just a test of ensuring that you are not utilizing deceptive advertising practices. This is an easy requirement to meet if you choose to do so.

In order to be effective, the empire requires that you devise a marketing approach that defines a fairly narrow market segment. This allows you to promote a unique product or service which is enticing and valuable. As an example, consider the broad range of services we defined earlier for our firm. This list, while proving valuable for our Fort Worth office, was too broad for our Austin location. Since the Austin office had only been in operation for a few years, at that time its client base wasn't large enough to support its two principals. Expansion was necessary. Therefore, the empire approach was adopted. The services were refined to suit a more targeted audience. For example, the Austin office promoted—

- Strategic and tactical business, technology, and marketing planning.
- Help in obtaining financing.
- Negotiation and arbitration of operational, financial, and personnel issues.

- Advice on how to improve internal controls and procedures.

Even though we provided other services, we publicized those services that *impacted small business profitability*. Some of the vehicles we utilized to communicate and demonstrate this concentration were—

- Publishing columns on management issues for local newspapers.
- Presenting lectures to various business organizations.
- Producing a television series called *You and Your Money*, which was aired by a local CBS affiliate.
- Writing several publications for the Small Business Division of the Texas Department of Commerce.

This kind of exposure helped us build a *business expert* image in our local community. From there, we have branched out on a national basis through a variety of vehicles—including nationally published articles, video and live television networks, and public speaking engagements.

The empire strategy is designed to sell niche specialty services to a broad marketplace while the fortress is designed to sell a broad set of services to a concentrated marketplace. Regardless of your approach, in order to fine-tune your market, you should consider how these strategies fit your organization. Once you have made that determination, the strategy itself will begin to dictate which alternatives to consider.

Marketing Segmentation

Market segmentation is simply the process of breaking a market into relatively homogeneous and identifiable groups.

According to the book *Principles of Marketing*, second edition, by Lamb, Hair & McDaniel (South-Western Publishing Co., Cincinnati, Ohio, 1994), here are some basics on this subject.

> The term *market* means different things to different people. . . . First, they are composed of people or organiza-

> tions. Second, these people or organizations have wants and needs that can be satisfied by particular products [and/or services]. Third, they have the ability to buy the products [and/or services] they seek. Fourth, they are willing to exchange their resources, usually money or credit, for the desired products and/or services.
>
> Within a *market*, a market segment is a subgroup of people or organizations sharing one or more characteristics that cause them to have similar product [and/or service] needs. [For example, on one extreme, you can define every client you have as a market segment. On the other extreme, every business in the world can be defined as a market segment.] The process of dividing a market into meaningful, relatively similar, and identifiable segments or groups is called *market segmentation*. [Segmentation can follow a variety of directions. Common bases are geographic (by city, region, country, etc.), demographic (by age, gender, income, etc.), psychographic (personality, motives, lifestyles), benefit (according to the benefits they seek from a product or service) or usage (divides a market by the amount of products or services consumed).]

The point of all of this is that in order to put together an effective marketing plan you have to pinpoint your market. The better job you do defining each market segment you are targeting, the better able you will be to create meaningful "action enticing" messages for that segment.

Notice the *Market Segmentation Worksheet* at the end of this chapter. It contains a picture of a box. Above the box is a bulleted list including clients, nonclients, business clients, individual clients, top 15 percent, bottom 85 percent, specialized industries, and so on. The top row of the box represents all potential clients. The next section below that subdivides "all potential clients" into "current clients" and "nonclients." The "current clients" section can be subdivided numerous ways. In this example, we chose "business clients" and "individuals." "Business clients" can be subdivided into even more categories, such as specialized industries and so on. The reason you should try to look at your marketplace this way before you put together your final exposure campaign is because the more relatively homogeneous and identifiable groups you can find, the less expensive and more powerful the advertising message is likely to be.

Managing Price per Contact

Managing price per contact is more difficult than it sounds. This is the process of determining the specific exposure vehicles that will do the best job of getting the attention of your target audience. One extreme would be television advertising where you could pay from several hundred to thousands of dollars for a 30-second spot during the local evening news. Another extreme would be a coupon stuck in a package of coupons for literally a few cents per thousand mailed. Paying the least money possible per contact is not the objective; making contact with your target audience in a way that motivates them to view your message for the least money is. The following scenario should shed some light on the complexity of this issue:

> Let's say your firm, in Austin, Texas, put together a newspaper advertisement announcing several new specialized services. Assume that you want to purchase a half-page ad, to be run for one day during the week, for $4,000. If the newspaper is delivered to a quarter of a million people, then your cost per contact is only $1.60 per hundred. This is an excellent price per contact. However, this assumes that you are selling a product or service that all 250,000 subscribers are likely to be interested in. In the accounting business, this just isn't even close to reality. So, in order to make this more realistic, let's say you were targeting general contractors. After a little research, you find out that there are only 200 general contractor organizations that subscribe to the newspaper. Now your price per contact is $20, which is a fairly costly price per contact, but still within reason if you know the 200 contractors always read the newspaper. So, in order to increase the odds of being seen, you put the ad in the paper for 5 days straight. Now your price per contact, assuming some volume discount for advertising, would be about $70 per contact. As you can see, it doesn't take long for this to get out-of-hand.
>
> Consider this. Instead of taking out a half-page ad in the newspaper, how about buying a full-page color ad on the back of the Associated General Contractors of Texas's bimonthly magazine called *Infrastructure*. This has an average circulation of 1,600 copies, and, for the sake of this example, is subscribed to by your 200 general contractor target audience. This ad would cost $950. Your price per contact is now $4.75 for full color exposure on the back of the magazine (which has a theoretical shelf live of several

months). With this alternative, you are also getting to the other out-of-market (but still viable) 1,400 general contractors for free. If the back cover of *Infrastructure* proved effective, you could advertise for a year (in all 6 issues) and still only be paying $28.50 per contact ($950 per issue × 6 issues / 200 local general contractors = $28.50 per contact).

Defaulting to mass media advertising to sell highly specialized products or services is usually taking the lazy way out. The fact is that it is easier and quicker to spend extra money than to try to identify the more cost-effective alternatives for contacting your particular audience. *Remember, the most common mistake regarding exposure is spending money on media targeted to a much more general audience than you are trying to reach.*

There may not be one best medium to advertise in. All we are trying to point out here is that you have to balance cost per contact with finding the best way to get the attention of your target market. Obviously, segmentation becomes key in helping you manage this complex issue.

Fine-Tuning Your Message

One of marketing's worst enemies is disorganization. Too often, marketing is done on a haphazard basis with little thought given to—

- *Overall theme.*
- *Creation of a consistent message.*
- *Achievement of a specific objective.*

This leads us to a question of paramount importance:

> *What is in your exposure proposition that will create enough urgency to prod your potential client into action?*

If the urgency generated by your proposition is lukewarm, then the results will most likely be marginal. Creating a message that motivates your client to action is what marketing is all about. Unfortunately, there is no magic formula to achieve this reaction. But there are some guidelines. Each message you send must be—

- *Simple.* (Make it easy to understand; being subtle here is wasted money.)

- *Concise.* (You probably get less than a second to get their attention, so net it out.)
- *Clear.* (Don't assume too much. Be clear about what you have to offer. You have a great deal invested to get attention, so don't let your audience walk away wondering what you're selling.)
- *Consistent.* (Your messages shouldn't change dramatically from one contact to the next. While you certainly can point out different features, services, and so on, you should provide a consistent message as to who you are and what your organization is all about.)
- *Repetitive.* (Marketing has often been referred to as a contact sport. It takes numerous contacts to make any impact at all.)

Make sure that your exposure messages meet these criteria. And by the way, be careful not to describe your services in jargon or accounting terms. A common mistake we encounter is firms using short descriptors in their advertising, as in this example:

> Below are some of the services we perform. If any of these are of interest, please contact us. We do:
> *Strategic Planning,*
> *Succession Planning,*
> *Personal Financial Planning, etc.*

Well, these descriptors are fine for communicating to another accountant, but they hardly deliver the kind of message or sense of urgency that's worthy of our advertising dollar. Business owners may turn away from your message, confident that they don't need—

- *Strategic planning* . . . but they might need someone to help them figure out how to double revenues in two years.
- *Succession planning* . . . but they might need to improve the communications among family members and make sure that the younger generation is ready to take over the business when the time comes.
- *Personal financial planning* . . . but they might want to make sure they have set aside enough money to pay for their children's college educations.

Yes, these are either one-and-the-same or a component of the service mentioned. However, while the message strategic planning is concise, it does not meet the criteria of simple and clear (because this service can be broadly interpreted as to scope, price, involvement required, output expected, and so on).

THE ROLE OF EXPOSURE

Even if your work is unsurpassed in creating the best messages, keep a perspective about the role exposure plays in this process. Exposure is like a quarterback. When the team wins, he gets too much credit. When the team loses, he is handed more than his share of the blame. Exposure by itself doesn't accomplish anything: your products or services have to be in demand; the clients have to be ready and able to buy; the exposure vehicles have to be seen or heard; and much more. This is one of the main reasons you have to be visible month after month—exposure relies on the timing of all of these factors coming together. Even if all of this works as planned, the best you can hope for is an opportunity to sell. If you are not prepared to capitalize on this opportunity, then the time and money spent implementing your exposure plans are wasted.

Exposure doesn't have to be expensive to be good. However, it does have to be well-thought-out to be effective. Creating an effective exposure plan is far from a science. However, the more facts you have, the more likely your efforts will result in profit rather than just another expense. With this in mind, let's take a look at the various exposure alternatives.

CHOOSING THE EXPOSURE VEHICLES THAT ARE BEST FOR YOUR ORGANIZATION

Exposure is a catch-all word to define any and all communication that gives your firm visibility. It is the subset of the marketing plan that lays out the who, what, where, when, why, and how of gaining visibility for the CPA firm.

Generally, exposure fits into these two categories:

1. *Institutional* exposure focuses on image and perception. This type of visibility sells features such as quality, competence, experience, uniqueness, and so on. But it rarely creates a sense of urgency. In other words, people become aware of your firm and the services provided, but you've given them no reason to call you today rather than tomorrow. The results of your efforts may not be visible for months or even years. This is a common exposure approach used by CPA firms.
2. *Promotional* exposure is built around an immediate response to some event or item such as a sale, a workshop, or a coupon. If immediate action isn't taken, the offer expires. This alternative is less often utilized within the CPA industry. But perhaps it is one that should be given further consideration.

With this in mind, let's look at our various exposure options and consider how each might be used.

Networking

The most obvious form of promotion, and always one of the best, involves the circle of people you work with or know. Most people call this networking. Webster's defines networking as—

> *The exchange of information or services among individuals, groups or institutions.*

Networking may include participation in professional associations, charitable organizations, specifically designated peer groups, loose associations with other professionals, and many other variations. The objective behind networking is to establish contacts that will—

1. *Provide access to additional or unique resources.*
2. *Refer clients.*
3. *Augment your knowledge through the sharing of ideas.*

Whether you have chosen the fortress or the empire, networking in some form should be the cornerstone of your exposure plan. With the fortress, your primary network is your client base. With the empire, since normally the client base is either not substantial enough or not centered around the desired type of services, your primary network will be other professionals, friends, organizations, specific industry organizations, and so on.

As an empire operation, our Austin office tends to focus its networking energy on professionals, such as CPAs (both in public practice and industry around the country), attorneys, bankers, and insurance agents, and a few professional associations. Our Fort Worth office, utilizing a fortress strategy, concentrates its primary energy on the client base, and occasionally, various professional associations and attorneys. One of the professional associations our firm sought out was one that would leverage both offices. It was Southern and Western Accounting Group (SWAG). This group of CPA firms provides a forum for partners to have an open exchange of ideas as well as to share information (not only financial, but strategies, compensation plans, organizational issues, and so on). There are many such groups both nationally and internationally, such as Accounting Group International (AGI) and Associated Accounting Firms International (AAFI).

There are literally hundreds of these kinds of organizations around the country, each with its own nuances and unique qualities which attract member firms. For example, gross revenue is often a distinguishing factor. In other words, one group might try to find firms throughout the world with revenues between $2 and $6 million, while another tries to find firms in the $250,000 to $1 million range. For example, SWAG is a group of CPA firms from various cities across Texas and Oklahoma that do not compete in the same geographic area with revenues between $250,000 and $2.5 million. Associations such as these meet several times a year to discuss business and professional issues and concerns common to the member firms. Often these meetings are held in resort environments to focus attention away from the everyday world back at the office. Of particular value is the open and informal sharing of members' financial results. This financial summary helps members to focus on each other's successes, problems, and even failures. The smallest firm members can anticipate growth problems and those a little larger are often reminded of what got them there. The group's agendas cover the gamut of administrative, practice development, and structural topics. We mention this type of network to emphasize that being able to discuss critical matters freely with peers can be very rewarding and profitable. One doesn't always have to re-invent the wheel.

One down side of networking is that it is often hard to quantify the results of your promotional efforts. But here's a motivational factor that eases this frustration:

> *Every time you make someone aware of why your firm is special, you create an outside salesperson.*

Not only can this salesperson freely introduce your firm to people you don't know, he or she does this without becoming a part of your firm's overhead. This situation is almost too good to be legal. Therefore, be sure that your exposure plan pays attention to the expansion of its "network sales force."

A common obstacle that hinders the effectiveness of networking is *ego block*. This occurs when the CPA performing the networking function doesn't want to appear too anxious to obtain new business, so he or she doesn't do much selling. Comments may be made as to firm size or current projects but the network is never really informed as to the skills and services that can be provided by the CPA firm. This aloofness is ridiculous! But it also is very common. It is almost as if there were an unwritten rule: *When a CPA shows interest in obtaining new clients, then he or she openly admits to a lack of success.* If you think this rule doesn't exist, then ask yourself this question: *Has anyone ever asked if you were interested in taking on another client?*

You're guilty, aren't you? What benefit can be obtained, except for some ego stroking, from sending the message that you have all the business you want? Remember, the point of networking is to obtain new clients. Everyone knows that. So don't kid yourself. The next time you or one of your staff members participates in a networking function, make sure some selling takes place.

Referrals

Referrals are the result of effective networking. As we discussed above, referrals are generated through the use of your network: your client base, employees, friends, family, associations, and so on.

After surveying thousands of CPAs participating in our training, we have learned that *most firms credit referrals for more than 80 percent (often more than 90 percent) of all new business.* Based on this response, it's obvious that the most effective marketing tool used by our profession is first-class client service. By keeping your current clients as happy as possible, you build loyalty. The marketing part comes in when these loyal clients become part of your network "sales force" and tell their friends how pleased they are with your work.

Developing an Effective Network "Sales Force." Due to the success of referrals, it makes sense that your exposure plan should be built around this resource. In other words, spend much of your exposure resources subtly educating and reminding those people most likely to refer you the different ways you can help. Why? Because most of the time, when someone asks for help, the cry isn't—

> *Hey Sue, do you know of anyone who can help me with some mundane accounting work?*

Instead, the inquiry will more likely be—

> *Sue, I'm trying to put together a financial package for my bank and need a little help. Do you know of anyone I can call?*

When people ask for help, they're usually requesting a specific skill or expertise. And while Sue may be your greatest supporter, she probably thinks of your organization from a narrow perspective; those services to which her organization subscribes. She most likely has no idea about the numerous other unique services you offer. So when someone is requesting help in an area in which she has no knowledge of your firm's skills, even if she has the confidence to refer you, the referral will most likely be weak (maybe to the point of being ineffective), such as—

> *I think the CPA firm of Jones and Smith has done that sort of work.*

The point is that your network of outside salespeople needs to know a few details regarding your operation. We are not suggesting that you immediately start pulling people aside to make a sales pitch. We are proposing that a sales pitch be made through a designed exposure campaign and whenever a suitable opportunity presents itself. And consider this approach when you do.

> Describe your services by telling a story that lets others know about a specific service, such as succession planning. Even if the story isn't an exact match with the discussion topic, it may lead to something. For example, if Bob, one of your clients, starts talking about being uncomfortable about who might replace him when he retires, you might say, "I recently prepared a plan for a doctor who was worried about the very same issue. He decided to sell his practice over a five-year period to his partner. While we looked at a variety of alternatives, here were some of the reasons . . . . "

This makes it clear that you know something about the subject and that you have experience in such matters. Using this technique, you've informed your client in a way that is clear and easy to understand. Many CPAs would respond with something far more obscure like, "Our firm does succession planning all the time. We should get together and talk about that sometime." Remember—people love stories. You don't have to give away any secrets to tell these stories either. And if you think your prospect or client might recognize the company you're talking about, change the facts—use a different industry, or change the family members from a father and two sons to a father and three daughters. Whatever you do, when you sell yourself in these networking situations, try to deliver your message through stories so that it is interesting to the listener and easy to follow.

Thanking Everyone Who Refers. The second issue surrounding referrals is recognition. *When members of your network refer business to you, what have they done?* The most important factor is that your network was willing to risk something for your gain. Each time a referral is made, that individual has put his or her good name and reputation on the line in order to put money in your pocket. What happens if your firm does sloppy work, gives bad advice, or charges more than expected? One thing you can count on . . . whoever made the recommendation will hear about it.

So what do these people gain by going out on a limb like this? The overwhelming majority of CPAs we polled commented, *We try to send them a "thank you" letter.* Our immediate response is, *You try or you do?* The most common rebuttal, *We send a letter most of the time.*

Let's pause here for a moment and review what we've covered so far.

> *Eighty percent or more of most CPA firms' new business comes from sources who might receive a thank-you letter for their high-risk, low-reward efforts.*

What's really odd about this is the fact that many firms will spend thousands of dollars developing a brochure, thousands again on various advertisements, thousands to sponsor events, and so on; yet the one resource that clearly generates the most new business *might* receive a thank-you letter.

Every firm should rethink its position on this matter. We have. In many business relationships, the best way to thank someone for a referral is to reciprocate. However, because this is not always possible, our solution was to make an arrangement with one of our clients who manufactures candy. We identified a variety of products (of different sizes and costs), presented them with our credit card, and set up a procedure for anyone in our firm to call in and initiate a referral package with an attached card. By the way, our thank you is not conditioned on whether the referred client does business with us, because whoever made the referral took the risk as soon as he or she mentioned our name.

There are hundreds, even thousands of ways to inexpensively thank those who are partly responsible for the growth of your business. So choose one that best suits your situation. You might send a novelty item (such as pens, hats, or shirts), movie passes, or a gift certificate. And whenever possible, use a client's product or service for this thank you because it not only sends a great message, it supports an organization that is already doing business with you. It's not what you send that matters, but that you clearly say, *Thank you, your referral means a great deal to us.* The gift demonstrates a little extra effort on your part to show how much you care.

Note: There are many advertising specialty agencies that can provide you with some interesting novelty items. For people who refer business to you and work on an ongoing basis with organizations within your target market, buy something especially nice that is likely to remain visible in their offices. By taking this route, you can print your firm name and logo inconspicuously on the item. Then when other people see and comment on it, a discussion about your firm is sure to follow.

Community Relations

This also is a form of networking. Typically, this kind of exposure is gained through involvement with civic organizations and charitable activities. Because the focus of these events is other than business-building, you have to be more subtle about selling. If it appears the only reason you are involved is to hawk your services, you are likely to do more damage than good. However, this doesn't mean that you should refuse conversation about your firm when asked.

By the way, it's easy to get someone to ask about your firm. The best way is to ask questions about your conversation partner's livelihood. After enough interested inquiries on your part, most people will respond appropriately and ask about your background as well. Yes, this sounds a little manipulative. But chances are that people have been doing this to you all your life; you just didn't know it. Learning to use techniques like this will help you better control and manage your communications.

Personal Sales Calls

Personal sales calls are the most effective method of selling. That's why a good portion of this book discusses ways to improve the skills used in this area. But, personal sales calls are also the most costly to make. One reason why this alternative is so expensive is because each minute a CPA spends selling is theoretically a minute that could have been billed. Another reason is because selling time is hard to leverage; you normally make personal sales calls one at a time, which takes an enormous amount of time. Because of the high costs associated with this alternative, you only want to use it when you have identified potential clients who are interested, qualified, and ready to buy.

Research and Development (R&D) Approach

This approach is like selling on-the-job training. It's called the research and development (R&D) approach because you know you are capable of doing the work, but you haven't actually performed the same kind of job the client is requesting. Therefore, while your existing experience is adequate to help you navigate successfully through the project, you know there will be times when you will have to do some extra reading, research problems, develop procedures, and much more. While almost every project requires some on-the-spot creativity and exploration, your inexperience will require you to spend a disproportionate amount of time working through such issues. So in order to make the client feel more comfortable with your inexperience, you either *give away a piece of the job, or perform the job at reduced rates.*

R&D is an excellent technique to use when attempting to provide new services. Enticing an existing client to allow you to perform work at a bargain price in exchange for a reference is a great deal for everyone involved. Why? Because it's hard to obtain new clients with a sales pitch like this:

> *Well, we've never done this kind of work before . . .but we've always wanted to. You would be a great organization to cut our teeth on.*

The R&D approach gives you a track record and confidence, which are both essential to selling consulting services.

Client Seminars and Workshops

These are excellent vehicles. They allow you to sell by offering education. Whether you are promoting new services, or reviewing old ones, teaching is marketing.

One of the requirements for success is that you offer something worthwhile. In other words, each seminar or workshop should be organized in a self-help fashion. If you put on a show that is clearly centered around creating new business, it will most likely backfire.

The fact is, when you teach someone how to do something, you sell yourself. Some will ask you to merely act as their consultant while they attempt to do the work. Others will get excited about the idea, but hire you to perform the work since they are too busy to do it themselves. And yes, a few will actually use the newfound skills you helped them develop on their own. But don't be afraid of giving away information for fear the participants will be able to handle the tasks without your involvement. Most problems are complex. Therefore, regardless of your thoroughness, you will not be able to address all the issues in sufficient detail to enable your clients to figure everything out on their own. In fact, it is typically a plus if they *do* attempt to proceed without you. This means your information was valuable to them. And when they inevitably hit a snag, they'll call you for assistance.

Everyone wins. By teaching a skill or identifying how to better use a tool, you gain two things—*enhanced client-base loyalty, and usually, additional opportunities.* Either one is enough to make client seminars and workshops a worthwhile effort.

Even if your clients do not take advantage of a value-adding service offer such as a seminar, your invitation reminds them of your existence and informs them of your capability to perform that service. For those who do not attend, consider following up after the event by offering the hand-out materials. This gives you one more contact. And as has been said before, marketing is a contact sport.

Joint Seminars and Workshops

These can create the same positive results as client seminars and workshops, with the added value of exponentially expanding your audience.

Joint seminars, in our opinion, are one of the most productive marketing vehicles used by professionals. You find lawyers, stockbrokers, insurance agents, psychologists, bankers, CPAs, and others forming strong alliances. These alliances are made in order to take advantage of the referral network and share client bases. So instead of referring business randomly, most opportunities are referred to those within the group.

These loose associations create two advantages:

1. Each firm has some access to the clients of the other through formal presentations, newsletters, and so on. This literally can double or triple the size of your available audience overnight. This temporary merging of client bases also gives you direct access to a great many people who would otherwise be difficult to contact.
2. These alliances form an umbrella of professional services. The combination of these services forms a protective wall (a fortress) that enhances client loyalty and satisfaction.

Joint seminars and workshops can be used by both fortress- and empire-minded firms since this vehicle facilitates both protection and expansion. Because those in attendance already have demonstrated an interest, marketing is not only easy but inexpensive as well. The trick is to find the right professionals to associate with. Even though this task may be time-consuming, the potential benefits of establishing such organizations are fantastic.

Writing

Writing rarely brings potential clients to your doors. However, when one does come, being published helps create an image that differentiates you from your competition. We estimate that we *close* more than 80 percent of the prospective clients we talk to about nontraditional services partially due to the perceived value created by exposure vehicles such as writing.

As for the marketing value of writing, this channel creates much more interest when the topics discussed are specific in nature and targeted towards a small group (such as addressing theft control for retailers). When you write specific pieces, you can expect them to generate more opportunities than general ones. Obviously, just being published isn't the key. The more important issues include—

- *Who publishes your work.*
- *Size of circulation.*
- *Target market.*

These become central to determining whether your writing efforts will impress prospects.

Writing obviously is an exposure vehicle in which we believe. An effort made in this area should pay off, but over a long period of time. Therefore, writing most often is selected as part of an empire-building plan.

Public Speaking

Public speaking, like writing, has a long-term payoff. Geared more towards an empire philosophy, speaking is a unique avenue to demonstrate your knowledge.

Speaking on general business topics gives you access to large audiences. The benefit here is the expansion of your network. Covering topics in specialized areas creates more immediate opportunities. However, in either case, if your speech is merely a sales pitch, you will not only insult your audience, but will lose its confidence as well.

There's one other issue you face with public speaking. You are taking on the role of expert. So be prepared and have a good presentation. Unlike writing, your audience can immediately challenge any comment you make. How you handle these potentially hostile situations often is more important than the speech itself. (Refer to the presentation guidance in chapter 11.)

Publicity

Used to promote image, publicity is both an empire and fortress alternative. However, the empire relies on this visibility much more than does the fortress.

Publicity can come in many forms. The most common is through news releases. Every time your firm decides to offer a unique service, or makes a contribution to the local community, a news release should be sent to all major television and radio stations and newspapers. The format of a news release is simple. The AICPA is a great source for this. Just look in the front of the materials of any seminar you attend. A short press release has been inserted for your use announcing the fact that you have gained new knowledge in a unique area. At a minimum, you can follow that format to create press releases of your own announcing different accomplishments.

Additionally, there are many other ways to achieve free exposure. As an example, we contacted a local television station, a CBS affiliate, and sold the idea of our firm providing advice in a business tip series called *You and Your Money*. It ran every weekend during the 6 P.M. news for over a year. This gave us excellent exposure, great credibility, but no short-term results. That's why this type of visibility belongs more in an empire strategy.

Along these same lines, several years earlier, we did the same thing with the local newspaper. We proposed a weekly column on small business. It was approved after about nine months of negotiation.

The point is that you have to be creative and find free ways to promote your business. Publicity not only gives your firm exposure, but enhances your credibility and image too. A word of warning though: alternatives like the television series or the weekly column are time-consuming commitments. Therefore, even though this visibility had no out-of-pocket costs, it was still expensive in unbilled time. This type of exposure has to occur over a long period of time for any benefit to accrue.

The good news is that publicity is free (except for your time). Therefore, something as simple as a news release should be incorporated as standard operating procedure and used extensively. Consider this: Being covered as part of the news gives you much more visibility than does a paid advertisement. So start a program right away to take advantage of all the free exposure you can get.

Cross-Selling

This channel of exposure has been widely used to generate business for CPA firms in the past. Because it is client-base focused, cross-selling is predominantly a fortress strategy. Cross-selling is the act of selling one service while providing another. For example, while performing audit services, you can drop a few premeditated hints about other expertise within your firm that could be of benefit. This is an effective technique because *the best time to sell future services is while you are solving current problems.*

It's important to note that the best chance we have for cross-selling is when we are in front of our clients. Tax practitioners have an enormous window of opportunity each year—Tax Time! During these few months, we have face-to-face meetings with a high percentage of our clients. Make sure you have a game plan for blending in a few sales messages during your client conferences. Look for occasions during these conversations to mention some of the other services your firm offers. When you consider the effort of communicating with your clients using other marketing methods (such as direct mail, newsletters, seminars, and so on), you simply can't afford to let this window of opportunity slip by.

Another important point that needs to be made is that effective cross-selling requires the creation of a *client service plan* for your major clients (at least the top 15 percent). This plan should identify the services you have or are delivering, as well as those you intend to deliver. The services you intend to deliver should be prioritized and scheduled on a time-line. The client service plan is a reminder to all within the firm as to what concepts are important to sell to each client, which in turn generates a smooth flow of opportunities. Your messages are consistent as to what the client should focus on because it's easy for members of your organization to stay tuned in to the client's current situation. This plan should have a horizon of a couple of years and is essential to maximizing your ability to cross-sell. A *Client Service Plan* form is included at the end of this chapter.

If you are not currently aware of a client's additional needs, consider making an investigative sales call. This commitment is easily justified for your firm's larger or more financially significant clients. Regarding the others, prepare occasional surveys or newsletters that solicit this kind of information on postage-paid reply cards or conduct a focus group or two each year.

Newsletters

Since we mentioned newsletters previously, we would like to take this time to make a few points regarding the fortress approach. First, newsletters are an excellent marketing and exposure vehicle. But they should be prepared with marketing in mind. Preprinted (canned) newsletters that just have your firm's name stamped on them don't sell. They do educate . . . which is good, but they don't tell your clients who you are or why you are special. Our rule of exposure is—

Don't send out any material or information that doesn't sell.

Don't just send out any newsletter; send out a selling newsletter. This can demand a great deal of work if you create it yourself. So consider incorporating some combination of canned and personal information into each issue. For instance, besides a few canned articles, discuss the benefits one of your clients has reported from a new service you provide, or introduce a new person you have hired and highlight one of his or her unique skills you want to showcase. Additionally, don't get bogged down in how elegantly this information is presented. Instead, make sure it always sells your firm and is sent out on a regular basis.

Promotional Pieces

Promotional pieces are image-building alternatives. While most firms develop them, too many spend an inordinate amount of money doing so. Their objective is to provide you with something tangible to leave with a potential client—something that will act as an inside salesperson.

Brochures, firm resumes, and so on are almost like business cards. They rarely generate business, but they're expected. We feel they are important and should be presented in a professional manner. We also feel that many firms place too much emphasis and spend too much money on vehicles such as these that do not generate new business opportunities.

Major Advertising Media

The media include television, newspaper, radio, and general audience magazines. Although these alternatives can be expensive, at times they may be your best logical alternative. The decision as to whether you should utilize mass media to promote your services lies in the answers to these questions:

1. *Can you obtain information that will narrow your target market?*
2. *If so, are there exposure vehicles more targeted towards the audience you are after?*

If the answers are *no*, then using general media is probably your best choice. However, you should make an immediate effort to start collecting demographic information about your clients and potential clients in order to find some common thread that can be used to better segment your market.

In an earlier discussion on mass media, we alluded to the fact that this channel often is a choice of convenience. For some firms, money is in greater supply than time. This makes the mass media alternatives very attractive. This is fine. But recognize that when you opt for convenience, when you analyze the cost-benefit of your exposure campaign, your price per contact is most likely much higher than it needs to be.

Direct Mail

This is a great alternative for both the empire and the fortress. However, it is much more cost-effective and productive when generating interest for the fortress. Even though this form of exposure is impersonal, it is still likely to gain your target's attention because your client will recognize who sent it.

Direct mail is typically used to promote an event or some special offering. Seminars would be an example of this. But don't limit yourself. Think of ways to create urgency other than by seminars—like sending money. That's right . . . money! As an example, if you are promoting a new consulting service, send out a hundred dollars of play money that can be used as payment against your newly offered service. Make sure the "money" has an expiration date of six weeks or less or it won't be as effective at generating an immediate response. Remember, the objective is to create some urgency for the client to call.

The act of sending "funny money" or coupons accomplishes a number of things. Besides creating urgency and calling attention to your new service, it does so without discounting it. Sometimes, when you discount a service, you create an impression that the service is not worth the full price. Sending "money" does not lead to the same impression. Besides, you would spend that same amount or more on a marketing call anyway.

Try to be creative and think of ways to take advantage of direct mail. One CPA firm told us that it had an excellent response from sending out a series of postcards (one each month for about six months) which dissected and discussed the firm's mission statement. Another idea is to create a series of postcards or brochures that sell your various services, one at a time. We and many others have purchased products from Paper Direct to help us create small but customized service announcements. You can buy preprinted brochure paper and even templates for your wordprocessor designed for use with your laser printer which deliver very professional marketing pieces. Call and get their catalog by dialing 800-A-Papers. If you don't have time to create your own sales materials, consider Mostad & Christensen (800-654-1654). This firm delivers marketing products and resources focused at supporting the sole practitioner gain quality exposure. If you are committed to marketing to the point that you are considering hiring a Marketing Director, call Alan D. Koltin, CPA, president of Practice Development Institute (PDI), LLC (800-227-0498). His organization not only helps with techniques like direct mail campaigns, but also in creating and implementing comprehensive marketing programs. Regardless of how you decide to implement this, there are an endless number of ideas that can be effectively communicated through direct mail.

As far as direct mail is concerned for the empire, you have to be persistent. If you are not willing to mail at least four pieces to the same audience, then direct mail is a waste of time. The empire audience is not intimately aware of your firm, at least not the way your clients are. So your first mailing most likely will be tossed into the trash can. The second might be held for a few seconds before the "file 13" decision is made. By the time the third or fourth mailers arrive, your prospective clients should at least start wondering who you are. They also should start recognizing your name. So with consistency and repetition, the odds begin to swing in your favor that your promotional piece will be carefully reviewed.

Another issue regarding direct mail is timing. People don't have good memories. Therefore, even when your mailers are read, if the prospective clients are not in need of your services at that time, the promotion or announcement won't produce any results. You have to mail to a group of people over and over again. When your message to provide help arrives at a time when your prospects perceive they need help, that's when the payoff comes. But since you'll rarely know exactly when that will happen, you have to remain visible month after month. Because of the requirements of repetitive visibility and presenting a meaningful message, you should segment your audience as much as possible before you start a campaign like this. This way the impact of your campaign is significantly greater due to targeted messages to a select audience.

Trade-Related

This vehicle includes magazines, other publications, convention booths, and so on. When you are targeting an industry or trade, look for ways that specifically focus on your target audience. By utilizing these vehicles, you can more easily get the attention of those who would be most interested in your products or services. This type of exposure is empire-oriented because it attempts to expand into a specialized area.

A note of warning: Any form of promotion needs to be exciting. Even though trade vehicles are addressing an interested niche market, your promotional material, trade show booth, or article, needs to stand out. Regardless of how, when, or where you publicize your firm, your potential clients always will be distracted by the thousands of other companies also trying to get their attention.

Signage

This channel includes billboards and exterior or interior promotional displays. As far as billboards are concerned, this is more like the mass media we discussed earlier. It is expensive because it is geared towards reaching a general audience. However, if your firm concentrates in an area like manufacturing and your city has a manufacturing district, then this general medium could become more targeted with careful placement. Even though billboard presentations can be expensive, when they are targeted they can be an excellent alternative to help you expand your empire.

Exterior and interior promotional displays should promote more than just your firm name. Interior signs, plaques, awards, and so on need to be tastefully done, but they should also help promote the kind of work performed by members of your firm. In other words, more selling emphasis should be given to the workplace, especially in the waiting and conference areas. A spin-off of this idea is to use one of your old computers in the waiting area to display firm propaganda through a presentation software package such as Powerpoint™, Astound™, Freelance™, or CorelDraw™. This way, you can tastefully let this waiting (and captive) audience better understand your firm's capabilities.

Telemarketing

Telemarketing is one of our industry's fastest growing methods for identifying prospects. Firms all over the country are finding this to be a profitable and productive vehicle. In the past, many organizations found themselves frustrated because the leads generated using this technique were much harder to convert into new business than those referred by clients. However, in the last few years, telemarketing has evolved into one of the tools of choice for middle-market and large firms. Why? Because while the cost of setting up a telemarketing program is too expensive for most small firms, this vehicle can generate a waiting list of prospects at a very reasonable price for larger organizations. But even more important, instead of relying completely on the more passive approach of generating leads through client referral, telemarketing is proactive.

Some firms have used a combination of telemarketing plus some giveaway to get in the door. For example, one firm calls up likely prospects (businesses in selected industries) and gives away a quick onsite review of previously filed excise tax returns. They then provide a written report of their findings. For those organizations that have overpaid their excise taxes, which include most of these targeted businesses, they also offer a variety of fee options to file the necessary amended returns. This is an example of a telemarketing giveaway that is turning out to be a great way to open doors and provide immediate value for this particular CPA firm.

Telemarketing is also an excellent method to maximize participation in some event. For example, a telemarketing follow-up to a seminar invitation should dramatically improve attendance. Many organizations are also using this technique to gather essential information, such as conducting client, market, and competitive surveys by telephone. Common offerings that are used to entice telephone prospects into opening their doors to an outsider include free tax reviews, a free hour of consulting, a free booklet (self-help on a specific topic), and free software, to name a few.

MONITORING THE RESULTS

Once you have developed an exposure campaign that defines your target markets and delivers appropriate consistent and repetitive messages to those markets through cost-effective vehicles, it's time to monitor what you have done. This is the step most often ignored by those who actually do create marketing plans. Monitoring the results is something everyone agrees is important, but a task that rarely receives much attention. A plan is significantly more effective if it is also monitored. So what does monitoring mean? Basically, you need to track the results of each exposure or promotion. Make notes as to what you did, whether it generated any phone calls or comments, if any new business resulted from it, time of year, day of week, and any other information that could prove pertinent (for instance, your biggest competitor staged a free workshop at the same time you offered your for-fee seminar).

Create an exposure notebook to record this information, including a calendar for recording the exposure schedule. The notebook also should include everything your firm does to create visibility, from mass media (such as newspaper or radio) to lectures, to networking meetings, to publicity, to articles published, and so on.

This information, over time, will help you identify what works for you. Also, note that interest or inquiries are a better indication of the effectiveness of exposure than are new clients or revenues. Remember, the objective of exposure is to prompt your potential clients into action—to get them to call you. If you judge your exposure plan by statistics, such as new clients, then you are assuming that your firm is able to convert 100 percent of the interest generated into requests for services. That assumption is not only invalid, but it may lead you to alter an effective exposure plan when the real problem may be the firm's marketing and communication skills.

The real benefit to monitoring results is it keeps everyone focused on fine-tuning the marketing effort. For example, let's say your organization pays a 10 percent commission based on the first year's billings to anyone bringing in a new client. Let's also say that your firm is proud of this commitment to marketing. However, the partner group is very dissatisfied with the number of new clients brought in by the junior partners. Rather than assuming that the 10 percent commission is in line and that you have ineffective junior partners, monitoring requires that you take a much closer look at the system in place. You may find that the only people who ever make any real money under this system are the senior partners. Are they just better marketers? They might be. They also have a great many more contacts than the junior partners. Therefore, just playing the numbers game alone, the odds of a senior partner bringing in new business are far greater than the odds of a junior partner doing the same. In addition, business owners without a contact name at a CPA firm will usually ask for one of the named or senior partners. This is because owners have found out over the years that they are almost always better served by working with whoever has the most influence. We bring this up because compensation systems are a definite part of the marketing plan. And on numerous occasions, we have found that the compensation system is rewarding behavior that is the exact opposite of what the firm desires. Take this junior partner-new business issue for example. What we have found several times is that the compensation system is structured in such a way that it is far more rewarding for the junior partners to bill work in-house than to find new business. If the firm wants junior partners to make the effort to gain more community contacts, then maybe junior partners should get an additional 10 percent (or 20 percent of the first year's billings) for all new business brought in. Why? Because, once again, junior partners typically have to work two to three times as hard to grow their contact network as compared to senior partners. So make sure your compensation system provides the greatest incentives for the behavior you really want to encourage.

Every aspect of your marketing plan has to be challenged as time tests it. If it is accomplishing what the firm desires . . . great! If not, change it. Regardless, note the details of what you are doing so that later, when you analyze what has happened, you have a better chance of determining what worked, what didn't, and maybe even why.

Don't Let Marketing Get Out of Hand

A word of warning on this subject. Marketing is like a bed of roses; it contains beautiful flowers and prickly thorns. One major thorn is that you can spend an endless amount of money performing the marketing function, with much of it proving to be of no value. You create twice the problem when you add the fact that the time you take to market is mostly nonbillable. These two issues make it easy to see why the abstract world of marketing often gets out of hand.

A good, first step to help keep things under control is to be honest about which resources are expended as part of your marketing strategy, and which are expended just for fun. This is a critical distinction because often you find CPAs talking marketing when they are really just playing. As an example, a golf outing with a client is only marketing when the firm can reasonably expect this time to deliver some increased benefit to the firm. That benefit should be identifiable before the meeting takes place. The next issue is, *Could that same benefit just as easily have been achieved through a less time-intensive activity?* For instance—

> If you are working on an extended project with a client, then the marketing benefit of playing golf may be the maintenance of ongoing rapport. If that client makes a substantial contribution to your yearly revenues, then spending the time and money to reinforce rapport is certainly valid and justified.
>
> When the possibility exists that a client may retain you to perform some additional work, then, once again, golf may be a productive use of time. However, the time involved should be commensurate with the potential reward. Spending $500 in unbilled time to take on a $300 project is playing!

The point is not to limit golf or any other activity, but to recognize these activities for what they really are. If you don't, then when you analyze the commitment to marketing versus its return, you'll quickly conclude that marketing just doesn't pay. And nothing could be further from the truth, especially if you do the right kind of marketing.

Financially, it's a great idea to mix pleasure and business whenever possible. So if you or some members of your staff enjoy sailing for example, then arrange an outing with an interested client. This kind of arrangement is not only good public relations for the firm, but a perk for you or the employee. Just remember to label it as such.

Managing Your Marketing Time

Because marketing, at times, is like a black hole, you can easily get sloppy with your time. We are not referring to lack of effort, but to misguided effort. To minimize this waste, everyone involved in marketing within your organization (which should be everyone) needs to undergo a crash course in time management. An old, but good, book on this subject was written by Alan Lakein, called *How to Get Control of Your Time and Your Life* (New American Library, New York, 1973, revised edition 1996). We make a special effort to practice many of the techniques set forth in that book. One particular technique Lakein suggests is simple, easy to implement, and effective. When it comes to marketing, just ask yourself—

Is this the best use of my time right now?

This question has several nuances. For example, it spawns the question, "Will the marketing effort I am making right now provide the firm with the greatest benefit?" For many, the answer would be something like, "No, but the things I can do that would have significantly greater leverage take more time than I have right now. So this is at least something positive." It's this kind of thinking that allows marketing to get out of hand fast. If you only have an hour, then spend it working on the high-leverage functions. Don't just attend a luncheon, work on that direct-mail piece you committed to send out. The problem is . . . the best use of your time is often something less appealing than what you are (or plan to be) doing. All of us are vulnerable to being sidetracked by unimportant time-consuming projects that have little or no impact on our goals. When this occurs, we need to quickly identify what is happening and stop it. Remember, time does not discriminate. Everyone, regardless of race, color, creed, wealth, sex, height, or foot size, has the same twenty-four-hour day. Learning to make the best use of your time has always been important. But as far as marketing is concerned, good time management is essential.

Marketing Must Be Planned

One reason why consulting has been difficult for CPAs to implement is due to our lack of internal planning. Consulting must be marketed. When the marketing effort isn't properly planned, it's not only very costly—but even worse—it's ineffective.

There are many ways to attract the attention of both your current and future clients. We have covered only a few. Selecting the best combination of alternatives is not something to take lightly, because marketing costs can quickly get out of hand. Creating a marketing plan is essential to ensuring that your exposure impact is high, yet financially manageable.

By becoming proficient at gaining visibility for your firm, you will be able to differentiate your services from those offered by the competition. This should translate into an abundance of new opportunities for you and your firm in the upcoming years, especially in the field of consulting.

Before You Move On

Now that you have completed this chapter, it's time to put it all together and decide on a strategy for implementing the growth of consulting in your firm. This is hard work and it requires a significant amount of thinking time. The forms that follow are organized so you can work through these exercises in a chronological fashion. Here are the steps to follow:

1. As needed, refer to the information in this book and your notes for ideas.
2. Fill out the *Consulting Questionnaire* at the end of this chapter, focusing on potential goals in areas such as growth, type of work you want to do, and marketing strategies.
3. Review your answers to the forms at the end of chapter 8—the *Skills Inventory Worksheet* and your lists of services, the *Requested Services List* and *Anticipated or Upcoming Requests.* Compare those answers to your answers to the *Skills Inventory Review* form at the end of this chapter, and match your firm skills to necessary services.
4. Use the *Consulting Skills Enhancement Worksheet* at the end of this chapter to develop a plan to enhance your current consulting skills (such as using training, role-play situations, or selling the R&D approach) as

well as for new skill development among staff. Remember to consider the skills needed for services you plan to provide in the future.

5. Segment your target market using the *Market Segmentation Worksheet* at the end of this chapter. Consider the fortress and empire as you segment your target audiences.
6. Complete the *Exposure Self-Assessment* form, noting what you think you should be doing that you are not, what you should change, and whether you should request additional resources.
7. Make copies of the *Client Service Plan* form at the end of this chapter and fill out one for each client that you consider in the top 15 percent of your total clientele.
8. Use the *Exposure Plan* form at the end of this chapter to help you decide on the exposure alternatives that are acceptable to you and your organization for the remaining 85 percent of your client base.
9. Based on the ideas noted in the *Exposure Plan* form, use the *Exposure Budget* form at the end of this chapter to help you establish an annual budget for your firm's marketing campaign.
10. Record the results of your plan by charting monthly revenues for new clients, appointments made, consulting revenue, new service revenue, or whatever criteria best suit your plans.
11. At least quarterly, review the effects of your marketing efforts and adjust or fine-tune accordingly.

Consulting Questionnaire

Think through and answer the following questions (guessing is good enough) in order to arrive at your consulting plan objectives.

☒ What were last year's annual revenues?

____

☒ What is our revenue goal (actual plus projected) for the current year?

____

☒ What is our projected revenue goal for next year?

____

☒ Of our current year's revenues, what annualized dollar amount would consulting represent, based on the way consulting has been defined in this book?

____

☒ Of our next year's projected revenues, what dollar amount do we anticipate consulting to represent, based on the way consulting has been defined?

____

☒ How many clients do we currently have? What is our goal as to number of clients?

Current # of clients ______ Goal # of clients ______

☒ What percent of our clients are businesses versus individuals (based on number)?

Business percentage ______ Individual percentage ______

☒ What would we like those percentages to be (based on number)?

Business ______________ Individual ______________

☒ What percent of our clients are businesses versus individuals (based on revenues)?

Business ______________ Individual ______________

☒ What would we like those percentages to be (based on revenues)?

Business ______________ Individual ______________

☒ How many clients make up 15% of our total revenue?

____

☒ What is average annual billings per client?

____

☒ Could this average easily be increased?

Yes/no ______________ If yes, what percentage? ________

☒ What are the strengths of our firm? (List the top three as they pertain to consulting)

1. ____

2. ____

3. ____

☒ What are we going to do to take better advantage of those strengths next year?

____

____

____

(continued on next page)

Consulting Questionnaire (continued)

☒ What are our firm's weaknesses? (List the top three as they pertain to consulting)

1. ______________________________

2. ______________________________

3. ______________________________

☒ What are we going to do to minimize the impact of those weaknesses next year?

____

____

____

☒ What four services do we want to focus on developing for next year? (List in confidence order)

1. ______________________________

2. ______________________________

3. ______________________________

4. ______________________________

☒ Estimate our firm's marketing and exposure budget for next year.

Skills Inventory Review

Consider the skills of those in your office as well as your own. Match those skills against your services list to insure that you are taking advantage of your strengths and minimizing your weaknesses. Use this form to list skills that your organization has but that are not being fully utilized, and work that could be re-organized to take better use of available skills.

Under-Utilized Skills

____

____

____

____

____

____

____

____

____

Re-Organized Work to Take Advantage of Existing Skills

____

____

____

____

____

____

____

Consulting Skills Enhancement Worksheet

Name: ______________________________ ***Year:*** __________

Current Skills Needed	Type of Training	Month	$ Budgeted

Future Skills Needed	Type of Training	Month	$ Budgeted

Total Budget: __________

Market Segmentation Worksheet

Identify How You Are Going to Segment Your Market

- Clients
- Nonclients
- Business clients
- Individual clients
- Top 15 percent
- Bottom 85 percent
- Specialized industries
- Retiring clients
- YUPies
- DINKs
- Generation X
- Estate clients
- Tax clients
- Financial statement clients
- Consulting clients

Segmenting Your Marketplace

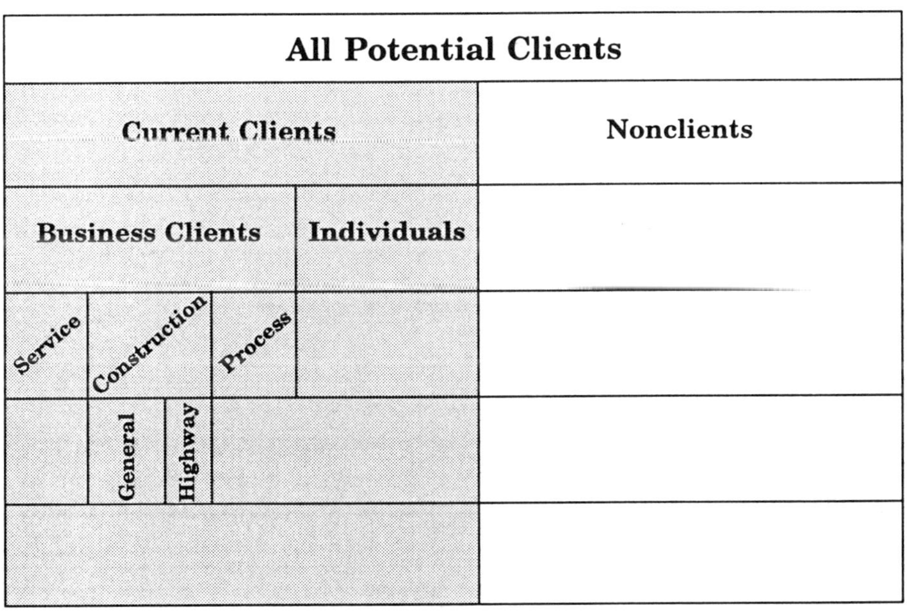

Segment Your Market As Much As Possible

☐ **Fortress** ☐ **Empire**

Exposure Self-Assessment

Based on your opinions about the way your firm markets its services, fill in your responses to the following questions:

What should we be doing that we are not?

- ______________________________
- ______________________________
- ______________________________
- ______________________________
- ______________________________
- ______________________________
- ______________________________

What are we doing that we should change . . . and how?

- ______________________________

-
-
-
-
-

What changes, if any, in resources should we be considering or requesting?

Client Service Plan

Fill out one of these for each client who represents a major client (top 15 percent) for your firm. It is important that you have a strategy tailored to each of these clients that outlines what services have been provided, what services you plan to provide, when, for how much, and how you are going to make it happen.

Client name: ______________________________

Client address: ______________________________

Contact name: ____________________ Day phone #: ________

After hrs #: __________ Fax #: __________ Email: __________

Services performed (current to past)	Frequency	Revenue
______________________	________	________
______________________	________	________
______________________	________	________
______________________	________	________
______________________	________	________

Future services to perform	Expected revenue	When start
1. ________________	________________	________
2. ________________	________________	________
3. ________________	________________	________

Strategy to create the urgency for the client to hire us for the identified future service.

1. ____

____

2. ____

____

3. ____

____

Exposure Plan

Based on the previous exercise, write down all the exposure alternatives your office should be planning on utilizing during the next twelve months.

- Networking
- Referrals
- Community relations
- Personal sales calls
- Research and development approach
- Client seminars or workshops
- Joint seminars or workshops
- Public speaking
- Writing
- Publicity
- Cross-selling
- Promotional pieces
- Major advertising mediums
- Direct mail
- Trade related
- Signage (outside)
- Telemarketing

____

____

____

____

____

____

____

____

____

____

____

____

____

____

Exposure Budget

Exposure Alternative	Month	No. of Contacts	$ Budgeted

Total Contacts: __________ Budget:__________

Expected Results

____ By ______________

____ By ______________

____ By ______________

____ By ______________

____ By ______________

____ By ______________

Section 4

Administrative and Organizational Issues

Chapter 10

Billing and Engagement Considerations

This is an area where personal preferences, organizational structure, and risk management all play a role. For example, even though consulting service collectability should improve by utilizing multiple billing cycles in a month, this administrative hassle may be deemed disproportionate to the gain (especially if collections haven't been a problem in the past). With this in mind, we would like to share with you our approach regarding a few billing and engagement issues.

Tracking Your Time for Billing Purposes

Accounting for hours and minutes has to be the most tedious and boring task associated with our profession. It is so hard to keep track of miscellaneous phone calls and other interruptions. But, over time, these minutes add up. This is especially true for consulting because you can easily find yourself delivering six hours worth of advisory services in fifteen-minute increments (that is, through telephone calls); an amount of time you can't afford to give away. So making an effort to record *all of your time* is essential if you want consulting to be profitable. However, because of the management policies of many organizations, while recording all of your time is administratively feasible, it is not politically practical. Let us explain.

The problem of recording time often is tied to that of billing it. Not all time is worthy of being billed, at least not at full rates. In a fair number of firms, certain time is not recorded because the worker does not want the time billed. More importantly, the worker doesn't want to argue with the billing partner as to why the time wasn't valuable. In other cases, partners might not log the time because they have already made the determination that the time wasn't going to be billed. Their theory is, "why create meaningless entries and paperwork?"

This dilemma can be solved by deciding to record all time, understanding that all time won't carry a full charge (if one at all), and then itemizing everything on the consulting bills. This includes billable and what we call *no-charge* time. By doing this, you will find that—

- *Clients will not call as often asking for an explanation of fees.*
- *Clients will pay on a more timely basis.*

Historically, the CPA profession has created bills that have a one- or two-line description along with a fee. In consulting, this can be deadly. Not only does this type of bill jeopardize your getting paid, but it can also impair your chances of being hired for future work. Why? Because traditional work is not completely understood by your clients, and therefore it is hard for them to judge if the actual time spent was necessary. Consulting is different. Because the client is usually very comfortable with the objectives and implementation plan of most management projects, he or she is more likely to scrutinize the manner in which the time was spent. By providing an itemized bill, you give your client an easy way to review your efforts and progress. For example, an itemized bill might look something like this:

For professional services rendered in connection with:

Lease of an office building: 4/21/97		
Telephone conference call regarding lease of an office building between Lynda, Sam, and Prominent Point leasing agent Jim.	1 hr	$150.00
Discussion with Lynda and Sam about conference call, pros and cons of leasing the building, various other issues regarding the same matter.	1.2 hrs	180.00

Meeting with Sam concerning: 4/25/97		
Americans With Disabilities Act requirements.	3.5 hrs	525.00
Telephone conversations with: 4/22/97–4/30/97		
Leasing agent regarding maintenance fee cap.	.3 hrs	45.00
Leasing agent regarding increasing the build-out allowance.	.2 hrs	30.00
Lynda regarding lease-versus-buy decision.	.4 hrs	60.00
Numerous quick conversations with Sam regarding various computer accounting system issues.	1.4 hrs	210.00
	Total	$1200.00

When there is price sensitivity, an itemized bill gives the client an opportunity to satisfy his or her concerns by reviewing the detailed time. This often triggers a reminder of the variety of events that happened to make up that time, such as that one phase of the project was more complicated than expected, or that additional work was requested.

Detailed billing is especially helpful in the worst-case scenario, in which the client challenges the value of some specific portion of your work. It's advantageous because, at this point, instead of arguing about the overall fee, you are now only discussing a few line items on the bill. This helps resolve issues expeditiously and, if concessions are made, they are based on smaller numbers.

For example, consider the bill above. Let's say that Lynda is upset by the $60 charge regarding the lease-buy decision conversation. She maintains that since no new information came out of that discussion, she shouldn't have to pay for it. We would then remind her, very politically of course, that we are paid by the hour, not by specific results, and that she initiated that conversation. Immediately after our "we bill for our time" explanation, we would likely continue with, "Would you like for us to remove that line item from the bill?" Lynda replies, "When I first called, I did. Now I'm not so sure that's fair." We would follow her statement with, "It's OK. We're glad you called. It would have been much worse if you would have been angry with us and we didn't know it!"

Consider what happened here. While this conversation is fictitious, it's based on many just like it that have occurred in our experience. There are several critical points to review. First, the argument was over $60, not the entire bill. Had the bill been summarized instead of itemized, we could have offered Lynda a 10 percent discount (which would have been $120) and had less impact than we had deleting an entire $60 line item. Keep in mind that the public is so numb from retail marketing that it takes discounts of around 30 percent or more to get people excited. So putting yourself in a position of having to discount an entire bill is a bad situation. By contrast, under our scenario you have the luxury of discounting a specific line item by 100 percent.

One last thought on recording detailed time entries. Either you can spend some time with your partners and staff outlining the kind of narrative they are expected to use when writing a time entry, or each billing partner can spend hours rewriting those entries at billing time. It is our experience that partners often procrastinate when it comes to reviewing and completing bills in the first place. Adding the extra laborious step of having to edit each line item on a consulting bill will only make matters worse. Therefore, it seems the logical choice is to spend time up front identifying the kind of work explanations you are looking for, and then training your staff properly, so the partner review effort required at billing time will be minimal.

Now that we've reviewed the issue of recording time, let's consider billing it. Our first topic of discussion is the time we code as *no-charge* or *gratis* time. Most billing partners attempt to charge it if at all possible. The perception is that if the time isn't billed, it didn't serve any purpose. We disagree. Our experience has been that gratis time is not only valuable, but a necessary part of the consulting business. When a bill is created, we specifically itemize any nonchargeable time. This enhances client loyalty, allows us to operate in a martyrdom-free environment, and indicates our commitment to the success of the project.

The idea of creating a martyrdom-free environment is critical because—

- *What your clients don't know, can and will work against you.*

- *If you expect to benefit from giving your clients something, they have to know you've given it to them.*

Any long-term arrangement with a client requires some give and take on both sides. This usually results in some discounted or free time somewhere along the way. Free time can have significant value as long as the client is aware of it. And the bill is an excellent forum to demonstrate this supportive commitment and attitude.

Discounting your bill or applying a credit against work you already have done can work in your favor too. The message is—

> *Time is money, but not all time is worth the same amount of money.*

In other words, you are communicating a quality control measure. When you perform premium-rate work, you expect to bill and receive premium rates. But since all work can't be of the same value, occasionally, when an inequity occurs, it makes sense to adjust your bill. This can be perceived as an attempt on your part to balance the relationship between rates and value. And this kind of perception is one of the keys to client satisfaction.

Frequency of Billing

The frequency of billing in most CPA firms is monthly. This cycle is not only in line with cash-flow requirements, but it's easier to manage (and requires less overhead) than weekly or biweekly billing.

With consulting projects, being paid, whether it is a retainer refreshment or regular billing, is an indication of management's satisfaction with your performance. Because the perception of your value as a consultant is usually more emotional than when you perform traditional work, you need to keep a close watch on the current feelings. Frequent billings are suggested.

Our time line is simple. Bill your consulting time often enough so that no individual bill exceeds the client's cash-flow comfort zone. For example, if a client feels $1,000 is a big project, bill before you accumulate that level of outstanding charges. Regarding large projects, because we are a small CPA firm, we tend to bill at intervals when the receivable becomes more than we want to carry. So, if after ten days we have accumulated $10,000 of work-in-process, we will bill it. As a general rule, other than the rare large consulting project which we might bill at any time (a $50,000 or greater project), we add a midmonth review of our consulting work. We send out an invoice to clients who have work-in-process that is either becoming too sizable for us to carry or for the client to pay. There's another way of saying this. *Bill in increments the client can afford.*

Additionally, if a project can be logically broken down into phases, an alternative to billing midmonth might be to send out an invoice at the conclusion of each phase (in addition to the monthly billing cycle). If you are working off of a retainer (normally a retainer should carry you to the end of the current phase), end-of-the-phase billing is merely a retainer refreshment to cover the next step of the project.

Billing your clients frequently also reminds them that you are hard at work on their behalf. If a number of weeks pass before you present your client with an invoice, he or she may get the impression that nothing is being done.

Finally, if the project is volatile, it may be imperative to bill weekly or—in some extreme cases where large resources are committed—daily. An example of a volatile situation would be performing a consulting engagement for a bank with imminent takeover by the FDIC. In such a situation, the agreement between the CPA firm and the client bank should be that an invoice will be prepared before day's end for that day's work, and submitted to the bank for payment, with the payment electronically transmitted to the CPA firm's account before closing.

Latest Pricing Trends—Survey Highlights

Now that we've talked about phasing, estimating, tracking your time, and frequency of billing, let's take a few moments to cover fees and pricing trends. The best way we know to address this is to present you with some highlights from a 1997 report called "Fees & Pricing Trends in Management Consulting," by Kennedy Research Group (KRG), located in Fitzwilliam, New Hampshire. The following extracts presented in this section are a combination of direct quotes and many times, for the sake of brevity, paraphrased findings of this study.

> KRG conducted an extensive survey of the world's leading consulting firms, with 92% of the respondents holding either managing partner or partner level positions with their firms. The sample distribution of firm sizes effectively mapped to the landscape of the management consulting profession. Respondents hailed from a wide variety of firms, from solo practitioners to 500+ employees, resulting in a representative sampling.

The report introduction had some information that immediately caught our attention because it discussed consulting utilization. This is a subject that always commands a great deal of interest. It said:

> The key to operating profitability in consulting requires attention to a multitude of details. Yet the widely accepted profitability model for the consulting profession can be reduced to three criteria: utilization, fees, and staff leverage. Each factor needs to be considered in relation to the other, and there is room for flexibility. For example, if fees can be significantly increased, then utilization can be reduced to attain targeted profitability.

While this position would receive little debate, it was what followed that caught our eyes. KRG commented:

> It is difficult to exceed 75% utilization rates with any consultant, regardless of the work available. Yet, if these rates fall below 60%, profitability becomes increasingly difficult, and perhaps impossible.

And in an example of survey-identified average hourly rates (included below), annualized revenues generated were projected assuming the following KRG-termed "typical" utilization rates:

	Average Hourly Rates	Utilization Rates (%)
Partner	$270/hr	59
Project managers	$212/hr	66
Consultants	$166/hr	70
Associates/analysts	$108/hr	70

Notice both the average rates and the utilization. Clearly, because of the level of marketing and nonbillable activity consulting requires, consulting cannot be expected to deliver the typically expected utilization rates found within traditional CPA services. As to the spread of billing rates:

> . . . while they ranged in the survey responses from $35 to $700, many partner level rates were $500/hr or more. Strategists commanded the highest average fee/hour rate at the partner and project manager level, marketing and sales consultants were a close second, with financial advisory consultants generating the lowest fee/hour rate of the group.

The survey went on to say that the fee per hour outlook for the financial advisory group was "relatively unfavorable" due to considerable competition. And as we have maintained throughout this book, it makes sense that those who help businesses plan a course for a successful future or help them create more revenue are the ones able to command the greatest fees. This idea is also consistent with the comments we shared with you from the AOMAR study back in chapter 1. As a side note, it should come as no surprise that "the highest fees were being charged by firms that cater to the largest corporations."

As to the question of most predominately used billing methods, KRG's study revealed:

> . . . hourly and daily billing rates are still used frequently (nearly 40% of the time combined), though mostly by smaller firms. Project-based billing was the most widely used billing method for consulting firms, garnering over 35% of the sample, most likely because the relationship between the service and price are linked by a defined deliverable. Value-based pricing strategies, though the darling of the trade and business press in recent years, are used minimally as the primary billing method (most groups reported using this method 10% or less for all engagements).

For our firm, considering the last year or two, we have been fairly evenly split between quoting hourly, daily, and project rates for services. However, our trend has been to quote daily rates more often, with project rates coming in second and hourly rates steadily declining.

As to mark-up rates, the comment was made that the study's findings "supported the benchmark that staff consultants must reach at least a mark-up rate of 3-times in order to achieve minimal profitability." The study also revealed average mark-ups to be as follows:

	Mark-Up Rates
Partner	3.0
Project managers	3.3
Consultants	3.5
Associates/analysts	3.6

Another interesting conclusion was drawn from the data:

> Consultants at firms of all types agree that "perceived value" is the #1 key criteria to clients when evaluating consultants. The "quality of the relationship" is a close second. "Price" placed 11th out of 15 criteria, but consultants agreed that most clients believe fees are too high. However, they also agree that rates will continue to increase at healthy rates into the year 2000.

There was one finding that was contrary to an approach we discussed in our book. It was "that there was no correlation between length of the project and average fees garnered." We expected to find that the longer the project, the more likely hourly fees would be discounted. As we discussed in the estimating section of chapter 6, there is good logic as to why project magnitude would have an impact on rates. It comes back to the idea that as utilization goes up, rates can go down and leave considerable room for profitability. We have come up with several reasons as to why *no correlation* between project length and rates was found, but they are purely speculation. We share this with you because this KRG finding has already made us rethink our pricing position on the rare occasion when we take on a $100,000+ job. It comes down to this. If a client wants us, a small firm, to commit a noticeable percentage of our resources to its project, it needs to pay a premium rate, or at least not a discounted one, for our time. Why? Because of the likely probability that we will be unable to react as quickly to some of our other clients' demands since our resources will be fully committed. Our modified philosophy was supported by the survey as it found that large projects, which it defined as $500,000 and over, commanded premium pricing in the marketplace.

We found a great deal of the information in the KRG study to be interesting and helpful to our planning. As you would guess, the research contains much more detail than what was discussed above, as well as more information. For your own copy of this study, contact Tim Bourgeous, Kennedy Research Group, at 603-585-3101, or by email at tcb@kennedypub.com.

Getting Paid for Your Involvement

Here are three key words to remember regarding the billing and collectability of consulting fees. They are—

Retainer, retainer, and retainer.

Traditional CPA work has been paper-oriented. For example, during tax season, we produce tax returns. When we perform audits, we deliver an opinion. For bookkeeping engagements, we compile financial statements, and so on. The point is, even though accounting is a service, the end result to the client is commonly a tangible product.

Consulting is just the opposite. The result is often intangible, such as the resolution of a dispute between labor and management or a new marketing approach. Therefore, there are many circumstances where adopting a retainer billing philosophy is critical to the success of the consultant. For example, after a consulting project has been completed, a client may begin to question whether the end result warranted the rate charged. It is easy, especially using hindsight, to rationalize why a fee is out-of-line. And once a problem has been solved, management's motivation to pay for its resolution often falls in priority. Even worse, as time passes, the perceived value of the consulting service diminishes or is taken for granted. These statements are partially true given the "beast" itself (consulting). A major part of the consultant's job is to facilitate necessary change. This means that the consultant helps management help themselves. By taking this approach of pushing management to solve their own problems through your facilitation, you direct the spotlight on their efforts. While this is the most effective approach for the organization, it often puts the consultant into the position of being taken for granted or viewed after the fact as unnecessary. Here's an example:

> Not very long ago, we conducted a planning meeting for an association that had been floundering in direction. After facilitating multiple days of sessions, and working individually with several small teams, a plan of attack for the group was mapped out. In one of the last days of planning, in one of the teams, a member commented, "We should have broken into small teams a long time ago. We are so effective when we work like this." The comment seemed to overlook the fact that our process and facilitation played a significant role as to why their small groups could gain the ground they did. The perception, by a number of the participants, was that the board members just magically got their act together and reached consensus. The reality was . . . had we not been there to facilitate the necessary exchange of information, to keep them on-track, and to have them follow a logical decision-making process, they would have floundered for many more months (maybe even years). By keeping the spotlight off us and our role, and the system focused around maximizing the talents of the management team (in this case, the association's board), we made it easy for some to minimize the value of our involvement.

This is why we maintain that with consulting, some of the collectability issues are inherent in the beast itself. Consulting is no place for the thin-skinned or the ego-maniac. The product we deliver is intangible, which is therefore constantly being challenged, interpreted, and misinterpreted. In addition, because of the high reliance and involvement of others, the success of our work is heavily dependent upon factors over which we have no control (such as the client's implementation of the action plan). Therefore, whenever possible, we want our fees to be based on performing the job . . . not the results thereof. Retainers are a tool that help facilitate the right perspective. Also, think of it as an insurance policy that protects the value of your time.

Note: We don't object to being held to results. However, in "results expected" cases, we either value-bill the job, add a premium to the project fee, or add a premium to our rates to cover additional work that might be necessary to secure the desired outcome. Given all of this, there are a number of reasons why retainers and consulting so often work hand-in-hand.

The Value of Consulting Fees Is More Subjective

Clients have a preconceived perception of a product's value, such as a tax return. This judgment as to what constitutes a *fair price* is usually based on two things:

1. *Comparison to a similar product.* Typically, accounting jobs are repetitive: tax returns are produced year after year, financial statements are generated monthly or quarterly. This repetition and past experience establishes an expectation as to a product's value.
2. *Experience and quality of work.* Most people assume that all CPAs have the same knowledge and therefore, that all similarly produced products, such as audits, are identical. This assumption, which doesn't distinguish between various degrees of experience and work quality, creates a commodity marketplace. Therefore, preparation of a tax return, financial statement, or audit is subject to being *shopped*. This theoretical comparability establishes an acceptable fee range.

Ideas, on the other hand, are not subject to this same kind of price rigidity. Each consulting project is unique, so comparison to the past is not as relevant. Even in a competitive bidding situation, it's often difficult to compare one proposal to another because factors such as experience and communication ability are key ingredients. In consulting projects, the consultant's skill—not time and effort—determines the value of the service. The bad news is that *value is often intangible and highly susceptible to interpretation*. Therefore, your client's perception of your work is of greater importance than the actual work itself. This makes consulting more political in nature than traditional CPA work. And if the internal politics aren't handled properly, the project is destined for difficulty, if not failure.

The good news is that this political environment and uncertainty allows for greater leverage in pricing, especially when the results are better than anticipated. But if the outcome of your effort is even remotely tainted, then your fees are at risk. As an example, if you were hired to obtain financing, and the approved loan amount is considerably less than expected, then the perceived value of your work diminishes even if the situation was beyond your control. Collecting a retainer before the work is performed protects you from clients who tend to place a subjective value on your time.

Project Deadlines Are Internally Generated

There is another issue regarding retainers. With tax returns, audits, and financial statements, compliance deadlines help focus management's attention to a project. These deadlines are often externally dictated, for example, by stockholders, banks, and vendors.

In the consulting arena, deadlines are most often internally generated. Management decides on a daily basis what issues are "hot." These priorities can easily shift if an externally imposed deadline appears. Internal deadlines are subject to change for many other reasons, such as a slowing economy or a new marketing opportunity. Many pressures can force management to reallocate available resources. Internally motivated projects are the first to be reviewed, shuffled around, or canceled. Since consulting projects are often internally motivated, holding a retainer protects your fees should a resource reallocation occur. Also, collecting a retainer ensures that your project at least starts out as a priority item—because clients don't pay in advance for low-priority work.

Client Commitment Is Imperative

Client commitment is the most important component in the success of a project, because almost all consulting requires a great deal of client participation. Since problems are rarely solved with simple solutions, the people (in your firm, your client's company, or a combination of both) who implement the ideas determine a project's success or failure. The payment of a retainer demonstrates commitment from the client, because once again, no one pays in advance for unimportant services.

There's one additional factor to consider. Ideas that are paid for tend to be more effective. This is because everyone likes to make good decisions. If your advice is bad, yet it was paid for in advance, then whoever hired you looks bad. So every time management refills your retainer, they increase their stake in the game. This intensifies management's commitment to the project as well as their support of your efforts.

Retainers Aren't a Panacea

Retainers have their downside too. Years ago, our firm started charging everyone a retainer for consulting work. As you will see in a minute, it's not hard to ask for a retainer. As a matter of fact, once you incorporate a few "retainer asking" tips into your repertoire, it's almost too easy to get paid a retainer. At one time, we found that we had been paid up front for about four months of work. While this sounds like a cash-flow jackpot, it created some other problems. As a result, we backed off on collecting retainers shortly after that. Now we collect them just for the reasons discussed above. Basically, we ask for retainers to—

- Verify management's commitment, both for starting the project and to secure continued support in order to complete it successfully.
- Ensure that our fees are protected should the project lose its high priority.

It's funny though, we tend to charge retainers to a few organizations you might not expect. The biggest example is . . . we are exponentially more likely to charge a retainer to a large organization, one that would have little to no problem paying us, over a much smaller one. Why? Because it's so easy to get caught in the middle with a large company. You may have support from one top manager, but not the support of another. Each may have verbally told consultants to start work, and when they find out what the other has done, a war breaks out. When this happens, even if we still get the job, either a significant amount of time winds up being lost (nonbillable) or the pre-everyone-approved work is heavily discounted. Where a mere phone call is ample to get started with smaller organizations, we use a retainer with large companies to make sure the *right people* have committed to the project before we expend a great deal of effort. One rule that has never failed us is—

If we can get a check in our hands before the work starts, we have the top-level visibility and project commitment we need.

On the other extreme, we tend to charge retainers to start-up companies and any time a project seems outside a company's "natural" capacity to pay. With start-ups, retainers are obvious. This group is willing to sign up for a multitude of services. Unfortunately, they are rarely able to pay for all of them. Charging a retainer does both you and the client a service; it matches high-priority work with capacity to pay. As to "natural" capacity to pay, we look for signals. For example, if we have a client who screams every time he or she receives a $1,000 or higher bill for services from anyone (whether it be from our firm, the lawyer, the brokerage house, and so on), then being asked to perform a $10,000 project is suspect. Or, if a retailer grossing $500,000 a year asks us to install a $70,000 computerized accounting solution, that also would be suspect. Other than the reasons stated above, we tend to just bill as we go (keep in mind that we might bill much more often than on a monthly basis).

Asking for a Retainer

After accepting the idea that collecting retainers is an important billing philosophy for consulting, your next step is to review the best way to ask for one. This is where a great many CPAs fail miserably. Here's a typical example of a CPA asking for a retainer for the first time:

CPA: Mr. Client, we would love to get started on your project. We usually require a retainer in advance . . . in a case like yours, oh, say . . . maybe $1,500?

Client: [*Doesn't say a word, just looks puzzled or stares*]

CPA: Is that all right? . . . ah . . . if it isn't . . . well, maybe we could make an exception and lower it a bit?

Client: [*More silence as the client ponders the words "usually," "maybe," "Is that all right?" and "exception"*]

CPA: How about $750 . . . could you afford $500?

By this time, the client has assessed several things. First, the collection of a retainer isn't a requirement because the CPA indicated that there are exceptions. Second, the client wonders why he or she is being singled out for this retainer policy, and becomes defensive regarding the issue. His or her perception of being singled out comes from the CPA's obvious discomfort with the idea. Third, even if the client believes that a retainer is in order, it is clear that the amount is negotiable. Fourth, the CPA's stumbling has relayed the message that the client can modify the rules.

To avoid this kind of confusion, ask for your retainer in a very positive way. The previous example was close, but see if this doesn't sound better:

CPA: Mr. Client, we would love to get started on your project. We require a retainer in advance, and on a project of this size, we could start work with $1,500.

The message is short, sweet, doesn't give the idea that this issue is negotiable, and says "we're ready to start as soon as you write the necessary check." By the way, the real mistake made above wasn't with the CPA's first statement, it was the fact that he or she made a second one before the client said anything.

Ask for your retainer with confidence. Don't hesitate in mid-sentence. Avoid "uhs" and "let's sees" and "maybes." The example above, if delivered in a steady tone of voice (and assuming you weren't sweating profusely), would illustrate to the client your confidence in the idea, and that it is important and necessary to collect a retainer.

After asking, don't say another word until the client responds. There is an old saying in the marketing game: *He who speaks first . . . loses.*

Ask for alternatives if necessary. If paying the retainer up front is a problem for a client, but you still want the business, ask them for an alternative:

CPA: I understand your situation. What do you suggest as an alternative?

This way, the client is committing first, which allows you to give a counterproposal if necessary.

Client: I set aside an amount of $750. I can write you a check for that amount today. Any additional amount would require a meeting with the rest of the management team and that would delay the project for at least a week.

CPA: I could work with a check for $750 today if we can bill you each Monday and expect to be paid by each Friday. Would that work for you?

Some might feel this scenario really is no different than the first one, but it is. In this case, the client understands that an exception is being made to accommodate his or her situation. In the first case, the retainer looks more like a *wish* than a *requirement*. Note: The bigger the project, the more important it is for you to follow up verbal agreements like this one with a letter of understanding. We rarely go to this level of formality, however, for projects under $5,000 (which represent the vast majority of our work).

How Much Retainer Should You Ask For?

This one is simple in theory, but difficult to pin down. The amount of retainer to request is really a risk and commitment issue. In other words, *How much risk are you willing to take that you'll be paid, and what kind of client commitment are you looking for in the project?*

For small projects, our firm requests half of the expected fee up front. If we work out a weekly billing arrangement (which we often do for small businesses), then a one- or two-week retainer is negotiated.

These rules aren't set in concrete. If the client is financially strong and you are convinced that management has a high level of commitment to the project, you can waive the retainer requirement conditioned on the fact that you can bill frequently and that they pay in a timely manner. This minimizes financial risk and constantly verifies management's attitude toward the project.

Final Caution: Stay Within the Limits of the Retainer

Most of us would rather not work at all (in other words . . . play golf or go fishing) than work and not get paid. Therefore, ask for retainers for consulting projects in order to minimize your financial exposure. This strategy also maximizes the value of your work because when management advances the retainer, they are demonstrating commitment to the project.

Before we leave this subject, there is one important rule to remember when a retainer is collected. *Work within the limits of the retainer.* Our experience is that firms charge retainers and then overwork them. For example, the client pays a $2,000 retainer to get started. A month later, that same client will get a bill for $3,000 more. CPAs often consider the retainer as a down payment. If that's what you are asking them to pay, call it that from the beginning. However, if you are collecting a retainer, you and the client have come to an agreement that you will work until the money runs out and then provide an update. While this update does not have to be a formal presentation, it is our belief that you have a responsibility to let the client know what you have done, where you are now, and generally what's left. By doing this, you don't overspend your clients' retainers, you keep them informed as to how their money is being utilized, and they tend to be much happier with your work. And the good news is, if there is a problem, you find out about it before you've done thousands of dollars' worth of uncollectable work.

Proposals

We have alluded numerous times in this text to the fact that we are not particularly fond of the proposal process. We even stated that our firm does not participate in most requests for proposals (RFPs). This is an odd position when you consider that proposals are the standard way of conducting business for large projects. But, practically speaking, our firm doesn't do large projects, which often start in the hundreds of thousands of dollars and range into the millions. One of the main reasons we are not enthusiastic about proposals is because it takes a great deal of unbillable time to create ones that are likely to win. In addition, oftentimes you are asked to provide some up-front evaluation or diagnostic services as part of the proposal process. Because of both of these issues, we are reluctant to get involved in too many of these efforts.

However, proposals definitely have their place. And depending on the magnitude of the project, a certain amount of free work is not only expected, but acceptable. To put this into perspective, remember the AICPA's MCS's work-in-process definition of consulting, that consulting is comprised of diagnosing, strategizing, constructing, implementing, and operating.

When you are creating a proposal for a million-plus dollar project, then the *diagnosing* step is often thrown in for a nominal fee or given away. Many times, firms will provide specialized research, all kinds of analysis, and even hire specialized consultants to help them win the project. For example, it is not uncommon in responses to RFPs to bring in consultants with the sole purpose of working with the project team to create resumes that best respond to bid specifications. Our point is, for large projects, proposal creation is big business in and of itself. The reason the *diagnosing* and sometimes part of the *strategizing* stages of consulting are given away in these sized projects is because the real money is made by leveraging large numbers of people for extended periods of time at good rates. The real plum is in performing the *construction, implementation,* or *operating* stages. However, for the kind of projects our firm typically handles, from several thousand to a couple-hundred thousand, with a normal big job being around $20,000, if we gave away the *diagnosing* phase, we would lose a significant piece of our revenue. Why? Because often, our clients or specialists will perform much of the constructing, implementing, or operating work.

So it makes sense that if you want to play in the skilled labor force delivery arena (which often means you have to be able to amass a large full-time staff in minimal time), then preparing quality customized proposals is essential. It also makes sense to give away expertise to demonstrate that you are the best firm for the project. However, this is not an environment for which our firm is typically well-suited. There are occasions when we make exceptions, as with the hospital example in chapter 7. But when the request for free advice becomes out of proportion with the overall project size, or when the proposal process is being used as a way to access free expertise, it's time to walk away.

Think of it another way. Many organizations pay partners 5 percent to 15 percent to bring in new projects. So we use 10 percent as a guideline. When the cost of proposal preparation (both time and expense) exceeds about 10 percent of the expected revenue, it's normally gone beyond our comfort zone of what we would consider a reasonable marketing investment.

There is an even more important factor that drives whether we are willing to create a proposal. It can best be explained by the answer to this question: *What are the odds that we will win the RFP?* Some of the criteria are:

- If we helped the potential client develop the proposal specifications, then we are certainly comfortable investing the necessary time and energy to prepare a proposal.
- If the proposal request is from a client with whom we have a good relationship, we will prepare a proposal.
- If we have a supportive ally who is one of, or close to, the decision-makers and will use his or her influence to sway the final selection, we will participate in the proposal process.

This last reason was why we participated in the hospital proposal. We could go on with specific situations, but the underlying key is that we are looking for much better than average odds of our proposal being selected.

One of the down sides of having a small firm with a good reputation is that organizations will ask you to be involved just so they can include your name in the list of candidates. The problem is, in many of these situations, management already has an inside favorite. They just want to do a little covering themselves before going public with their decision. These are the situations we try to avoid. But we want to make one thing clear before we move on. We are not against preparing proposals, we are just against spending valuable time doing make-work. If we feel we have a real chance of winning the proposal, most likely, we'll participate. Even with this attitude, we still lose a few. The good news is that we haven't had to waste the time and money to establish a proposal department just to respond to requests that we have virtually no chance of winning.

ENGAGEMENT LETTERS

Whether or not to use an engagement letter is a risk-management question that we cannot address for you. Every firm decides where the line should be drawn regarding this issue, and it is drawn everywhere from no engagement letters for any clients to engagement letters for every client. We have put together the following guidelines for our organization regarding this issue.

Our firm's guidelines as to when *oral engagement understandings* are appropriate with the client include—

- When the consulting situation is narrow in focus with few stages.
- When the engagement primarily consists of meetings and discussions with the client.
- When the engagement costs are not significant to the client company.
- When the opportunity for misunderstanding the nature and scope of work is minimal.
- When the consulting delivered is primarily demonstrating knowledge possessed prior to the engagement.
- When the consultant and the client are very familiar and have a good existing relationship.

Conversely, *engagement letters* are appropriate and important when—

- The consulting situation is complex.

- Misunderstandings are likely or highly possible.
- There are a variety of stages required to perform the work.
- The project will take place over a long period of time, for example, months or years (people forget as time passes).
- The future stages of work can significantly vary based on the findings of each stage.
- The level of knowledge required to perform the work is beyond that currently possessed by the consultant (data gathering, information analysis, and research are all terms that signal a need to consider formalizing the engagement with a written understanding).
- There is little to no existing relationship with the client.
- The firm's professional liability carrier requires formal understandings (or at least strongly encourages this formality for fees in excess of some designated amount).

These are not the only issues to consider. We also view the size of the client organization before making a final decision as to whether engagement letters should be prepared. For example, the larger the organization, the more formal the agreement, because—

- It's consistent with the corporate culture; the way they do business.
- Upper management wants the engagement letter to minimize the potential for misunderstandings between contractor and contractee.
- The client company wants to avoid being trapped into paying for worthless services or products (it sees formalized engagement letters or contracts as protecting its rights).
- The person hiring the consultant wants protection from rebuke from upper management.
- The larger company demands greater formality in order to better protect its assets.

On the other hand, smaller companies will more likely be threatened by engagement letters because—

- They want to avoid being trapped into paying for worthless services or products (they see formalized engagement letters or contracts as limiting their options).
- Engagement letters are not consistent with the way they normally do business.
- They are more comfortable building personal relationships with customers and vendors. To many small organizations, these relationships should not start off with legal babble. (Note how many prenuptial agreements never get signed.)

As we stated earlier, engagement letters often fall into the risk management zone—what is at risk versus what is to gain. The majority of the time, we do not ask for or prepare engagement letters. Why? Because much of our work is for small business owners (who dislike the formality of legal stylized paperwork) and is performed primarily with knowledge currently possessed by the consultant. Large projects—$10,000 or greater—are usually accompanied by letters of understanding or contracts. For example, if we were to facilitate a strategic planning session that carried a price tag of $7,500 to $15,000, we would typically send out a letter confirming the price along with outlining our approach. In such a situation there would be no requirement for the client to sign or return our letter. However, when we perform technology consulting (finding the best software, determining what areas of the organization should be automated, software support, and so on) we have the client sign an engagement letter or contract. Why? Because technology is an area where misunderstandings are not only predictable, but expected.

By considering the elements identified above, the decision as to whether or not to use engagement letters becomes fairly straightforward. When in doubt, or if the situation is borderline, don't take unnecessary chances. Prepare an engagement letter and don't give it a second thought.

There is one last point to keep in mind. Don't overfocus on the engagement letter and lose sight of the engagement itself. An engagement letter should be used to clarify responsibilities and create a layer of protection between your firm and litigation. *It is not a selling tool* and if interjected too early, it may kill the deal. That doesn't mean you shouldn't use it. We are just saying to weigh the risks you are taking, the client situation, the work you are performing, and make a decision that is comfortable for you and your organization. If the project is borderline, feel the fear and send out the engagement letter anyway. If a borderline deal is killed by the use of an engagement letter, the odds are high that you should never have considered doing the work in the first place.

Chapter 11
Client Communications

With consulting, often what you do is not as important as keeping the client updated and involved in what's going on. For many consulting engagements, oral presentations and meetings are your best tools for facilitating the information exchange desired. This chapter addresses fundamentals and techniques important to both.

Meeting Management

Why is it that business people dislike business meetings? John Kenneth Galbraith, a noted economist, was quoted as saying, "Meetings are indispensable when you don't want to do anything." Dr. Peter Drucker, in his book *The Effective Executive*, sarcastically comments, "One either meets or one works. One cannot do both at the same time."

If there is such a genuine belief that meetings are a waste of time, why do we keep conducting them? Dr. Peter Drucker says, "We meet because people holding different jobs have to cooperate to get a specific task done." In today's fast paced environment, decisions have to be made quickly, and then communicated even quicker. Meetings, which can be held for all kinds of reasons, are an effective way to gather, decide on, and disseminate important information. The trick is to make sure that every time you meet, there is an identifiable and appropriate reason for the gathering.

In the book *How to Run Better Business Meetings*, authored by the 3M Meeting Management Team (McGraw-

Hill, Inc., New York, 1987), several important issues are addressed. We have summarized and paraphrased many of the book's concepts in the paragraphs below that we believe need to be essential knowledge to the practicing consultant. As consultants, it is imperative that since much of our time is spent in meetings with our clients, our skills are exemplary in this area. This section identifies what it takes to run a productive and effective meeting.

3M's book cites thirteen "good reasons" for calling a meeting. We will elaborate on three that are common to the advisory function. You should call a meeting—

1. *When you need to reach a group judgment or decision.* This is the kind of meeting called when the participants are expected to express opinions regarding a subject or action in order to reach a consensus as to direction. However, many people call these meetings when the decision has already been made. Therefore, the meeting is not only a waste of time, but it is an insult to those attending.
2. *When you need to analyze or solve a problem.* Group dialog regarding problem resolution brings unique insight and experience to the table, and simultaneously instills solution commitment and ownership. Yet in many companies, problem-solving meetings are really witch hunts in disguise. In the typical meeting, it's not as important to fix the problem as it is to find someone to blame it on. Obviously, this type of meeting is often mismanaged.
3. *When you need to ensure that everyone has the same understanding of the information.* It is so easy for management's actions to be misinterpreted. As an example, let's say an employee is suddenly let go due to unique circumstances. By the end of the week, the masses are expecting a companywide layoff. A timely informational meeting is a good way to keep the negative impact of the grapevine in check.

Informational meetings need to be concise and to the point. All too often, those conducting the meeting either aren't prepared to explain the issues simply and clearly, or they arrive with a week's worth of charts and are unwilling to skip over a single one.

Since meetings are such an important tool to help facilitate organizational success, it is important to know not only when to call them, but how to run them as well. Unfortunately, meetings with legitimate purposes often become disasters because they are run so ineptly. This happens because there are entire corporate cultures that rarely conduct a good meeting, and the employees climbing the rungs of their corporate ladders continually absorb poor meeting management skills from people who never knew how to run meetings in the first place.

What are the characteristics of a well-run meeting? A meeting needs—

- A purpose, one that everyone knows and understands.
- To occur at the right time and place.
- To be called only when other less expensive, less time-intensive alternatives won't provide a satisfactory solution.

One of 3M's points that really hit home with us was, "The real issue isn't that meetings are a waste of time. It's just that too much time is wasted in meetings." Assuming there is a legitimate reason to have one, there are several issues regarding conducting a productive and effective meeting that need to be considered.

Who Should Attend?

In order to make a contribution, attendees should have one or more of the following:

- A working *knowledge* of the business to be discussed
- The *power* to make a decision or approve an agreed-to action
- The *responsibility* for project continuation or implementation
- *Responsibility* to a group that will be affected by any meeting decisions
- The *need* to know the information presented

The bottom line is, never invite anyone to a meeting who doesn't need to be there.

How Many Should Come to the Meeting?

Keep in mind that too many people is the easiest way to ensure that an otherwise quality meeting ends up in disaster. For example, experts suggest—

- Five or fewer participants for decision making and problem solving.
- Ten or fewer for problem identification.
- Less than thirty for informational meetings (in order to maximize a sense of intimacy and therefore promote personal participation).
- Fifteen or fewer for training.

The point is, depending on the objective of the meeting, the optimal and maximum number of participants changes.

How Do You Set a Positive Climate?

This is another critical focus to good meeting management. Here are some key considerations that ensure a positive climate:

- If key people can't attend, cancel the meeting.
- Start and end meetings on time. You have an obligation to honor those who work with you by ensuring their time is not wasted due to poor meeting management.
- Regarding levity, humor can be an asset in establishing a positive work environment. However, if it becomes too pervasive, it could easily undermine and derail the meeting.
- The 3M Meeting Management Team's primary meeting commandment: *never* begin a meeting without a written agenda. Regardless of the informality, every meeting should attempt to accomplish something within a specific period of time. An agenda formalizes that objective.

How Often and How Long Should the Breaks Be?

If your meeting is less than an hour-and-a-half, breaks are not essential. But for every minute you push beyond this hour-and-a-half window without a break, the likelihood of losing someone goes up exponentially. Also, studies have shown that beyond this time frame, productivity starts to decline, exponentially eroding as you surpass the two-hour mark. In all-day meetings, breaking on the hour becomes important in the afternoon if you want to maintain the group's energy and interest.

As for the length of the breaks, they should last about ten to fifteen minutes. Remember that we are talking about breaks relative to hour and hour-and-a-half sessions. For example, breaking on the hour with a ten-minute break works well. However, whenever you are breaking often you need to be diligent about getting people back together and continuing your sessions on schedule. Keep breaks under twenty minutes or people will get involved in other activities. If the breaks are too short (five minutes or less) there is not enough time for your participants to get refreshed and re-energized.

There is a great deal to consider if you want to run productive and effective meetings. It requires planning, organization, and effort. Without all three, you're just one of the nine out of ten companies that just call meetings—which tend not only to waste the company's money, but also to steal one of its scarcest resources, management's time.

Effective Group Presentation Techniques

Besides putting in the necessary planning, organization, and effort that is required to run productive and effective meetings, there are certain skills that play a large part in this process. These skills are the same as those required for group presentations. Therefore, we have included a high-level review of the skill set your group facilitation tool kit should contain.

Often in consulting, meetings consist of one or two CPAs and several members of the client's organization. This kind of setting usually is more formal than one-on-one dialogue. It's more of a presentation than a conversation. The skills required to conduct this kind of meeting are similar to those used in public speaking. In fact, as scary as it may sound, this environment *is* public speaking. Therefore, we're including a few important group communication techniques. With just a little practice, you should quickly become more comfortable and effective in a one-on-many dialogue. The following ideas and techniques were shared with us by Communispond, Inc., a Dallas, Texas company that focuses on communication training.

Controlling Your Eyes

Controlling your eyes is the act of focusing on, and talking to, only one person at a time. At the end of each thought (usually about five seconds), find someone else to address. Controlling your eyes helps you avoid *brain overload*, a condition that usually results in losing your train of thought, appearing nervous, and repeating yourself.

Brain overload occurs because your brain receives too much simultaneous stimulation (like looking at five people, the room, and trying to come up with an intelligent thought within the same three- to four-second period). Focusing your eyes on one person at a time seems too simple to be the answer, but it is. A side benefit in the more formal group setting is that this direct eye contact gives your words a personal touch. Mastering this technique is imperative; it is the foundation for group speaking. Even though it may be uncomfortable at first, you'll get used to it within a short period of time.

Controlling your eyes has another meaning to us, which we mentioned in chapter 5. The listening exercises at the end of that chapter focus on this. Getting the consultant to share eye contact with either the observer in the first exercise or client 2 in the second exercise is rare. Why? Because CPAs tend to focus on the decision maker or the person with the highest authority. This causes them to fixate on one person and exclude everyone else. While this conversational style doesn't seem to have a negative impact on highly technical matters, when it comes to management-related issues, it is a catastrophe waiting to happen. There are countless stories of one CPA firm being chosen over another because an apparent observer in a conversation was a powerful influencer who felt disregarded. There are just as many stories about quality ideas that were covertly sabotaged for this same reason. In the facilitation, persuasion, and consensus-building business of the consultant, it is essential to be aware of inclusive eye contact and develop it as an instinctive skill.

Being Aware of Your Posture

Stand squarely facing the group, with your arms relaxed at your side. This is called the *neutral position*. It gives the appearance of confidence and sincerity. However, if you're like most people, the neutral position will feel horribly awkward.

Most of us naturally do one of the following. We put our hands in our pockets, behind our backs, or in front of us (the fig-leaf position). Additionally, we often stand with one foot in front of the other. Any of these combinations of hands and feet look bad. As a matter of fact, almost every position besides the neutral position is displeasing to the eye. If you don't believe us, videotape yourself and witness the effect of these different stances on camera.

Using Gestures to Give Emphasis and to Avoid Appearing Stiff

Gestures should be in line with the group size. As an example, when you are conversing with one or two people sitting at a table, gesturing in front of you at table top height is very appropriate. However, with a group of seven or eight, these gestures need to be exaggerated to have the same impact. For example, you might stand up and use gestures that extend beyond the frame of your body. And when you talk to a very large group, consider gesturing to the side of your body. Gestures made in front of you to groups of fifty or more can be negatively impacted by the depth perception of your audience.

Also, don't abuse gestures by overusing them. If you do, people will get distracted and tired from watching you. The best tip we can provide is, before you start talking, take a second or two and muster some excitement about your topic. Then, just let your natural energy flow into gestures. Don't try to confine that energy—use it to your advantage.

Projecting Your Voice

In communication studies, speaking with a strong voice has been rated *as the single most important ingredient to appearing confident.*

You want to talk loudly enough for people to hear what you're saying. Generally, if you project your voice at a level you think is appropriate . . . it isn't. The right volume often is a notch or two above your instincts. In groups of fifteen or more, the appropriate level may be about the point you feel you are shouting. Don't worry, you're not.

The reason you should go to all of this effort of monitoring your volume is very simple. Your clients shouldn't have to struggle to hear what you're saying. They're paying good money for your time and talents; allow them painless and easy access to your knowledge.

Clearing Your Visual Aids

When a visual aid is first shown, such as flip chart, slide, transparency, or marker-board, the reaction of your audience will be to read it from top to bottom. During this time, you have momentarily lost control. In order to regain everyone's attention, mention each point shown on the visual aid with only a brief comment. This technique is called *clearing your visual aid.* This satisfies the curiosity of your audience and allows them to refocus their attention back to you. At this time, you can return to the first point and begin elaborating in more detail, one point after the other, until you have fully discussed the references on the visual aid.

Also, avoid using the overhead projector peek-a-boo technique, where you put up an overhead and then cover up the part you don't want the audience to see just yet. This can be very distracting. Your audience is likely to spend more time wondering what's being covered up and why than paying attention to what you are saying. At best, it's awkward for the speaker to try to manage the cover-up:

covering up too much, not enough, "oops, they saw something they weren't suppose to see," and so on.

Looking, Then Turning and Speaking

The proper way to clear your visual aid is to (1) look and point to the item with a full hand, not just a pointed finger, (2) turn toward your group, and finally, (3) speak. This tip is to remind you to speak to your audience, not to your visual aids. So, look at your chart, but before you say a word, turn to your audience. By doing this, you keep everyone involved, you are easier to hear, and you maintain better control of your group.

Using the Power of Silence

What often seems like an eternity in front of a group is really only a few seconds . . . time hardly noticeable. If you are not sure of what to say next, look at your notes or flip through some of your paperwork. But whatever you do, don't stand in front of your audience saying "uh." While we know it is hard to get rid of that ugly sounding noise altogether, you *can* minimize its use.

The ideas above are only a few tips that promote effective public speaking. And with just a little practice, your speaking capabilities should improve dramatically.

Handling Questions

Even if you have mastered speaking and presentation skills, you're not out of the woods yet. How you handle questions is the next area that can make or break your entire presentation. Communispond, Inc. has some suggestions to help simplify this process too.

Effective question-and-answer sessions can be achieved by focusing on the following rules:

- *Never lose control of your session*
- *Always show absolute confidence*
- *Be courteous—even if someone in your audience is out of line*

Maintaining control of your audience is the key to a strong positive finish. After you finish your talk, say, "What are your questions?" and raise your hand. This subtly demonstrates the etiquette expected for asking questions. And this can be used effectively in small groups as well.

If your audience doesn't respond, be prepared to make a transitional statement such as, "Raise your hand if you're ready to start using teleconferencing at your office." Then you can call on individuals and ask why they do or don't see teleconferencing in their near future. Regardless of whether meeting participants raise their hands or not, they are now involved. And that's the trick . . . because once involved, talking is the next natural step. However, this also creates a new set of problems, which leads us to our next topic.

Dealing With Questioners

If you are asked a question and don't know the answer—say so. You can always tell the questioner that you'll find out and get back to him or her later. On the positive side, saying that you don't know something adds credibility to the issues you do address.

If a question is asked that is outside the scope of your discussion (too technical for the rest of the group) make the comment, "If you don't mind, I'd like to discuss that with you right after this session." This treats the questioner with respect, but doesn't allow the conversation to get sidetracked on unimportant, confusing, or inappropriate topics.

Speaking Out of Turn. Let's say someone speaks out of turn. How do you stop that? One technique is to hold up one hand, palm towards the interrupter, as if you are stopping traffic. Then point with the other (pointing in this context refers to using a full hand, never just a finger) to someone whose hand is raised. Follow this by saying something like, "Excuse me, the gentleman in the corner had his hand up first." This politely but firmly says that you are in control and re-emphasizes the proper question-asking etiquette. Of course, if the top dog of your client's organization speaks out of turn . . . well . . . that's a different story. While we don't want people to be cut off when they have used the proper technique to take the floor, cutting off the CEO after he or she has interrupted an employee can carry a high price tag too. When this happens—and it will—just remember who was interrupted and as soon as possible, go back and say something like, "I believe you had something else to say on this subject. Would you mind sharing that with us now?" If the issue has been addressed, or the participant no longer wants to make a statement, he or she will just say so.

Calling People by Name. This is a common mistake. Don't recognize a questioner by name unless you can do so with everyone in the group. Why? Because the person whose name you call aloud feels special, but those you don't know feel left out. Alienating part of your audience is not an effective communication technique. If you feel it is important to call people by name, then use name tags or name cards so you can treat everyone the same. By the way, when you are conducting a meeting, it is always your job to learn everyone's name. Use whatever techniques work for you, but make sure that by the end of the meeting, you have personalized your conversation by being able to address everyone individually.

A technique that we use is to write down everyone's name at the start of a meeting. If you didn't do this right away, get the names down on paper as soon as possible. While it may be embarrassing fifteen minutes into a conversation to say, "I'm sorry, what's your name again?" that's not nearly as bad as asking that same question when the meeting is wrapping up. After you write down the names, try to incorporate them into a couple of your directed comments early on to help you memorize them.

A Question That You Plan to Answer. Let's assume a question has been asked that you plan to answer. What's next? First, paraphrase it back to your audience. Here's an example:

Questioner: Do you feel pre-printed newsletters are an effective marketing tool?

CPA: Are pre-printed newsletters an effective marketing tool? Well, we believe . . .

This technique buys you time to think and keeps everyone involved. However, don't start off with, "That's a good question." This comment subtly categorizes every other question as being a "bad question." Also, you normally don't need to say, "The question is" because a well-executed rephrase makes it clear to the audience that you are repeating the question.

If the question is antagonistic, paraphrase it to restate it more positively; then answer it. For instance:

Questioner: Our firm has been using pre-printed newsletters for years and it works for us. I don't think you know what you're talking about.

CPA: Why are we so adamant about personalizing your newsletters? Well, our experience has been . . .

This takes practice to do really well, but it is an exceptional tool for controlling your audience. *Never verbally attack a questioner,* no matter how far he or she is out of line. You don't want to become the bad guy. Using your power as the group leader to embarrass someone is a good way to become the villain.

What do you do if one person is monopolizing the question-and-answer phase of your talk? That's easy. During the first part of your answer, look at the questioner. Then turn and look at someone else and give the remainder of the answer. This break in eye contact from the original questioner allows you the chance to call on someone new.

Finally, when you're about ready to wrap up, or more importantly, out of time, say, "We have time for one more question." Take the question, answer it . . . and quit. You do this as a meeting management technique. Obviously, there are many times when you want to keep answering questions as long as the client is interested in asking. However, when you have asked management for a forty-five-minute audience, and they state up front minimal time flexibility, make sure the meeting is over on time by controlling the questioning phase. Otherwise, you may find it much more difficult to get on their calendar for the next meeting.

Practice Is the Solution to Comfort

The techniques discussed in this chapter form the basics of successful one-on-one and group presentation management. In the field of consulting, your success depends on your ability to communicate to both individuals and groups. So a little work in this area should go a long way towards developing your client base . . . and then keeping them satisfied.

In order to become more comfortable with public speaking, consider examining the numerous books and courses available. However, nothing is as effective as practice. Toastmasters is a good forum for improving your skills. Another good way to improve is role-playing with a peer, one acting as client and the other as consultant.

If these concepts are already familiar to you, then we hope the material has served as a refresher. If this information is new, remember that you are not alone if you feel a little overwhelmed. Regardless of your current level of expertise in this area, improving these skills should be a part of your itinerary to better prepare you to compete in the twenty-first century.

Before You Move On

Giving presentations to a group, especially to your peers, has to be one of the most stressful situations you can imagine. But as consultants, this is an imperative skill to develop in order to facilitate the level of change our clients are demanding. Therefore, a *Group Presentations* exercise is in order. This is a group exercise where each person takes a turn both as presenter and as observer.

We've also included a *Self-Assessment* exercise. No doubt this exercise will elicit plenty of areas you feel need work.

Group Presentations—Presenter's Role

Take about ten minutes and think of a story you enjoy telling about yourself, a member of your family, or a friend. This story should be less than three minutes. Outline your ideas below.

Be aware of the issues covered earlier in this chapter:

- Controlling your eyes
- Being aware of posture
- Using gestures to give emphasis
- Projecting your voice

Notes or outline for talk

Group Presentations—Observer's Role

Observers (or put another way, those waiting their turn to make a speech) should use this sheet to take notes on each lecturing consultant. Notice how each speaker controls his or her eyes and posture, uses gestures, projects voice, uses silence, uses visual aids (if any), and "looks, turns, and speaks" (if appropriate). Remember, your turn will be next; keep your criticism constructive.

Self-Assessment Time Line

Based on the materials covered in this chapter, please take a few moments to assess your strengths and weaknesses. Then, using the form below, note any skills you plan to work on as well as a time frame to re-assess your progress. In addition, if there are activities or exercises you plan on attempting, jot them down and note your intended completion date. This form is provided solely as a self-improvement tool.

The following are ***Skills*** *I plan to* ***Improve:***

______________________________ By when: ______

______________________________ By when: ______

______________________________ By when: ______

______________________________ By when: ______

______________________________ By when: ______

______________________________ By when: ______

______________________________ By when: ______

______________________________ By when: ______

______________________________ By when: ______

The following are ***Activities*** *I plan to* ***Attempt:***

______________________________ By when: ______

______________________________ By when: ______

______________________________ By when: ______

______________________________ By when: ______

______________________________ By when: ______

______________________________ By when: ______

______________________________ By when: ______

Section 5

Consulting Packages

Chapter 12
Facilitating Your Client's Planning Process

Of all the value-adding services a CPA can offer, helping an organization plan its strategy should top the list. Why? Because planning is an essential ingredient to success. Theodore Roosevelt said it well, "*When you aim at nothing, you'll hit it every time.*"

The kind of companies we tend to work for already perform this function to some degree. The problem is, for many, planning is not accomplished through a formalized procedure. Therefore, the employees, including the management team, are informed of the corporate direction only through casual conversation or occasional comments. This lack of communication is often the key difference between performing at a marginal level versus becoming extremely successful. Think of it this way:

> *Picture fifty ants carrying a small twig with the objective of maneuvering in a northerly direction. What happens when forty ants push north and the other ten are attempting to march west?*

The answer ... chaos. The ants moving west cause two problems. First, they slow the progress of the overall group. Second, within a short period of time, the entire group will be way off course. They might even find that their movement has been circular.

Companies can suffer from this same kind of confusion. It's easy for several people or even entire departments to operate in a vacuum when they are uninformed. Even though these people or groups may be operating very efficiently, the overall progress of the company can be hindered. In many ways, the more efficient and effective these misguided splinter groups are, the worse off the company, because the impact they make is so inconsistent with the goals of the leadership. These unintentionally wayward decisions could easily have the same negative impact as those ten misdirected ants.

In order for an operation to continuously improve performance, the workers need to have a clear sense of direction or mission. The theory is simple:

> *The more people working towards a common goal, the greater the likelihood of its achievement.*

By formalizing the planning process, you better inform the people. Since the planning process defines the corporate targets and identifies the actions required to reach them, everyone has a better understanding of their roles. This understanding synchronizes individual efforts, thus promoting departmental achievement, culminating in the accomplishment of corporate objectives.

Our experience is that most businesses fail due to the lack of good basic business practices. Here's what we mean. We've all heard that undercapitalization and poor management are held responsible for many going-out-of-business sales. If this is true, then why are so many companies undercapitalized? Couldn't this problem really be a matter of overspending? And why does a company overspend? Two answers come to mind: lack of a clear direction and unrealistic expectations. Planning addresses both of these. And what about poor management? Doesn't it stand to reason that poor planning leads to poor management? The point is that inadequate planning may be the cause of most failures, whereas undercapitalization, poor management, and so on are merely results of this neglect.

If our premise is accurate and the lack of planning is the root of most problems, then making sure that you and your client's organization consistently spend quality time planning may be the most important function you can serve. This includes both short-term and long-range planning. Short-term planning is essential to today's survival. Long-range planning is critical to business continuation. Therefore, you need to consistently consider both in your daily business decisions.

Planning Versus Reality

Planning is dynamic. Today's plans affect tomorrow's reality; tomorrow's reality influences tomorrow's plans; tomorrow's plans impact the future's reality, and so on.

In a perfect world, planning and reality pictorially could be demonstrated as two straight lines overlapping each other. In a controlled world, plans could remain constant because we eventually would fine-tune reality to match the plan. But in our world, which is more often than not out of control, both plans and reality are moving targets. So our expectations need to be put into perspective.

First, don't expect reality to emulate the plan. The best we can hope for is that the two begin to parallel each other at some point in the future. The net of this is, plans continually need to be monitored and adjusted so that they are consistent with the resources available. Operations need to be continually monitored and adjusted so that the end products and services approximate the plan.

In the absence of planning and plan monitoring, companies are likely to zig and zag too often . . . and for too long. This, in turn, stifles any significant forward movement. Scarce resources such as cash, capability, and capacity are often wasted on efforts that do not contribute to the organization's long-term survival and profitability.

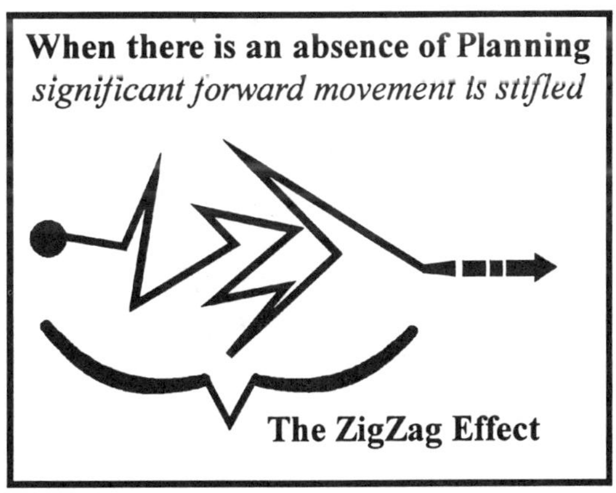

One example is the ladies clothing store my wife and I founded in 1980 called "Suited for Success." It was the second clothing store in the United States to cater exclusively to professional working women. The concept had several advantages in its favor. Market demand was present. The business catered to a group with money, that wanted personal service. The product line was narrow and deep. All of this added up to a situation which spelled success.

Was it successful? Yes and no. When the store stayed true to its original concept, which was depth in tailored career clothing, it made money. However, all to often, in an attempt to take advantage of short-term opportunities, critical resources were tied up on fringe areas (such as casual clothes or expansion of the dress line into evening wear) inconsistent with the store concept. This not only had an impact on the amount of backup stock in inventory, inventory turns, and profitability, but most important, it confused the customer. This confusion and inconsistency caused the business to limp when it should have sprinted. Based on surveys and interviews, it was apparent that customers came to the store specifically for the purpose of purchasing professional business attire. While in the store, these customers were typically very focused on accomplishing their mission (completing their business wardrobe).

So the question of success often boils down to whether management can remain focused on its goals. Every time a company veers off course, it can take months and even years to reverse the momentum. In many circumstances, long recovery cycles are too much for a business to support. Therefore, many course direction deviations wind up being deadly. By planning, and planning often, you can avoid decisions that spread your organization in conflicting directions. Thus, you minimize the mistake-recovery cycle or the zigzag effect, thereby making a significant contribution to your bottom line.

How do you go about doing this? Get your own firm as well as your clients involved in both *strategic* and *tactical* planning.

Strategic Planning Overview

Strategic planning consists of a long-term view of the corporate objectives. The span of time covered will vary based on each company's unique situation. A three- to five-year planning window is common, but certainly not etched in stone. Two rules of thumb which help dictate the period covered by the strategic plan are—

1. Twice the product development cycle.
2. The half life of obsolescence.

To put these in perspective, if it takes two years to develop a product, the strategic plan should cover at least four years—two years to create the product and two years to capture market share. Looking at this from the other direction, if your client's product will most likely be obsolete in six years, the strategic plan horizon should be about three years. Why? Because in this case, in three years, your client needs to be planning its replacement product or service within a window of time sufficient to accomplish this task. This horizon also has to be one that doesn't allow market share to be lost during the transition.

Another way to look at strategic planning is that it is the mental positioning of a company at some specific point in the future. By helping your organization formalize this mental position, you can begin to build the bridge linking today with the future.

Tactical Planning Overview

Tactical planning, the counterpart of strategic planning, is a look at a company from a short-term perspective. This process is often broken into two phases, mainly because each has a different purpose.

In the first phase, the annual plan, management establishes the new year's targets. The intent is to create goals, plans, objectives, budgets, and incentives for the coming year. This helps to focus on today's tasks, which in turn need to be consistent with the strategic plan.

The second phase of tactical planning, usually held around midyear, is for management to monitor the progress towards achieving these yearly objectives. Logically, shortfalls are identified and adjustments are made. These might include alterations to the commission structure, production schedules, budgets, personnel, and so on.

There's a third form of tactical planning that we should mention. Unfortunately, it's the one most often practiced. We call it *"Grab a bucket matey . . . there's a hole in the boat."* This is not the kind of planning we encourage, but at least it's a step in the right direction. If your client is struggling through a crisis, get the management team together quickly and facilitate daily and weekly planning sessions. Once the crisis is averted or at least disarmed, you'll have an open door to move the planning horizon back to its proper distance.

To summarize, tactical planning considers the ideas and direction of the strategic plan along with the current situation and resources of the company. This combination requires balancing today's requirements with tomorrow's opportunities.

Developing a Mission

The first step in the planning cycle is for you to revisit the purpose of your company or your client's company. In other words, *develop a mission.* Why does the company exist? What is its focus? Notice that these questions are focused on the customer because the corporate mission, in order to achieve the maximum effectiveness, should be *customer-driven.* The issues are not, *"Where am I?"* and *"Where am I going?"* but rather, *"Who are my customers?"* and *"Where are they going?"* One of the main objectives behind defining the corporate mission is to think through where your market will be in the future. By performing this exercise, you can help your organization devise a plan that will allow it to deliver demanded products or services to this future market.

MTV is a good example. Assume for a moment that MTV segmented the "music-video-watching-market" into age groups (one of many probable demographics). Let's further assume that MTV's customer profile was kids from the ages of twelve to nineteen. How successful would MTV be today had it chosen a strategic direction purely by answering the questions *"Where am I?"* and *"Where am I going?"* We maintain it would be out of business. When you consider the questions *"Who are my customers?"* and *"Where are they going?"* then questions, opportunities, and obstacles more clearly come to mind. If the true customers are now twelve to nineteen, then next year they will be thirteen to twenty, the year after fourteen to twenty-one, and so on. However, if the customers are an age group, then each year, whoever is twelve to nineteen would fit the profile.

On one hand, this distinction seems too obvious to mention. On the other hand, it is the kind of subtlety that organizations miss every day, that eventually puts them in bankruptcy. For example, if MTV decided that its product served the original twelve to nineteen age group, then MTV would be playing the music now aired by VH1, and in the year 2020, the music would likely be classified as "The Golden Oldies." However, MTV decided its market was the age group twelve to nineteen. So every year, it probably researches the music tastes of those from eight to eleven years of age in order to begin preparing for the format shifts required to maintain its market share.

The Planning Cycle

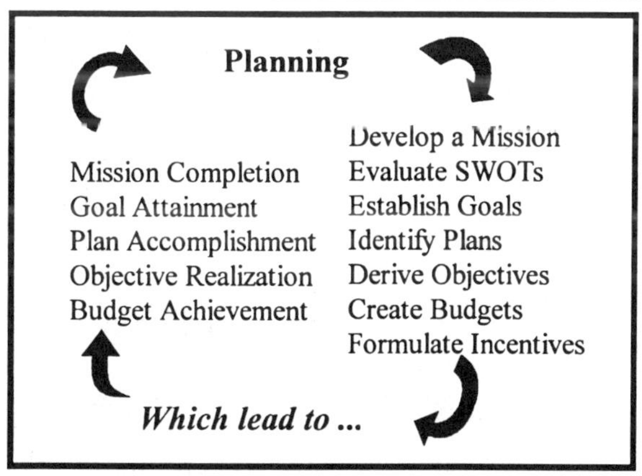

As soon as the mission statement is complete, the emphasis shifts towards identifying the steps which will facilitate its achievement. As highlighted by the graphic to the right, the traditional approach is to break the mission into goals by considering the SWOT analysis. This is an acronym for *strengths, weaknesses, opportunities,* and *threats*. Then, plans are laid out to accomplish those goals. If further breakdown is required, plans can be divided into objectives or tasks. Once an idea becomes measurable, monitorable, assignable, and accountable, you're done; it's time to move on to the next topic of interest.

Once the details as to how your clients are going to go about accomplishing each goal have been identified, establishing a budget is in order. And establishing budgets is one area CPAs can do in their sleep. Finally, no budget should be considered complete until incentives are developed and put in place that will reward those who achieve or exceed expectation. Without incentives, there's no clear thread connecting the beginning of this process to its end.

By implementing an incentive program, your clients begin to create an environment that holds people accountable. *Accountability leads to accomplishability*. Creating a system where people are held responsible for their work is such a simple principle, yet few companies implement it. How do we know? Once again, through our informal surveys of corporate controllers, one fact (which used to be startling) is always revealed: *most businesses don't hold their personnel accountable for achieving their budgets.* Since the budget is the numerical representation of the goals, plans, and objectives, achieving or over-achieving the target is important. However, the common scenario is . . . if you come in over budget, you get a light slap on the wrist and an increased budget next year. If you come in under budget, you get a light pat on the back and a reduced budget for the next year. Talk about a system that promotes the exact opposite behavior it is looking to achieve. This widespread lack of accountability and disincentives only re-emphasizes that there is a real need to pay more attention to this area.

If you are a little hazy about the distinction between goals, plans, and objectives, you're not alone. Thinking of an outline may help clarify this:

- The overall message = The business mission
- The roman numerals = The goals
- The A,B,Cs under the roman numerals = The plans
- The 1,2,3s under the A,B,Cs = The objectives

Remember that all roman numerals don't have A,B,Cs and all A,B,Cs don't have 1,2,3s. Just like an outline, some goals may be broken down into many plans. Some plans may be further divided into a variety of objectives. On the other hand, some other goals may require no additional definition at all. How do you know when to stop trying to break down a goal? It's as soon as all of the lowest level items identified are defined to the point that they are measurable, monitorable, assignable, and accountable. And by the way, depending on the group you are with, these terms will change. For example, some switch the term strategies for goals, others use initiatives instead of goals. When this happens, the term goals typically replaces either plans or objectives. The point is, you could toss up the words goals, plans, objectives, strategies, initiatives, tasks, and several others, and find an organization using them in almost every order they could possibly land. The key is, whatever the order, thinking of them as an outline helps everything fall into place.

Now that we have summarized the planning cycle, let's consider the role you are likely to play.

Our Role in Planning

Small business planning varies significantly from that done for larger operations, the main difference being our role. While we are valuable to both, large companies will generally ask you to perform only a small part, such as taking on the job of budget analyst, financial information preparer, plan writer, "gofer," and so on. The good news is that these larger operations can afford to pay us to perform whatever level of detail they assign. In addition, it is common for them to hire numerous consultants, each fulfilling some special piece of the project. Small businesses do not have this luxury. The detail work often has to be done by internal personnel. Your role is typically going to be a combination of facilitator, advisor, and visionary, which means you might need to provide guidance and assistance to those gathering information for the planning meeting.

With large businesses, plans are usually written, formal, and elegantly presented. Small businesses rarely write plans. And if they do, they are only two or three pages long rather than two or three inches deep. Remember, with small businesses, if you take on much more than the role of planning facilitator, advisor, or visionary, you'll spend the client's entire planning budget before the first meeting begins.

This chapter does not discuss how to perform the detail work, such as preparing budgets, gathering organizational data, performing client surveys, and so on. Each of these topics could be several chapters all by themselves. What we do focus on is conducting the planning meeting, which provides the highest financial return to both the client and the CPA firm. We've learned from experience that, for the small to mid-sized business, budgeting falls way below planning. As the client grows and becomes more successful, the budgetary process will take on a more dominant role. *But the right place to start your emphasis is on planning, planning, and planning.*

Planning From the Marketing Perspective

Besides the fact that clients benefit from formalized planning, there are also two selfish motivations for performing this function. The first is, planning sessions allow the CPA to build a stronger relationship with the client. This occurs because your involvement now centers around its future, not just its past. Second, and most selfish, is that by participating in the client's planning process you become privy to the future objectives and resource requirements. As an example, let's say the planning session identifies the following focus areas for the upcoming year for your client:

- Upgrade computers and accounting systems to accept and submit EDI and EFT transactions
- Develop a compensation system that will generate revenue growth commensurate with plant capacity
- Re-engineer all departments in order to be ISO 9000- and 14000-compliant

Armed with this kind of information about the client's priorities, you can ascertain quickly the areas in which your firm can be of service. Therefore, planning usually offers a gold mine of opportunities for your firm.

The Difficulty of Planning

So how hard is it to pull off this planning role? It's simple—you do it every day informally. We're just talking about taking what you do informally and formalizing it.

Basically, every time you ask your clients questions about their future, you are helping them plan, such as by asking, *What do you envision your company doing three years from now?*

And just as we discussed in chapter 7, by listening to your clients' answers, follow-up questions will naturally come to mind. For example:

Client: We would like to be the largest answering service in town.

CPA: What's another way to describe the word *largest*?

Client: Biggest. (Since these conversations are often relaxed and informal, bantering like this is common. However, your own style and the specific circumstances will dictate the appropriate level of seriousness.)

CPA: Thank you for that insightful comment. OK, let me ask the question differently. Describe *largest* in a more measurable context. As an example, do you mean number of customers, total revenue, services offered?

Client: I think we would like to take care of the small business owners. The people I'm thinking about generally have annual sales of less than two million. We would like our firm to provide these people with more than just telephone answering. We want to be thought of as part of the business. What do you think, Mike (his partner)?

Client: I agree, but I also think we need to help these businesses stay in close contact with their customers. I feel we need to be on the leading edge of technology with pagers, e-mail, faxes, and maybe even expand into areas such as mobile phones and televideo conferencing.

And the conversation goes on. While this reflects an informal conversation between a CPA and two owners, conducting a planning session is very similar in many ways. The difference is that instead of reacting to a comment made by a single individual, you instead react to the comments made by planning break-out groups (we will get into the detail of conducting a planning retreat in just a few paragraphs). This process, referred to as a planning retreat, is usually held off-site to facilitate a relaxed and uninterrupted environment. This emphasis is on inviting or encouraging a creative exchange of ideas. Be aware, however, that this loose, informal atmosphere also can create problems. Many times, things are said that normally would have been stifled. Therefore, this free exchange of ideas can promote a discussion that reveals dramatic differences of opinion. That's okay . . . and most of the time, exactly what you want to happen. But as the planning facilitator, you have the responsibility of keeping the discussion moving and on track, provoking thought, and holding tempers in check.

Conducting the Planning Session

As a starting point, note that planning sessions should include all key personnel within your client's organization and someone to take notes. The meetings should be conducted in an interruption-free setting, preferably for a day and a half to two days. If this is not possible, then set up a series of sessions, with each lasting two to three hours. Two to three hours as your minimum duration is important because it takes thirty to forty-five minutes for everyone to relax and begin a meaningful dialog. With this in mind, let's begin our review of the basics.

Mission Statement Exercise

The first step is to visit the mission statement. After you have an understanding of who you are and who your customer is, it's time to arrive at a couple of sentences or a paragraph that describes the organization's mission succinctly. Consider this example:

> *The Mission of the IBM Texas Employees Federal Credit Union is to provide personalized member service through secure, convenient, and sound financial and complementary alternatives.*

Short and sweet, the first focus of the organization is personal service. And with that personal service comes secure, convenient, and sound financial alternatives. Think about what this does. While it gives guidance to the management team, it also empowers the employees. For example, since personal service is a primary focus, then committing funds to implement "home banking" would have a higher priority than attempting to expand the profit margin. The words secure and sound provide very specific guidelines as to the kind of investment alternatives that should be considered for unloaned funds. Don't misunderstand us—we're not saying that a mission statement is the answer to an organization's problems, but it does mark the beginning of plan accountability.

> Plan accountability is a framework that promotes consistency between all the elements of a plan, from the mission through specific goals, plans, objectives, tasks, and so on.

Consider our credit union example. If one of the goals of the organization was to create a high-risk, high-yield loan fund, then the first question someone in management should ask is, "How does a high-risk, high-yield loan fund fit with the mission of the credit union?" Assuming the answer was to increase loan income, while the idea still may be plausible, according to the mission statement, this focus is not a high priority. On the other hand, if the high-risk, high-yield loan fund was an attempt to service members with marginal credit, that members without this fund would be turned down, then the story changes.

While it seems we are dealing with semantics, the reality is that too many businesses today get sidetracked because of short-term opportunities and thereby lose their long-term strategic advantage. Plan accountability is the process used to verify that the mission, goals, and plans of an organization are consistent, and when they are not, to either change the goals, or change the mission. For example, if a primary focus of the credit union is to maintain a certain level of profitability, then that idea should be reflected somewhere in the mission.

How do we go about creating, modifying, or testing a mission statement to bring it in line with current thinking? We use a simple strategy. Years ago, we were glancing through an AICPA publication called *Strategic Planning, A Step-by-Step Guide to Building a Successful CPA Firm* (AICPA, New York, 1993) and we spied an exercise that has proven quite useful. Instead of asking management teams to come up with a mission statement, the author, Sheryl Barbich, suggested this approach:

> One "game" that has been very successful in helping participants envision the future is to suppose that it is now five years from the current date, and the firm has just won a national award for being the most successful firm of its size. Each group is to write a press release identifying exactly what the firm has been recognized for and what the firm did in the intervening years to achieve that success.

We have used a version of this exercise for years. First, we shorten the horizon to usually three years. Second, we tell the planning participants to describe to the rest of their management team what their organization has accomplished that has resulted in winning this national award. This takes the focus off the award itself, and the press release wording, without losing the creativity and flexibility this exercise offers. Third, we break the planning participants into groups of three or four. At times, we allow groups of up to six people, but above that, you begin to lose efficiency and creativity. Why? Because with larger groups, the existing personality dynamics and hierarchy stimulate a more traditional meeting dialog, which stifles the brainstorming or think-tank environment we are trying to create. Also, we optimally are looking for four to five groups. So, if you have eighteen people at a meeting, we would probably break this down into three groups of four and two groups of three. If our planning meeting is only a day and a half, we would try to condense presentation time and create two groups of four and two groups of five. (Even if there are only three people in a meeting, we'd keep them together for some exercises, but for many of them, such as the mission statement exercise, we would break into one group of two and our facilitator would join the remaining person to brainstorm various ideas.)

Once the planning participants have been broken into break-out groups, we give them twenty-five minutes to come up with ideas, and then another ten minutes to commit those ideas to flip chart paper. The time for this exercise is flexible. If everyone is working hard, we extend the time in ten-minute increments, up to about an hour maximum. In addition, we insist that each group's ideas be written down on flip charts. We do this for numerous reasons. First, it forces participants to commit to their own ideas. Second, flip charts allow you to write large enough so that everyone can see whatever each group has decided to share. Third, once written, it is difficult to pretend a belief, issue, or problem doesn't exist. The whole point of planning is to break out of the day-to-day "this is the way we wash our clothes" and challenge the norms.

After the clock runs out on the break-out exercise, we have each group present their winning ideas to the rest of the management team. This update requirement keeps everyone honest and allows each group a chance to sell their vision of the corporate future. Once again, committing ideas to flip chart paper is critical to this process. Why? Well, here's what happens when a group's thoughts are just written down on someone's notepad or computer (using computers is OK if you connect them to an overhead panel). When it comes time for group reporting, since no one but the group spokesperson can see all of the points identified, issues that are confrontational or challenging are often skipped over. And common spokesperson statements are made like, "we came up with the same ideas as the last group except one. It was . . ." If you allow this level of noncommittal sharing, you're wasting people's lives. Think about it this way, as the facilitator, what can you do with information this vague? Did Group 2 really agree with everything Group 1 said? Or did they just agree with some of the ideas Group 1 shared. There is a big difference as to the weight of an idea if four groups came up with it independently versus just one. And more important, *what about those ideas that were discussed that challenged the status quo*? If you didn't insist that each group's ideas be committed to flip charts before the reporting begins, many of them will *not* be shared, and the planning process will lose a significant amount of power.

Once each break-out group has made its presentation, all the planning participants should work together to identify the best ideas, ethics, principles, and so on that should be part of the guiding philosophy of the organization. Often, the exercise ends here (once general feedback has been gathered) with the commitment that we (the facilitators) will pull together the beginnings of a mission statement based on the information gathered. We then tell the participants that they will get a chance to review what we synthesize and can fine-tune it later. This way, we don't get caught micro-wordsmithing the mission as a group. If you do, you not only waste a significant amount of valuable meeting time, but you can quickly destroy the creativity of the planning session as well. If you don't want to take on the task of mission statement synthesis yourself, then assign a few people to a mission statement task force and give them time during the retreat to develop a version they can share with the entire group.

SWOT Analysis

In our approach, SWOT analysis immediately follows the mission statement exercise. This section of the planning meeting is focused on an open and honest evaluation of the company's *strengths*, *weaknesses*, *opportunities,* and *threats.* It is during this phase of the planning retreat that participants will be examining factors such as the—

- Viability of the organization's products or services.
- Demographics, buying criteria, and changing demands of its customers.
- Expansion, evolution, and success of its competition.
- Management team's skills or lack thereof.
- Organization's financial position, leverage, and options.
- Organization's marketing capabilities, plans, and commitment.

Strengths and weaknesses are internally focused (on areas such as management, personnel, products, services, quality, and timely delivery). By the way, in company after company, the most common weakness we find, based on confidential employee surveys, is the criticism that there is no communication between management and workers. But what's really interesting is that most of the time, management thinks there is good communication between themselves and the workforce. To be fair, poor communication encompasses a huge area, from strategic direction to job expectation, which leaves plenty of room for disillusionment.

The opportunities and threats analysis focuses on issues and factors that are externally directed, such as new competition, a changing marketplace, potential regulation, or deregulation. For example, in the health care industry, health care reform could be considered a potential threat, but it is also an opportunity for those who position themselves to leverage the changes that occur.

As with the mission statement, we have the management team break into groups for the SWOT analysis too. We usually pre-plan break-out groups so that the members can quickly be rotated to their new assignments at the beginning of each new exercise. We pre-plan this for three reasons:

1. It minimizes the control factor. Higher ranking managers often dominate lower ranking managers, potentially squelching good ideas.
2. It prevents the group from taking on a dynamic of its own. The longer people are together in a group, roles and responsibilities start developing, and creativity along with freedom of expression declines.
3. It gives everyone a chance to work with everyone else. This not only facilitates greater synergy among the management team, but it gives the owners (or executive management team) a greater appreciation for the values and perspectives of others.

Surveying Client's Staff Before the SWOT Session. In order to leverage our time and gain a more honest or critical view of the organization, we recommend that a confidential survey be performed prior to the planning session. The survey typically not only includes planning participants, but other managers and key employees too. While it is difficult to conduct planning sessions with twenty or more participants, it is often a good idea to get input from thirty to forty of the company's personnel. So after we review the survey with executive management and modify the questions to their liking, we send out the confidential survey with our firm's return envelop to the approved personnel list. The survey responses help us better facilitate the planning meeting because we gain significant insight as to the organization's strengths, weaknesses, opportunities, and threats before the meeting starts.

After we organize and review the survey results, we prepare summary slides (using presentation software) for each element of SWOT analysis. For example, we will summarize the strengths outlined in the survey responses, usually with one section dealing with the company and another focused on management. There are only a few times that we actually modify the survey responses. For example, if the comment itself would incriminate the respondent, we try to make the point more general in scope. Also, comments are sometimes very hostile towards certain individuals. If there are several pointing to the same person, we name the individual specifically. If negative comments are random in nature but point to a specific department, we identify the problem group. If the personal attacks are random, but too numerous to ignore, we just point out that employee infighting and positioning is common. Sometimes we can't help ourselves and we provide a quick lecture offering reasons why this kind of infighting occurs. We do this under the guise of providing food for thought during the break-out sessions.

Presenting negative information is a tough part of the planning facilitator's job, and therefore sometimes avoided. However, it's our belief that our role regarding surveys is to share the information and not to act as judge, jury, or sensor. Then again, it's not our role to unnecessarily hurt people's feelings either. So you have to decide what information to use, what to ignore, and, if there is an unusual set of circumstances, what to discuss with management beforehand (without revealing where the comments came from). On the brighter side, we try to leverage the negative comments, especially if they refer to top management. If the information available allows us to take a few shots early on at the highest level positions, this can really open up the planning session for some great positive discussion. To throw off the tendency of the potentially insulted to "seek out and destroy" the informant, we tell the participants that a point on a slide might not have come from the survey at all, but from our own observations. And if something is important but negative, appeared numerous times, and is an idea we feel management will try to slough off as an anomaly, we might verbally embellish the point by stating that it was a recurrent theme. The bottom line is we do everything we can to elicit frank and open discussion of the SWOT analysis. However, when it comes to sensitive areas, plan your strategy well. If you get sloppy and careless, the egos and defense barriers of those involved can destroy the entire planning effort. That's why you, the facilitator, are there—to maintain the necessary intricate balance between searching for ways to leverage the organization and conducting a witch-hunt.

A sample planning letter, survey, and sample slides are included at the end of this chapter.

Conducting the SWOT Analysis. Now, back to the planning meeting. Explain the concept of SWOT analysis and that participants should work through it one letter at a time. Then show the slides that focus on company and management strengths. After you have introduced the survey responses, provide everyone with printed handouts of these slides. Next, create new break-out groups (usually by reshuffling the mission exercise break-outs), and assign the tasks of—

1. Re-thinking the organization's strengths.
2. Culling that list so that it only includes the top ten strengths.
3. Putting the top ten strengths in priority order.

Allow thirty minutes or so to do this. As the facilitator, part of your job is to monitor the progress of the groups. So walk around the room and listen in on the discussions. As the exercise timer nears thirty minutes, if the groups are not wrapping up, then once again, extend the exercise about ten minutes or so. The reason your exercises are timed in the first place is because you want to keep the planning session moving and avoid getting bogged down. If you observe lively discussions, then take advantage of the positive effort. If the reverse is taking place, bring the exercise to a close. Once the groups have committed their ideas to flip charts, have each provide an oral report. Also, remember to have someone from your client's organization at the retreat to type up each group's responses so the information can be distributed at day's end for people to think about. By the way, we typically ask that everyone, at least once, be the group reporter. This forces even the shyest of participants to take on the role of group leader, which we believe increases creativity because everyone stays energized and involved.

After everyone has given their report regarding company strengths, it's time to move to the next step—review your client's weaknesses. The drill is the same. First, discuss the survey responses. Then hand out a printed copy of the slides. Reshuffle the break-out group members and give them another thirty minutes. Once the reports have been given, conduct the same exercise for company opportunities, then company threats.

Remember to give the planning participants breaks (refer to chapter 11 for useful advice on conducting a quality meeting). Warning, warning, warning ... don't try to squeeze an extra hour or two of work into each planning day. We strongly discourage more than an eight-hour planning day; six-and-a-half to seven hours is much better. As a matter of fact, a successful and leisurely itinerary is a seven-hour day of planning, followed by a half day of planning combined with some organized fun activity, and concluded with a half day of planning. While this sounds more like play than work, note that planning retreats usually demand high energy and produce high stress (because the topics discussed impact each individual's livelihood and include sensitive subjects). If participants work hard in each exercise, you can expect them to be brain-dead by late afternoon. If you force everyone to keep working, very little will be gained. So breaking up the planning agenda to include organized relaxation revitalizes the participants and improves overall performance.

Once SWOT analysis is complete, it's time to consider everything that has been done so far in order to identify corporate goals. Usually, this is as far as we get in the first day. It's also a great place to break for the day because it gives everyone a chance to reconsider the wealth of information discussed.

Goals, Plans, Objectives (Strategies, Initiatives, Tasks)

At this point, the emphasis shifts towards identifying steps which will achieve the mission, take advantage of the company's strengths and opportunities, and minimize its weaknesses and threats. This leads us to the goal-setting portion of the planning retreat.

Re-establish break-out groups and pose the question, "What should our company's top three or four goals be?" Why just three or four? Because goals have very broad definitions, such as, "open new profitable distribution channels," or "gain a competitive advantage utilizing technology." These are not easily or quickly accomplished, and they usually take numerous actions to complete. When you open up planning to as many goals as you can identify, you will not only end up with a wide disparity between their relative importance, but you will also overload the management team with more work than can be realistically completed.

When looking for your three to four goals, give careful consideration to the mission statement. For example, the Credit Union's mission statement contains the phase "provide personalized member service," which is most likely a goal all by itself. By taking the time to decide what this phrase really means, you begin to break this goal down into plans, objectives, tasks, and so on.

Answering questions such as the following will help Credit Union management uncover how they want to go about positioning the organization for the future:

- What do the members want?
- Will members still want to come into the Credit Union to do business two to three years from now?
- What factors do they consider important when choosing a financial institution for their loans?

Staying with this same logic, after the break-out groups have identified goals, challenge them to propose an action plan (plans, objectives, and so on) for each one.

In a two-day meeting, it is almost inconceivable that complete action plans will be created to address each of the identified goals. At a minimum, though, you want to take this process far enough to define the goals. With whatever time you have left, pick one of the goals and try to take it as far as you can. If time remains, pick another. Or if you want to cover ground more quickly, assign different groups to different goals to speed up the brainstorming process.

The Planning Retreat Wrap-Up

One of the last steps before adjourning your planning retreat is to assign teams to continue work on any unfinished areas. Before you do this, pull the owner or executive management team aside to solicit how to proceed. Sometimes, they want to take a week or two to think through the information generated before taking any further action. That's fine. Other times, they will ask you to solicit volunteers to further refine each action plan. If this is the case, consider incorporating some nonplanning participants into each team to enhance acceptance of proposed changes as the plans develop. And just because an idea gained consensus during your planning session doesn't mean it will receive any attention after the retreat. We bring this point up early on in one of our slides in order to set the right participant expectation level.

A "sanity check" is a good idea before the meeting is adjourned. As the planning process progresses, you, the facilitator, are supposed to compare the goals to the mission statement as a sanity check. If the mission statement is focusing on areas totally different from the identified goals, then ask your participants to either change their goals or re-define the mission. This sanity check ensures that your marching orders are in sync with the direction you have chosen.

Remind the person responsible for taking notes to send you a copy of the meeting notes as soon as they are completed. You can add, delete, modify, and make suggestions regarding the planning retreat summary's final content before companywide distribution (at a minimum, distribute the summary to the planning participants). From this point, the action plans will evolve into tactical plans, which will likely require more assistance from your firm to implement. Regardless, however, make sure you stay involved at a level that doesn't allow the energy, effort, and ideas shared at the retreat to dissipate. Otherwise, even if your planning retreat was flawless in its presentation, it will prove worthless in its implementation.

Baby Steps May Be Your Best Start

Every planning session is unique because each client's needs are different. As you can see, planning can be pretty straightforward and easy too. The first time you conduct one of these sessions, you'll most likely be nervous. But once you get rolling, you'll have a great time. Since most people don't plan regularly, if at all, the fact that you will be leading these discussions in an organized manner will not only be beneficial to the participants, it will be impressive as well.

One way to get committed to this process is to conduct a planning retreat for your own firm. Once you see the benefits, it's easier to sell your clients on them. If you can't persuade your clients into committing to a two-day retreat, then create little baby steps to get there. Your first session can be a couple of hours focused on one specific topic. The point is, you can implement this process immediately. And the best part is you can start seeing the results of your efforts just as fast.

One last caution: Planning doesn't amount to much without action. Before concluding a planning meeting, be sure to identify the next step. Consider how you can motivate the participants to fulfill their commitments. Determine what sort of follow-up is appropriate. Conducting quarterly review sessions is a good way for you to monitor progress and stay involved as a catalyst, so the enthusiasm generated during the planning and goal-setting sessions leads to meaningful accomplishments.

Before We Move On

Included for your review are forms and slides we have used in the past when facilitating planning sessions. We have included a sample introductory letter, a sample questionnaire, and copies of Powerpoint™ slides.

You may wonder why the *Sample Questionnaire* includes spaces for the respondent's name and title. Yes, the survey *is* confidential. But I don't want a bunch of anonymous comments made to me. I want to know who is saying what, what position he or she holds, and so on. And people *don't* hold back once I tell them, as I do in the letter, that my staff and I will be the only ones that know. And *we do not ever tell!* (And trust me, people ask all the time.)

If you can use any or all of this, that's great. At a minimum, it gives you a perspective of the way we approach our projects.

Sample Letter

Date

⟨⟨FirstName⟩⟩ ⟨⟨LastName⟩⟩

⟨⟨Address1⟩⟩

⟨⟨Address2⟩⟩

⟨⟨City⟩⟩, ⟨⟨State⟩⟩ ⟨⟨PostalCode⟩⟩

Dear ⟨⟨FirstName⟩⟩:

I am writing this letter as an introduction to your firm's strategic planning retreat. We will focus on better defining, fine-tuning and internally communicating your organization's strategic direction. Logically, your participation and input play a critical role, which is why I am contacting you now.

Enclosed is a questionnaire. I am sending this to your home with a self-addressed return envelope because I wanted to assure you of the confidentiality of the information you provide (only my organization will have access to your specific responses). Like any successful organization, ABC Company is doing many things right. However, in order to capitalize on your organization's strengths, and minimize its weaknesses, I need some insight into what you know and think. Your answers will also help me better organize and facilitate the limited time I have with the management group.

As Theodore Roosevelt once said, "*If you aim at nothing, you'll hit it every time.*" And while your company clearly has been aiming at something all along, the feedback you provide through this survey will provide valuable input in defining your organization's future. In summary form (anonymously), I will share the results of my analysis at the meeting.

I would like to thank you in advance for your cooperation.

Sincerely,

William L. Reeb, CPA

Sample Questionnaire

Name: ______________________________

Your job title: ______________________________

How long have you worked at ABC Company? ____________

How do you spend the majority of your time? ____________

____

In about twenty words, describe what ABC does.

____

____

____

____

What are three strengths of your organization?

1. ______________________________
2. ______________________________
3. ______________________________

What are three weaknesses of your organization?

1. ______________________________
2. ______________________________
3. ______________________________

Identify two strengths of the management team.

1. ______________________________
2. ______________________________

Identify two weaknesses of the management team.

1. ______________________________
2. ______________________________

Consider your top two competitors. What does either of them offer that gives them a competitive advantage over your organization?

____

____

____

____

____

____

____

List three reasons why your organization has been able to achieve such rapid growth.

1. ____

2. ____

3. ____

List the two most important reasons why you like working with ABC.

1. ____

2. ____

If you were given total control over this company tomorrow, what changes (up to three) would you immediately make regarding day-to-day operations?

1. ____

2. ____

3. ____

If you were authorized to alter your job in some way, how would you change it so that it would be more enjoyable?

____

____

(continued on next page)

***Sample Questionnaire* (*continued*)**

More productive?

____

____

How much input do you have in what you do every day? Circle your choice and explain.

Very little   About average   A great deal

____

____

What do you see as the two greatest threats to the future success of this organization? Explain.

1. ____

____

____

____

2. ____

____

____

____

Diagram the way you see the organizational chart.

Planning Slides

The following are many of the slides we used when facilitating the AICPA's Information Technology Division's (IT) planning meeting several years ago. Samples of each slide type have been included for your reference. Every meeting flows a little differently, so we modify our base slides to suit each unique situation. The actual IT planning session slides incorporated some information not included here. We omitted them because, out of context, they wouldn't make much sense. However, all of our planning meetings basically follow the format discussed in this chapter and demonstrated by the slides that follow.

As for the goal-setting phase, by that time in the meeting, everyone knows the drill. We often then use the overhead projector in combination with a word processor to display the notes being taken regarding each group's presentation.

AICPA
Information
Technology
Strategic
Planning
Session

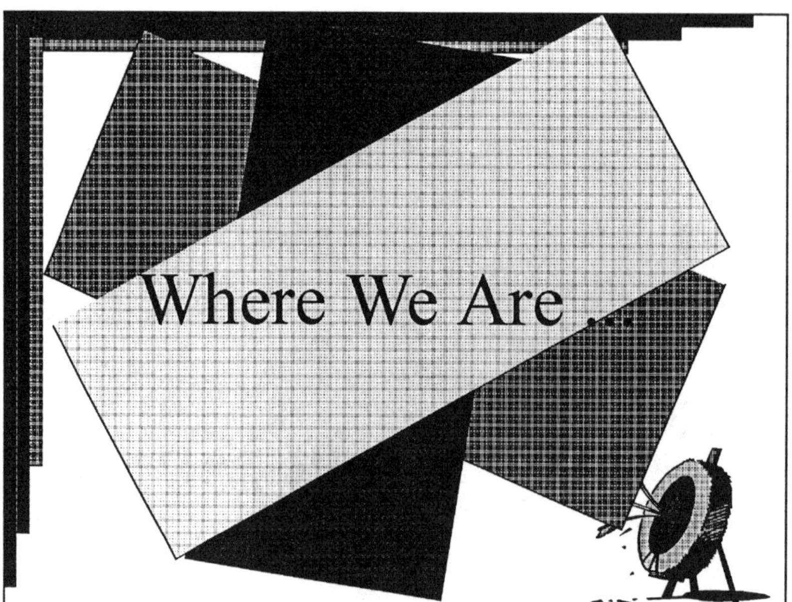
Where We Are ...

Setting the Right Expectation

- Provide input to the President and Board
- Identify the most important issues to be considered
- The output may be totally ignored
- But, this is your chance to influence the organization's priorities

The Ground Rules

- Be Open
- Be Honest
- Speak Up
- Remember that No One Really Knows What the Future Holds

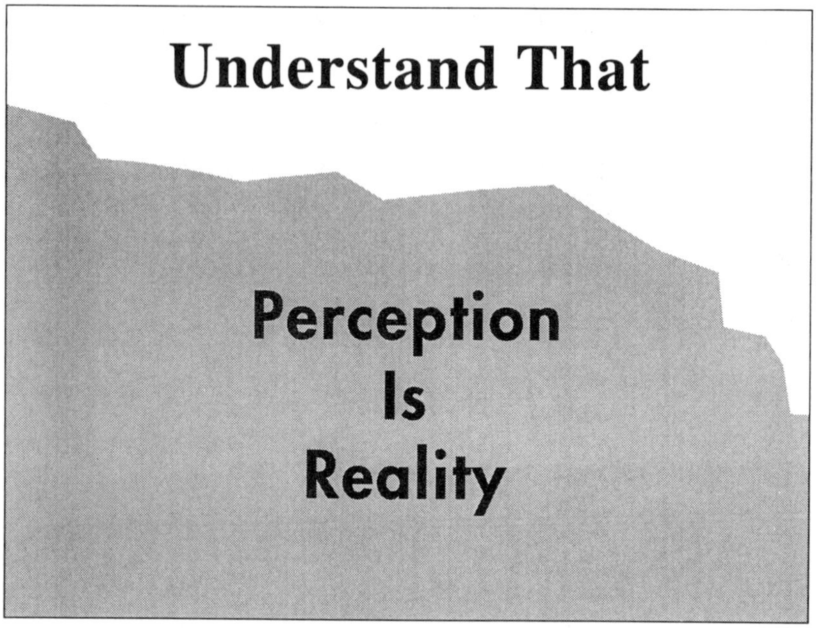
Understand That
Perception
Is
Reality

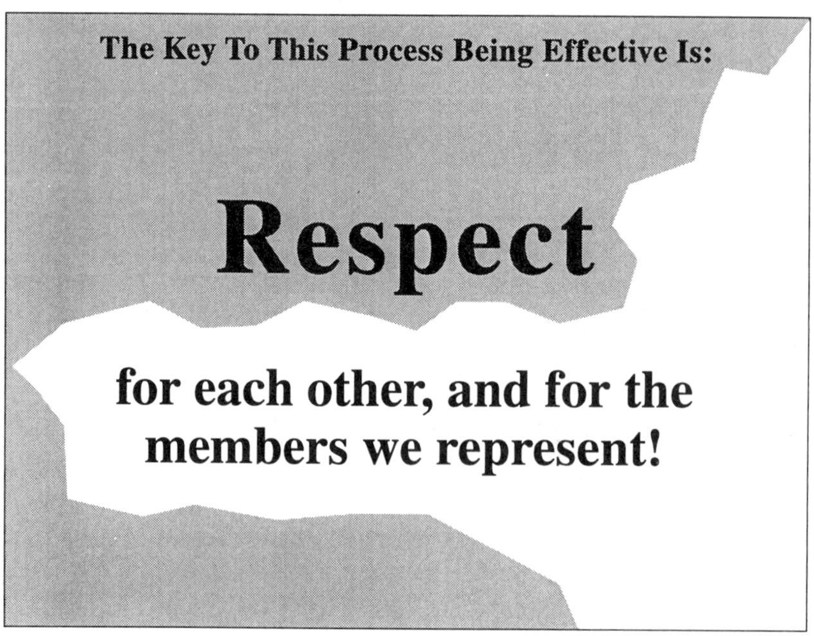
The Key To This Process Being Effective Is:
Respect
for each other, and for the
members we represent!

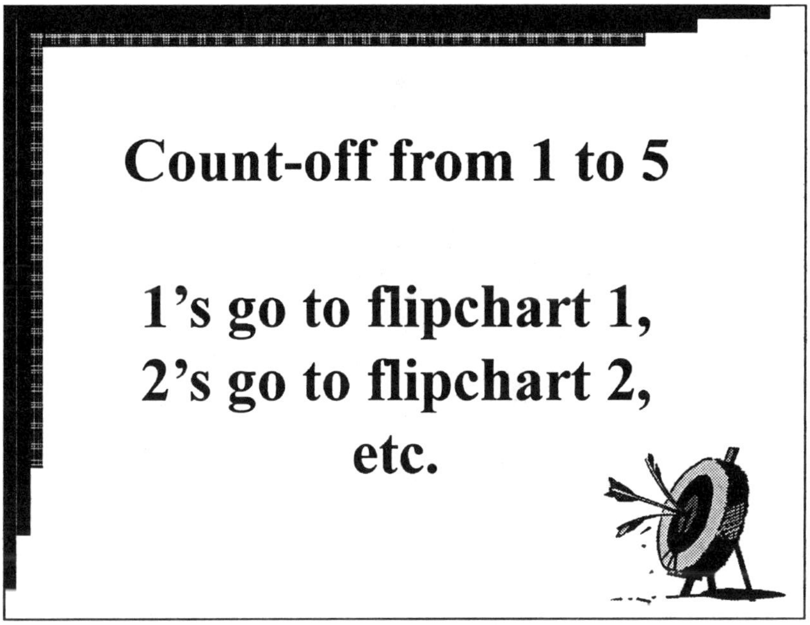
Count-off from 1 to 5
1's go to flipchart 1,
2's go to flipchart 2,
etc.

Vision Exercise
Consider that it is three years from now and the AICPA has just won a national award for its role in Technology.
Describe what the AICPA accomplished to warrant such an award!

Group Exercise
You have 30 minutes to think and prepare your answer to this

Where We Want to Go

What Are We Looking for From This Meeting

Planning Agenda

- Mission Statement Review
- SWOT Analysis
  - Strength Assessment
  - Weakness Discussion
  - Opportunity Review
  - Threat Identifications
- Goal(s) Identification
- Plan(s) Development
- Objective(s) Determination

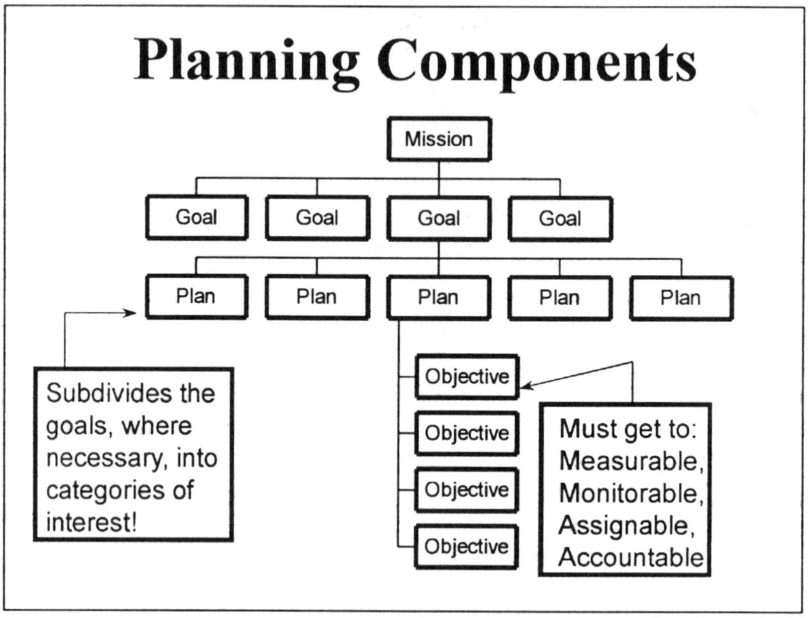
Planning Components
Mission
Goal
Goal
Goal
Goal
Plan
Plan
Plan
Plan
Plan
Subdivides the goals, where necessary, into categories of interest!
Objective
Objective
Objective
Objective
Must get to: Measurable, Monitorable, Assignable, Accountable

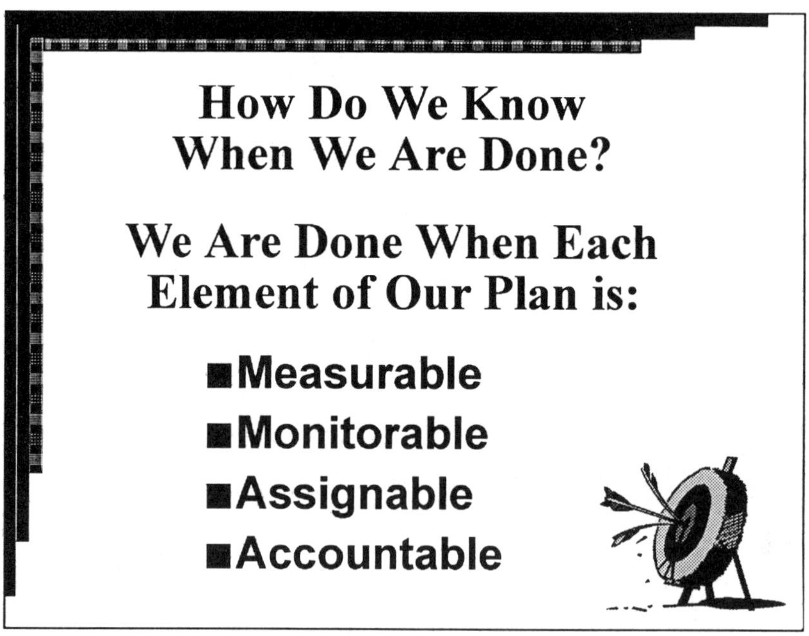
How Do We Know When We Are Done?
We Are Done When Each Element of Our Plan is:
■Measurable
■Monitorable
■Assignable
■Accountable

The AICPA's IT Mission Statement Is:

To enable all members to provide value to their clients and employers through effective application of current, emerging and future information technologies

Who Are We Planning For?

- We Are Creating an Information Technology Strategic Plan for?
  - –the Entire AICPA Membership
  - –the IT Division
  - –the IT Executive Committee as well as the other IT Committees

IT
Strengths

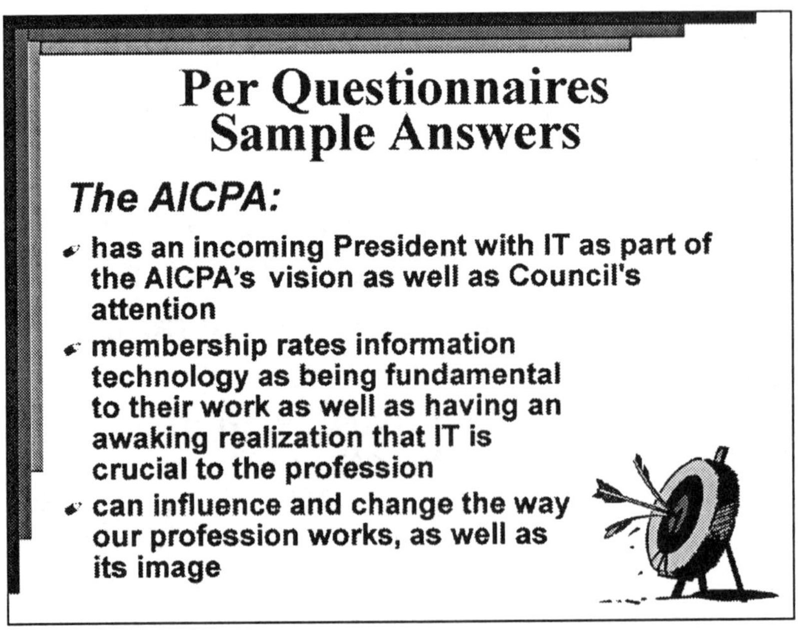
Per Questionnaires
Sample Answers
The AICPA:
has an incoming President with IT as part of the AICPA's vision as well as Council's attention
membership rates information technology as being fundamental to their work as well as having an awaking realization that IT is crucial to the profession
can influence and change the way our profession works, as well as its image

Per Questionnaires Sample Answers

CPAs:

- still have a positive image in eye's of the public
- have a broad business experience which gives them a valuable perspective regarding best practices in IT
- are control oriented regarding IT
- have a financial understanding of costs/benefits of technology

Per Questionnaires Sample Answers

The Profession:

- has younger members entering with a greater awareness of IT
- offers committee members who genuinely want to help the profession
- has a well educated and motivated ($) membership with a diverse pool of talents, technical knowledge, financial know-how, business savvy and leadership ability

Group Exercise

You have 30 minutes to identify the AICPA's or the Profession's top 10 Strengths

Here are the new work-groups for this exercise

Weaknesses

Per Questionnaires Sample Answers

- ☹ It's belief that compliance work, accounting, audits, F/S, are the future services of our profession
- ☹ The powerful and most vocal part of our membership has the approach that if they ignore the changing professional environment, it will go away
- ☹ Belief that technology is an optional tool, rather than an evolutionary change in the business climate
- ☹ We are way behind industry/client needs

Group Exercise

You have 30 minutes to identify the AICPA's or the Profession's top 10 Weaknesses

Here are the new work-groups for this exercise

IT
Opportunities

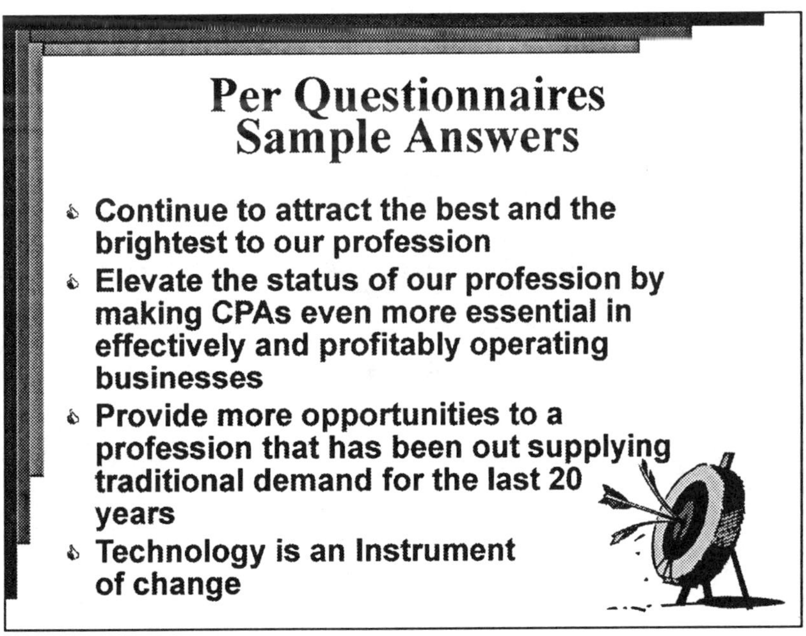
Per Questionnaires
Sample Answers
Continue to attract the best and the brightest to our profession
Elevate the status of our profession by making CPAs even more essential in effectively and profitably operating businesses
Provide more opportunities to a profession that has been out supplying traditional demand for the last 20 years
Technology is an Instrument of change

Group Exercise
You have 30 minutes to identify the AICPA's or the Profession's top 10 Opportunities

Here are the new work-groups for this exercise

Threats
IT

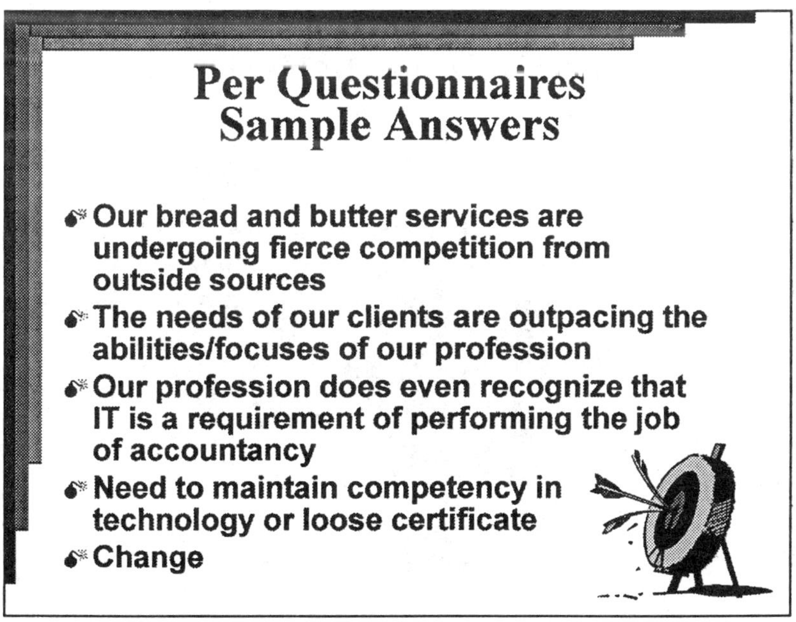
Per Questionnaires
Sample Answers
Our bread and butter services are undergoing fierce competition from outside sources
The needs of our clients are outpacing the abilities/focuses of our profession
Our profession does even recognize that IT is a requirement of performing the job of accountancy
Need to maintain competency in technology or loose certificate
Change

Note That Threats
Often Have
Counterbalancing
Opportunities,
and visa-versa

Group Exercise
You have 30 minutes to identify the AICPA's or the Profession's top 10 Threats

Here are the new work-groups for this exercise

This Is As Far As We Will Take This Today

IT
It's Time To Determine
Our Goals
(Strongly consider the information
identified during the SWOT analysis)

Here are the new
work-groups for this
exercise

Group Exercise
You have 30 minutes to identify the IT Division's top 3 to 5 goals

Now, let's work on our Goals 1 Goal at a time
IT

IT
It's time to further define our
first Goal by breaking it down
into more bite-sized pieces
(plans, objectives, actions, etc.)

Here are the new
work-groups for this
exercise

Group Exercise

You have 30 minutes to identify steps that should be taken in order to accomplish this goal

This process continues for each Goal until you run out of time

That's It For Today

Conclusion

It seems fitting that our last words complete the full circle and take us back to the beginning of the book. As we mentioned in the beginning, Anne Drozd's article published in *CAmagazine* listed seven key skills all consultants should have:

1. Ability to learn quickly
2. Proficiency in asking questions
3. Ability to patiently listen and observe
4. Possession of people skills
5. Adeptness at analyzing information and situations and drawing conclusions
6. Creativity
7. Competence as a communicator

It is our contention that as a CPA, before you even opened this book, you possessed all you need of the first skill, expert's version (rather than advisor's version) of the second, and more than enough of the fifth and sixth skills. This book was focused on providing you with a different approach to asking questions relative to consulting. Traditional services, in order to be proficient, force us to develop skills in asking questions that rule out information. With consulting, our questions need to help us find information. And often, it is the way we ask those questions that helps our clients uncover and define what is really bothering them. We talked a great deal about the importance of improving listening and increasing patience, for both you and your client. As far as possession of people skills, CPAs have always been people who care about other people. However, many times we ignore those little communication techniques that convey just how much we care. All of these factors combine to contribute heavily to our competence as communicators. We hope our book has provided value in these areas.

Another key to the success of consulting is proficiently obtaining, managing, and executing the engagements in a manner best suited to your clients' needs. We discussed numerous techniques to help with this, from project estimation to billing, from selling to specific implementation techniques, from meeting management to presentation skills and more. Once again, we hope the ideas we have shared will prove helpful.

With any firm, organizing and administering the practice plays a large role in the profitability of service delivery. We hope our discussions on marketing, on our fortress-empire methodology, and on how to formalize consulting within your firm gave you some new ideas as to how to refine what you are doing.

There is no question that much of this book is basic stuff. However, our experience is that when you want to improve a process, profitability, delivery, or almost anything, a back-to-the-basics review is the best place to start. So as a parting comment, if there is anything else we can share, it is to go back and complete all of the forms and exercises in this text. The key is not the forms themselves, but the fact that you take the time to think about all of the issues this book raises. And don't forget the exercises. Many of them require the involvement of others. It's worth the effort to get together with a couple of your peers (even if they are from other firms) and go through the process. You will likely find that you can revisit these exercises every year and build on the efforts of the past. If you do all of this, you will find that the entire experience will not only help you create a vision of what your firm should look like three or four years from now, but what you should start working on now to facilitate the desired transition.

As a final word: Thank you for the time you have given us and we wish you the best of luck in the future!

Appendix

Statement on Standards for Consulting Services No. 1

Consulting Services: Definitions and Standards

Introduction

1. Consulting services that CPAs provided to their clients have evolved from advice on accounting-related matters to a wide range of services involving diverse technical disciplines, industry knowledge, and consulting skills. Most practitioners, including those who provide audit and tax services, also provide business and management consulting services to their clients.

2. Consulting services differ fundamentally from the CPA's function of attesting to the assertions of other parties. In an attest service, the practitioner expresses a conclusion about the reliability of a written assertion that is the responsibility of another party, the asserter. In a consulting service, the practitioner develops the findings, conclusions, and recommendations presented. The nature and scope of work is determined solely by the agreement between the practitioner and the client. Generally, the work is performed only for the use and benefit of the client.

3. Historically, CPA consulting services have been commonly referred to as management consulting services, management advisory services, business advisory services, or management services. A series of Statements on Standards for Management Advisory Services (SSMASs) previously issued by the AICPA contained guidance on certain types of consulting services provided by members. This Statement on Standards for Consulting Services (SSCS) supersedes the SSMASs and provides standards of practice for a broader range of professional services, as described in paragraph 5.

4. This SSCS and any subsequent SSCSs apply to any AICPA member holding out as a CPA while providing Consulting Services as defined herein.

Definitions

5. Terms established for the purpose of SSCSs are as follows:

Consulting Services Practitioner. Any AICPA member holding out as a CPA while engaged in the performance of a Consulting Service for a client, or any other individual who is carrying out a Consulting Service for a client on behalf of any Institute member or member's firm holding out as a CPA.

Consulting Process. The analytical approach and process applied in a Consulting Service. It typically involves some combination of activities relating to determination of client objectives, fact-finding, definition of the problems or opportunities, evaluation of alternatives, formulation of proposed action, communication of results, implementation, and follow-up.

Consulting Services. Professional services that employ the practitioner's technical skills, education, observations, experiences, and knowledge of the consulting process.[1] Consulting Services may include one or more of the following:

a. *Consultations,* in which the practitioner's function is to provide counsel in a short time frame, based mostly, if not entirely, on existing personal knowledge about the client, the circumstances, the technical matters involved, client representations, and the mutual intent of the parties. Examples of consultations are reviewing and commenting on a client-prepared business plan and suggesting computer software for further client investigation.

b. *Advisory services,* in which the practitioner's function is to develop findings, conclusions, and recommendations for client consideration and decision making. Examples of advisory services are an operational review and improvement study, analysis of an accounting system, assistance with strategic planning, and definition of requirements for an information system.

c. *Implementation services,* in which the practitioner's function is to put an action plan into effect. Client personnel and resources may be pooled with the practitioner's to accomplish

[1] The definition of Consulting Services excludes the following:

a. Services subject to other AICPA Technical Standards such as Statements on Auditing Standards (SASs), Statements on Standards for Attestation Engagements (SSAEs), or Statements on Standards for Accounting and Review Services (SSARs). (These included services may be performed in conjunction with Consulting Services, but only the Consulting Services are subject to the SSCS.)

b. Engagements specifically to perform tax return preparation, tax planning/advice, tax representation, personal financial planning or bookkeeping services; or situations involving the preparation of written reports or the provisions of oral advice on the application of accounting principles to specified transactions or events, either completed or proposed, and the reporting thereof.

c. Recommendations and comments prepared during the same engagement as a direct result of observations made while performing the excluded services.

the implementation objectives. The practitioner is responsible to the client for the conduct and management of engagement activities. Examples of implementation services are providing computer system installation and support, executing steps to improve productivity, and assisting with the merger of organizations.

d. *Transaction services*, in which the practitioner's function is to provide services related to a specific client transaction, generally with a third party. Examples of transaction services are insolvency services, valuation services, preparation of information for obtaining financing, analysis of a potential merger or acquisition, and litigation services.

e. *Staff and other support services*, in which the practitioner's function is to provide appropriate staff and possibly other support to perform tasks specified by the client. The staff provided will be directed by the client as circumstances require. Examples of staff and other support services are data processing facilities management, computer programming, bankruptcy trusteeship, and controllership activities.

f. *Product services*, in which the practitioner's function is to provide the client with a product and associated professional services in support of the installation, use, or maintenance of the product. Examples of product services are the sale and delivery of packaged training programs, the sale and implementation of computer software, and the sale and installation of systems development methodologies.

Standards for Consulting Services

6. The general standards of the profession are contained in Rule 201 of the AICPA Code of Professional Conduct [ET section 201.01] and apply to all services performed by members. They are as follows:

Professional Competence. Undertake only those professional services that the member or the member's firm can reasonably expect to be completed with professional competence.

Due Professional Care. Exercise due professional care in the performance of professional services.

Planning and Supervision. Adequately plan and supervise the performance of professional services.

Sufficient Relevant Data. Obtain sufficient relevant data to afford a reasonable basis for conclusions or recommendations in relation to any professional services performed.

7. The following additional general standards for all Consulting Services are promulgated to address the distinctive nature of Consulting Services in which the understanding with the client may establish valid limitations on the practitioner's performance of services. These Standards are established under Rule 202 of the AICPA Code of Professional Conduct [ET section 202.01].

Client Interest. Serve the client interest by seeking to accomplish the objectives established by the understanding with the client while maintaining integrity and objectivity.[2]

Understanding With Client. Establish with the client a written or oral understanding about the responsibilities of the parties and the nature, scope, and limitations of services to be performed, and modify the understanding if circumstances require a significant change during the engagement.

Communication With Client. Inform the client of (a) conflicts of interest that may occur pursuant to interpretations of Rule 102 of the Code of Professional Conduct [ET section 102.03],[3] (b) significant reservations concerning the scope or

---

[2] Article III of the Code of Professional Conduct describes *integrity* as follows:

"Integrity requires a member to be among, other things, honest and candid within the constraints of client confidentiality. Service and the public trust should not be subordinated to personal gain and advantage. Integrity can accommodate the inadvertent error and the honest difference of opinion; it cannot accommodate deceit or subordination of principle."

Article IV of the Code of Professional Conduct differentiates between *objectivity* and *independence* as follows:

"Objectivity is a state of mind, a quality that lends value to a member's services. It is a distinguishing feature of the profession. The principle of objectivity imposes the obligation to be impartial, intellectually honest, and free of conflicts of interest. Independence precludes relationships that may appear to impair a member's objectivity in rendering attestation services."

[3] Rule 102-2 on Conflicts of Interest states, in part, the following:

"A conflict of interest may occur if a member performs a professional service for client or employer and the member or his or her firm has a significant relationship with another person, entity, product, or service that could be viewed as impairing the member's objectivity. If this significant relationship is disclosed to and consent is obtained from such client, employer, or other appropriate parties, the rule shall not operate to prohibit the performance of the professional service . . ."

benefits of the engagement, and (c) significant engagement findings or events.

8. Professional judgment must be used in applying Statements on Standards for Consulting Services in a specific instance since the oral or written understanding with the client may establish constraints within which services are to be provided. For example, the understanding with the client may limit the practitioner's effort with regard to gathering relevant data. The practitioner is not required to decline or withdraw from a consulting engagement when the agreed-upon scope of services includes such limitations.

Consulting Services for Attest Clients

9. The performance of Consulting Services for an attest client does not, in and of itself, impair independence.[4] However, members and their firms performing attest services for a client should comply with applicable independence standards, rules and regulations issued by AICPA, the state boards of accountancy, state CPA societies, and other regulatory agencies.

Effective Date

10. This section is effective for engagements accepted on or after January 1, 1992. Early application of the provisions of this section is permissible.

---

[4] AICPA independence standards relate only to the performance of attestation services; objectivity standards apply to all services. See footnote 2.

About the Authors

William L. Reeb, CPA, *author,* has been consulting for seventeen years to all sizes of businesses, from mom-and-pop operations to Fortune 100 companies, primarily in the areas of organization, automation, and revenue generation. He decided to add the credentials of CPA behind his advisory work and became a CPA in 1986.

Prior to his life as a CPA, he worked for IBM in sales back in the late 1970s. As an entrepreneur, Bill has founded seven small businesses in the retail, software development, and services sectors. One of his businesses developed the computer-based training software called PASS (Professional Automated Self-Study) which has been sold by most state societies as part of their CPE offering.

As an award-winning public speaker, Bill lectures throughout the U.S. to thousands of executives and CPAs each year. In addition, he has been featured on numerous videotaped and live television programs. As an award-winning author, Bill is nationally published, with over 200 columns and articles in magazines, journals, and newspapers, on a variety of management topics.

Bill is an active volunteer with the local, state, and national CPA organizations and has served or is currently on numerous committees, including AICPA's Management Consulting Services Executive Committee, AICPA's Information and Technology Executive Committee, the Texas delegate to the AICPA's Vision Project, the Texas Society of CPA's (TSCPA) Executive Committee, and the TSCPA's Strategic Planning Committee. He serves as chair of the TSCPA's Technology Oversight Committee, which is managing a million-dollar technology improvement project. He has also served on a number of boards of directors, including chairman of the board of the IBM Texas Employees Federal Credit Union, a $130 million financial institution.

Stephen L. Winters, CPA, *technical editor,* has served companies during the past twelve years as a management, financial, and computer consultant. Steve also has a background in accounting and tax, and was an investment broker with Lehman Brothers. He has published articles nationally, produced a business and tax tip series for a CBS affiliate, has taught and authored various continuing education courses, and is an active volunteer for the CPA profession.

Stanley E. Winters, CPA, *consulting editor,* has practiced public accounting for thirty-seven years. As managing partner of Winters, Winters and Reeb, he brings an essential ingredient to the firm—experience. In addition to his traditional accounting skills, Stan has built a reputation in the areas of litigation support, business acquisitions, and valuations. Stan has also served his profession in numerous roles on state and national councils and executive committees.